The Social Dynamics of Schooling: Participants, Priorities and Strategies

F. J. Hunt

The Falmer Press

(A member of the Taylor & Francis Group)
London · New York · Philadelphia

UK	The Falmer Press, Rankine Road, Basingstoke, Hampshire, RG24 0PR
USA	The Falmer Press, Taylor & Francis Inc., 1900 Frost Road, Suite 101, Bristol, PA 19007

© F. J. Hunt 1990

All rights reserved. No part of this publication may be reproduced, stored in a retrieval system, or transmitted in any form or by any means, electronic, mechanical, photocopying, recording or otherwise, without permission in writing from the Publisher.

First published 1990

British Library Cataloguing in Publication Data
Hunt, F. J. (Frederick J.)
  The social dynamics of schooling: participants, priorities and standards.
  1. Schools. Social aspects
  I. Title
  370.19
  ISBN 1-85000-747-0
  ISBN 1-85000-748-9 (pbk.)

Library of Congress Cataloging-in-Publication Data is available on request

Jacket design by Caroline Archer

Typeset in 10½/13pt Bembo by Graphicraft Typesetters Ltd

Printed in Great Britain by Taylor & Francis (Printers) Ltd, Basingstoke on paper which has a specified pH value on final paper manufacture of not less than 7.5 and is therefore 'acid free'.

Contents

Acknowledgements		vi
Chapter 1	The Examination and Appraisal of Schooling	1
Chapter 2	Schooling as a System of Activity	17
Chapter 3	The Student Experience	45
Chapter 4	Parenting	67
Chapter 5	Teaching	85
Chapter 6	Programming	103
Chapter 7	Servicing	125
Chapter 8	Managing	147
Chapter 9	Steering	167
Chapter 10	Interpretation	189
Chapter 11	Strategies for Developmentalism	213
Bibliography		233
Index		247

Acknowledgements

This book represents one major outcome of a long involvement in the practice and understanding of schooling. That association has included many forms of participation such as student, teacher, parent, lecturer, researcher, curriculum developer and observer in several societies.

The task of articulating a more systematic understanding was taken up in a period of study leave in the late 1970s but put aside to pursue what emerged initially as an incidental interest, namely the relevance for education of changing economic circumstances. With the completion of that study and its publication in *The Incorporation of Education* (Routledge, 1988), findings such as the similarities in policies of governments of quite different political commitments restimulated my interest in the dynamics of schooling.

In the course of pursuing that interest, I have studied the discussions and interpretations of many others and invariably found them helpful, with some contributing much more to the extension of my understanding than others. But of considerable interest have been the different perspectives from which people work and which influence their perceptions and concerns, the questions they ask, the interpretations they make, and the strategies they offer for further action and which, incidentally, are often a most valuable guide to the usefulness of their analyses and interpretations.

In coming to present this discussion, I am conscious of considerable indebtedness to many authors and, at the same time, of the difficulty of identifying many important influences on my work. Some obvious sources can be readily identified but they are not necessarily the more interesting or significant ones. These latter include people whose work may have been particularly significant at a particular time but sometimes became lost from consciousness with the passing of time. So although considerable effort has been put into acknowledging the work of specific

Acknowledgements

scholars throughout the discussion, I am conscious that important influences remain unacknowledged.

In addition to those of course are people and institutions more directly involved in my work and life and so in the production of this book: Monash University and its Faculty of Education which have provided a situation and resources, including study leave time for observation and discussion, reading, reflection and writing, and increasingly in recent years constituted illuminative situations in themselves; London University Institute of Education and its library where some study leave time was spent, and its helpful staff; Elaine Scott who transformed my draft into the final manuscript and thereby considerably enhanced the appearance of the statement; Peg, my wife, who lived with my preoccupation with the project but continuously and generously supported my 'developmental' activity.

Despite such assistance and support, the work remains my responsibility, particularly for its limitations. At the same time, one remains hopeful that some positive features may help with the work of building better systems of schooling and, even perhaps, a better world, thereby joining with others in these important tasks.

Chapter 1

The Examination and Appraisal of Schooling

The present is a period of considerable social change, with profound implications for schooling. In many societies substantial efforts are being directed to change fundamentally the priorities of school activity at all levels and in all sectors. In the main, economic priorities are dominant and the thrust is to make schooling more responsive to the requirements of productive systems of activity, and even to be an integral part of those systems, both generating income and producing a profit by operating as a service in the improvement of human capital and in the production of commercially usable knowledge. Indeed, primary concerns could be expressed as to use schooling increasingly in instrumental and even exploitative ways, rather than developmentally. However, while the present may appear to have evolved straightforwardly from the recent past, and so be unproblematical, there are some inconsistent, even contradictory features of recent developments that indicate they reflect social and political as well as economic initiatives and imperatives. Such trends and incongruities indicate the need for a close and critical appraisal of the undertaking of schooling, and this study is an attempt to examine current practices and establish the social dynamics of what is happening. It may be useful to begin this discussion with a brief review of developments since World War II when three main periods can be discerned with possibly a fourth, involving concerns about the environment, aspects of modes of production, and the conservation of natural resources, currently emerging.

First was a period of widespread and sustained economic growth, with many societies experiencing near to full employment and people enjoying increasing prosperity, with considerable social mobility. Associated with the economic circumstances were moods of optimism, liberality and even generosity, with a considerable readiness to accept and even support projects for disadvantaged groups both in one's own and in other societies. Schooling was widely seen as an important factor in providing access to opportunities and in contributing to economic, political and other aspects of development, and efforts were made to expand substantially and improve the quality of school facilities. In particular, attempts were made to 'open up' arrangements with progressive reforms in programs, school, classroom and system organization, and in examination practices and teaching strategies to remove obstacles to students' progress through schooling. In retrospect, those efforts can be seen to have been less progressive than they were thought to be and that, in quite important ways, arrangements changed in form rather than in substance. Nonetheless, there was something of a 'trickle down' effect in the distribution of benefits.

That period ended suddenly in the early 1970s when a sharp increase in the price of oil was followed by rapid inflation, economic recession and a dramatic growth in unemployment, particularly among youth. Again, it can now be seen in retrospect that the oil crisis sometimes exacerbated trends that had been developing for considerable periods of time, with established producers in particular fields finding themselves less effective than hitherto, and being displaced by often newly established producers, giving rise to changes in status and relationships and in prospects of prosperity. But it is also evident that the turbulent economic period of the 1970s was accompanied by other developments such as a revival of conservative forces, and used by them and other groups for purposes significant to themselves. Conservative reactions to educational developments of the 1950s and 1960s can be traced back to the Black Papers in England and similar expressions of concern in Australia, the USA and other societies from around the late 1960s. Then, with the onset of economic difficulties, some politicians, business leaders, academics and media specialists, together with some special interest groups also vigorously attacked schooling, claiming it to be inefficient and contributing by inadequate or inappropriate activity to producing unemployable youth. A significant and disturbing factor in both sets of claims was a lack of substantiation so that unsustained diagnoses were accompanied by recommendations that highlighted conservative structuring of modes of undertaking schooling. Particular features were a concentration of the attacks on progressivism in publicly operated schools, a phenomenon that in reality scarcely surfaced, and recommendations of 'back to basics', vocationalism and the greater structuring of school processes, along with greater accountability of schools and their staffs. Pervading those strategies were concerns to exercise greater control over and direction of schooling, and generally in ways compatible with the conservative criticisms.

The situation has again changed substantially since the early 1980s. One important factor has been a recognition that problems in the productive sector of a society often reflected long-standing trends which had been exacerbated by the difficult circumstances of the mid- and late 1970s. A second has been the recognition of changes in the relative status of societies as producers, with some declining and others rising in significance and displacing others. Associated with that has been the growth in the interrelationships between economies as the world has come to be seen as essentially a single economy. But of fundamental importance have been developments in technology which have had profound implications for productive, communicative and managerial processes in particular. One consequence has been for political, business and other societal leaders to decide that educational activity is central to the development of productive efficiency, and work to transform school systems to make them more effective in the development of human capital and as producers of commercially usable knowledge. A consequence is some remarkable similarities between societies in their policies for the reorganization of their school systems, despite important ideological differences between governments, and differences in strategies used by ideologically similar governments.

However, despite such evidence of consensus regarding goals and strategies in educational transformation, a number of puzzling features exist concerning those developments. For example, while considerable emphasis has been given to the vocationalization of schooling, available evidence indicates that it has little significance for increasing the quality of human resources and thereby of productivity; more likely, the workforce is better served by more general educational experiences that produce people more able to adapt to changing situations and technology, and more resourceful with available technology and in existing situations. Again, much has been made of a necessity to use existing resources more efficiently but it is clear that in ongoing arrangements substantial resources achieve no additional educational return and so can be said to be used ineffectively, a situation that is not remarked upon.

Probably the most significant issue, however, concerns relationships between the two major social entities of societies and privately operated corporations. Societies and their associated states are the social entities through which people have sought to establish and operate support and development systems such as education, with the accompanying need to mobilize resources to sustain those services. In contrast, corporations have been developed in the productive sector as exploitative mechanisms, and become increasingly preoccupied with growth and profit. As such, the very large multinational corporations give little or no loyalty to societies, and indeed are concerned to reduce their regulatory activity and limit contributions to and maximize benefits from them as means of reducing costs and maximizing profits. Thus they can be seen as inherently oppositional to societies. Correspondingly, they have been prime movers in seeking deregulation and restructuring societal arrangements to achieve an international market place. A cost of that to societies is that achievements in standards of practices that form parts of a standard of living, and which have been built up over extended periods, are placed under threat in attempts to compete with goods and services coming from societies that do not observe those standards of operating. In addition, technological developments that open up opportunities to exploit education as an economic activity favour particular kinds of business corporations in displacing schools and other institutions as producers and suppliers of programs. That in turn raises questions concerning how educational activities will be undertaken in commercial organizations, and the impact of exploitatory values, priorities and modes of operating upon the undertaking of education. Certain aspects and areas of education are not amenable to profit-making modes of operating and, in situations of increasing competition, appear likely to be neglected or inappropriately serviced. One likely prospect is that certain more profitable sectors will be undertaken by the private sector and public 'socialized' sectors continue to provide for economically unattractive groups and programs, as with slow learners and 'difficult' students. Another is the vitiation of pedagogic and academic integrity and the perversion of educational practice as educators increasingly find it necessary to gain or maintain sponsors' support.

A further closely related issue is that while societies should control corporations as they do individuals, communities and other social entities to ensure mutually responsible behaviour, the corporations and the megacoalitions in which they operate constitute entities that are far larger and more powerful than many societies so that the latter are substantially dependent on their operation. As such, they are sometimes able to influence societal policies on such matters as education so that they become the major beneficiaries, even to the extent of subverting a society's efforts in relation to its population.

It is in relation to that general situation that this study has been undertaken as an attempt to examine and appraise the undertaking of schooling. It reviews evidence on what schooling does and how it is operated, and seeks to interpret why it is operated in those ways and with those outcomes, and to indicate how it may be influenced to operate in other, more desirable ways. As such, it is an ambitious study and arguably presumptuous in aspiring to appraise where so much rests on personal or subjective judgment. Yet such judgments are commonly and necessarily made, and an important task is to develop appropriate strategies and procedures or methodologies for undertaking such tasks. Central or basic in such a project is the issue of perspectives for they are crucial to what is taken into account, the questions that are asked and responded to, and the interpretations and judgments that are made, points to which I will return later in this chapter.

It may be of interest to note that this study was not initially undertaken with such a goal in mind, but evolved towards such an outcome. It was initiated several years ago as an attempt to review a wide range of social research in schooling, and out of which might emerge a 'Sociology of Schooling' type of report. In the course of that work I became interested in the relevance of economic circumstances and undertook a series of case studies of societies which were published first as a set of journal articles and then, revised, updated and extended, in a book entitled *The Incorporation of Education* (Hunt, 1988).

A major observation that emerged from that work concerned the exceptional efforts being made to transform the character of school activity. On the one hand, strong efforts had been made to ensure that schooling operated to promote personal development in a more open or general educative sense, as institutions of personal and also societal development. While those efforts had been made in the main by teachers, they had also been supported or even encouraged by other groups, as testified to by the patronage of institutions with such emphases or orientations. At the same time, business, political and other groups, together with some people within schooling, had acted to direct schools to be more instrumental or utilitarian and even exploitative, and provide more practical programs with short-term and even sectional benefits. It should also be noted that the issue can be seen in terms of impartiality and discrimination, involving whether schooling serves all educationally or only some, and is used to shape others according to the purposes of more powerful groups in societal activities.

It will also be evident that these themes are not new ones, but are very much the traditional uses of schooling. What is special about the present situation is that the efforts to influence the operation of schooling are more intensely pursued and undertaken as part of a world-wide process of transformation. For such reasons, the present is a most appropriate time to study and appraise the undertaking of schooling. It is also a time when sound insights and proposals can be especially useful.

The Study of Schooling

As a complex and dynamic activity, the study of schooling entails a diverse array of techniques and strategies. Because studies are often carried out in quite limited projects, it may be useful to indicate what is entailed in a more comprehensive conception of schooling, and how it must be approached if we are to grasp and make sense of what is going on. At the same time, the techniques and strategies used relate to more general or basic perspectives from which social reality is viewed, so that it is also necessary to consider perspectives or the sets of basic assumptions about the nature of social reality from which people operate.

In identifying aspects of schooling, a most obvious feature is the activity of teachers and students, interacting in classrooms within schools. That situation has also been much studied, particularly in recent years, largely reflecting the development of appropriate perspectives such as interactionism and the adoption of ethnographic research techniques. Closely associated activity involves the organization and operation of schools, made particularly complex and dynamic by the practice of bringing together large numbers of students and staff on to particular sites, often with limited resources and facilities. Further important but less obvious features include the systems of schools within a society, usually systematically differentiated by level, and often by type, to deal separately with girls and boys, or to serve children who differ by religious affiliation, socio-economic circumstances or ethnic identity, or in rural, suburban or inner city locations. That is, schools relate to characteristics of particular populations, and vary markedly on the basis of those differences in terms of staff, the allocation of resources, and the programs and experiences they offer students.

Somewhat less obvious, but again crucial to teaching and learning and the operation of schools, are the activities of specialists who operate in the background, as it were. These work in curriculum development and research, the testing or examination of students, the pre- and in-service education of teachers, the guidance and counselling of students, and the management of those activities. They constitute a diverse array of support, control or other types of activities, often undertaken in specialized organizations, and while not so apparent to the observer, are often of major significance in the operation of schools.

Beyond these again, other areas of activity involve the provision of school plants and facilities, the allocation of financial and other resources, and the appointment and employment of staff. There is, too, the formulation and implementation of policies to steer the operation of schooling and, inevitably with that, the activity of many interest groups —

teachers, parents, administrators, politicians, employers and managers, bureaucrats and others — who seek to influence the determination of school policies.

Currently, too, interrelationships between schooling and economic, political and other areas of activity are exceptionally visible. In many societies, national policies have been devised to achieve closer complementation of efforts, particularly between schooling and economic activity. In turn, the location of a society's economy in the world economy, and the relevance of international political and social issues, are important connecting points by which circumstances and developments in the world at large affect activity in schooling.

However, it is not so much the areas of activity in themselves as the perceptions and interpretations of them by particular groups of participants that influence school activity. Hence, it is necessary to take account of participants' values, assumptions and beliefs that constitute cultural phenomena and come together in cultural systems. In that those relate to particular circumstances and associated interests and the undertaking of some particular areas of responsibility such as the operation of business, the conduct of political activity, or the position of employees or parents, they are sectional, and so to a degree give rise to partial or biased views which come to be expressed as particular ideologies or rationalizations in schooling activity.

If we are to understand schooling in the fullest sense, it is also necessary to examine it in different societal contexts such as in developed and developing, socialist and capitalist, traditional and modern, and in prosperous and impoverished periods. In examining these, it is also important to recognize that the activities and circumstances of particular societies may be interdependent, whether in the ways argued by dependency theorists or otherwise, and not simply in terms of schooling but through the operation of economic, political, military or other strategies. So to understand what is happening in schooling in one society, it may be crucial to study what is happening in other societies, or in some set of societies of which the one of particular interest is a part.

The study and interpretation of these aspects of school activity entail, as a second task, the identification of techniques employed in the enquiry process. Clearly, a vast and diverse array of techniques is required for the observation of interaction in the classroom or in administration and management, the analysis of language and other modes of interacting, the undertaking of interviews with participants in all sectors of schooling activity, surveys with samples and forms of analysis that enable relationships to be established, together with techniques for the examination of the allocation and use of resources, of participation and achievement patterns, the operation of labour markets, political activity, the identification and operation of values and systems of beliefs, and the undertaking of education in different societal contexts, and in its system and international relationships.

However, while these examples constitute an extensive array of techniques for studying schooling, they still fall short of being comprehensive. In fact, they derive in the main from work by social scientists and largely exclude the complementary interests and techniques of other approaches. For example, specialists in genetics, biology and psychology focus on the attributes, dynamics and activities of people, historians examine personal and social realities in temporal contexts and how they evolve, develop or change over time, while philosophers focus on questions about the nature of reality and how it may be studied, and about ethical and moral issues in education, and incidentally contribute to the examination and analysis of concepts, theories, techniques and strategies used by other specialists. As disciplined approaches, reflecting the theoretical assumptions and modes of operating developed in those areas of enquiry, these contrast with a more restricted set of essentially atheoretical and atomistic approaches that examine education not simply in isolation from other systems of activity but separate out and focus on specific sectors of activity such as teaching, curriculum, examinations or administration. As such, these latter reflect the 'practical' or technocratic orientations that have considerable appeal to managers, particularly in the current turbulent and conservative period, but lack comprehensiveness and a capacity systematically to interrelate analyses of issues, and are correspondingly superficial and unperceptive.

Collectively, then, in identifying aspects of schooling and how they may be studied, one generates listings that are substantial in their number and diversity, and daunting in the difficulties they raise in any attempt to assemble the 'pieces' into some overall view. It is that problem to which we can respond by considering a third facet of the study and practice of schooling, namely the perspectives from which people operate. These constitute sets of assumptions about the nature of reality and how to operate in respect of it that people generate and use in their lay or professional activities to steer the formulation and undertaking of courses of action, whether that be research, teaching, management or otherwise. Often they are unconsciously and so uncritically formed, operating as 'taken for granted' assumptions and, as such, can be quite unsound, inconsistent and even contradictory within themselves, and so inadequate and even counterproductive for the users.

At the same time, considerable effort has been made to develop critically appraised sets of assumptions and formulate sound, coherent and consistent perspectives. And while a common tendency is to see these as the preoccupation of theorists and researchers, and of little relevance to 'practitioners' such as teachers and administrators, it is apparent that the latter employ such sets of assumptions and perspectives. Often theirs may be differently identified, as in terms of progressive or traditional approaches to teaching and the operation of schooling. Nonetheless, such conceptions can be related to the perspectives from which researchers operate, and it is arguable that similar conceptions are employed by all who act in relation to schooling in one way or another, and that differences lie in the scope and explicitness of their articulation.

However, not only has considerable effort been put into developing approaches, including the elaboration of new developments and the critical appraisal of established positions, but a substantial 'secondary industry' has emerged involving the categorization and delineation of major positions, and the illustration of them with contributions by their exponents (e.g. Karabel and Halsey, 1977). More recently, a further development has involved the analysis of particular positions to identify key ontological and epistemological assumptions that underlie them. Thus Burrell and Morgan (1979) argue that all theories (or perspectives) are based on 'a philosophy of science and a theory of society' (p. x). They selected *objectivity* and *subjectivity* as alternative responses to a key issue in social science, and *regulation* and *radical change* as alternative responses to a key issue in theories of society, and interrelated the polarities to generate the four positions of functionalism, interpretivism, radical humanism and radical structuralism. Subsequently, they related an extensive range of conventionally conceived perspectives to their four positions and so offered a concise and promising statement of possibilities. Nonetheless, their analysis remains an unsatisfactory response to the problem they addressed partly because, in dealing with the nature of social science, they separated human nature from ontological issues rather than seeing it as a particular aspect or form of reality. Indeed, distinctions regarding the ontological character of humans are used to separate social from other aspects of reality, and justify distinctive epistemological approaches to social research and practice. Again, with the nature of society, Burrell and Morgan's selection of regulation versus radical change as the crucial issue also derives from the nature attributed to people, with regulation having relevance only where voluntarism is a reality.

The contrasting interpretation argued here upholds an evolutionary development among perspectives, with refinements or modifications of earlier positions made to take account of additional factors. Passiveness has thus been complemented with activeness, compatible with incompatible characteristics of individuals and groups, and so acceptance of the inevitability of conflict, and the relevance of differential power. Necessary, too, has been an extension in epistemological approaches to include a more diverse range of techniques with which to study social reality. More recent developments again include recognition of the reality of human attributes with their potentiality to develop, and with consequential questions about the significance of experience and environmental conditions. That aspect involves the role of the researcher as well as of the educator, and suggests close connections between theory and practice. Ultimately these issues pose questions about concern for others, or of the relevance of a sense of justice, particularly in the use of power.

Hence the basic issues involve, first, an ontological one of the nature of social reality, including the person and, second, a moral one concerning opportunities for people to develop. The first includes the voluntarist-determinist dichotomy and also takes account of the potentiality of humans to develop. The second, focusing on whether or not people have scope for development, leads on to other issues of power and justice, and whether or not the more powerful limit the scope for the less powerful to develop. That issue is basic to the nature of relationships in social entities and is essentially a moral one that confronts the social researcher and the practitioner.

The Appraisal of Schooling

I have developed this discussion of bases for appraisal elsewhere (Hunt, 1986) and grouped positions into four. The first, identified as *scientism* (e.g. Eisner, 1985: 27), includes behaviourism which is an adaptation from the physical sciences, and functionalism which is an adaptation from the biological sciences. Although developed and modified into a number of forms, essential features of behaviourism continue to involve beliefs in the monistic nature of reality and in the adequacy of particular approaches to the study of all forms of reality. In addition, an atomistic approach is taken to the identification of problems and the study of situations. A contemporary example is a study of some London primary schools by Mortimore and others (1988) who measured many aspects of schooling and correlated their results but lacked a general social theory by which to interpret their findings. In consequence, they did not identify basic dynamics of schooling or provide a coherent rationale for responsive strategies. Again, structural functionalism, inspired by the concept of the organism drawn from the life sciences to serve as a model for society and other social entities, has had considerable appeal but is now generally regarded as inadequate if not unsatisfactory. Ironically, however, it continues to be used by managers for whom it offers a convenient metaphor for the organizations they manage, and by researchers and other specialists who unwittingly employ somewhat naive and simplistic functionalist conceptions to guide both the identification of policy implications and the modes of operating employed in promoting them.

A second form of structuralism derived from Marxist thought emphasizes incompatible elements in competing and even conflicting relationships that develop over time (e.g. Althusser, 1972). Major elements include the state and the economy, labour, capital and the class structure and, more recently, race and gender (e.g. Apple, 1986). While differing from functional structuralism in emphasizing incompatible elements and even conflict, the two are similar in minimizing the significance of individuals and groups as participants in activities. Rather, they involve mechanistic conceptions that encourage expectations of predictability while disregarding the significance of subjective orientations, priorities and interpretations.

Humanistic *interpretive* positions constitute a second set of positions that distinguish between social and physical reality. For example, interactionism has been useful in the examination of face-to-face situations such as classrooms and schools (e.g. Woods, 1983). However, it has not been fully explored in relation to more remote interactions as from within and between organizations, and has been seen as insensitive to powerful structural forces that operate upon people (Sharp and Green, 1975). Nonetheless, it has considerable potential and is drawn on extensively here within a more inclusive framework.

A third set of positions, identifiable as *conflict theories* (e.g. Collins, 1975), incorporates incompatible elements from the other two, locates them in historical and contemporary contexts, and requires a diversity of approaches to understand those realities. Thus the active-passive nature of human participation is accepted but interpreted in terms of relative power. People are seen to pursue interests with different levels of resources, competencies and other elements of power so that some establish dominance and assert their claims, and subjugate and possibly exploit others who are obliged to be compliant or at most resistant. The use of power also means that such relationships can be regulated or made mechanistic, although the unlikelihood of achieving complete dominance means that degrees of initiative and innovational actions regularly occur. A more inclusive stance also means sensitivity to historical and contemporary contexts and to patterns, trends, strategies and other, often quite fundamental processes. Such comprehensiveness, together with recognition of distinctive human attributes such as rationality, fosters and sustains a critical perspective so that situations and events are appraised rather than taken for granted.

An interesting feature of conflict theorists' positions are differences in the locus of incompatibilities. Psychoanalysts locate incompatibility in psychic forces, giving rise to intra-personal conflict and the use of such mechanisms as repression, sublimation, displacement or projection. Social theorists commonly locate conflict in groups pursuing class interests, although ethnicity, gender, religion and other social characteristics also serve as bases for conflict. A third set of theorists locates conflict in such structures or forces as the modes of production or cultural styles and sees these as essentially impersonal. Common to all is a perception of the impact of particular forces upon people and the generation of diverse patterns of acting, such as domination and exploitation, alienation, depersonalization, resistance, compliance, frustration or sublimation.

Even though conflict theories entail a substantially more viable set of assumptions than the others, at least for examining large complex social entities such as communities, organizations and societies, it is necessary to go further in order to accommodate assumptions about other aspects of social reality.

Hence we come to *developmentalism* as a fourth position. It incorporates many of the facets of other perspectives, including objective and subjective forms of reality and the active nature of people. It also recognizes the existence of differential power with some being constrained and experiencing regulation and possibly exploitation by more powerful people. It accepts, too, the coexistence of incompatible attributes, groups and forces, and requires comprehensive views incorporating historical and contemporary realities. In addition, however, humans are recognized as beginning life with attributes that develop, possibly through stages, in relation to circumstances and experiences, and so of having potential to develop. Indeed, cognitive, moral, physical, social, religious, communicative and other aspects of the person have been explored along those lines and it is evident that a person at any point of time reflects biographical, social and cultural experiences. Moreover, personal development, together with social aggrandisement in such terms as identity and status, resources and influence, as well as the development of one's group, community, organization or other social entity, constitute personal and social interests that are pursued individually and collectively. Finally, because social arrangements and processes are constructed, they can be devised or reconstructed to foster or inhibit personal and social development, making it important to consider them in their developmental significance.

Consistent with that position is the view that concepts such as social structure, culture, the economy and the polity are essentially ones of convenience. The reality involves people interacting as parts of dynamic, complex, changing situations. Of course, some of these situations are ongoing and enduring, and buttressed by laws and regulations; even so, they endure only while they are affirmed and their procedures enforced or accepted, and so reproduced. For particular purposes we may need to analyze and tease out what has been going on, as in historical and ethnographic studies, and depict situations as unique, and constantly changing. But in general, such situations are too complex and dynamic to deal with in those ways, and it is convenient to conceptualize sectors of reality as schools, culture, teaching, the economy and other forms of activity and modes of operating. The crucial point is to recognize that they are concepts of convenience and not to reify them into social phenomena with a life and force of their own and as forces or structures against which we are relatively powerless and ineffective.

It is also important to recognize that power is not the only determinant of how research or other activities are undertaken. The taking up of the problems of others, as in some programs of research and action concerning discrimination, exploitation, political persecution and oppression, and practices involving unequal rights and obligations, and including the well-being and developmental prospects of other species, indicates a sense of compassion or awareness of the rights of and obligations towards others, and so of a sense of justice. Hence, justice has to be placed alongside power, establishing a necessity to go beyond conflict theories for a basis for research and other kinds of activity.

Central to developmentalism, then, and distinguishing it from conflict theories are ontological assumptions that recognize the developmental nature of people (and other species), and a moral conception recognizing their right to develop. Following Scheffler (1985: 34–40), this position can be related to Kant's categorical imperative to act to treat humanity, whether self or other, as an end and not as a means, and to similar exhortations in Christianity and other major religions, thus requiring a society 'normatively ordered by a democratic ideal, commitment to which has radical and far-reaching consequences, not only for basic political and legal institutions, but also for the educational conceptions that guide the development of the young' (p. 122). That is, accordance of rights for all to develop entails counterpart responsibilities for others, and so establishes the basic requirements for a system of social arrangements. Thus we also have a basis for appraising existing arrangements and for devising more satisfactory alternatives.

Several positions are compatible with a developmental orientation. Maslow, Rogers and others have argued possibilities of realization of attributes and the experience of fulfilment and satisfaction, while Erikson, Piaget, Kohlberg and others have argued conceptions of evolving development, possibly through stages so that, collectively, a notion of personal destiny has meaning. In a second position, critical theorists conceptualize situations and processes in ideal terms and explore factors giving rise to deficiencies or constraints, with Habermas (e.g. 1978) giving particular attention to communicative processes. These invariably recognize limiting consequences for people but also include recognition of the significance of developmental achievements for ability to share in communication. New areas and approaches in science such as environmentalism, together with genetic, reproductive and other forms of engineering, are also at least partially compatible with developmental concerns in adopting critical positions, and in seeking to improve attributes and processes and so enhance development and performance. However, they are incompatible when involving the other as means rather than as ends. Similarly, developmentalism has meaning for more idealist approaches such as psychoanalysis which has long recognized developmental capacities and patterns. Indeed, some critical theorists recognize psychoanalysis as an exemplary case of the practice of critical theory, distinguished by its focus on the individual, and relative neglect of structural arrangements, and the lesser significance given to physical aspects of reality. Finally, Giddens (1984) accommodates the objective and subjective by incorporating them into the dualism of structures and recognizes the active nature of actors who use the structural properties of social systems in reproducing or transforming social relationships.

The thrust of developmentalism and, in particular, recognition of the relevance of social arrangements and processes for developmental opportunities and experiences, also raises some important issues for researchers, as for other types of practitioners. Styles of research are an obvious feature because conventional research is a process of some acting upon others, with the latter being held passive, or at most reactive, and gaining little or nothing in skills or competence, or possibly even in knowledge or insights from the research process. Less obviously, the thrust of questions can be to focus on the problems of some rather than others, as for example, in focusing on the problems of researchers rather than the researched, or where research is commonly part of the process of management, and so an instrument of the more powerful in the management of the less powerful.

Finally, it should be noted that the assumptions underlying developmentalism justify an approach that is comprehensive and even holistic. For example, it requires theoretical positions on the person and on social reality, and entails historical and contemporary comparative studies. However, it is not necessary for any particular practitioner to be expert in all these but it does require that they have conscious assumptions which are stated and can be subjected to critical appraisal. As a consequence, a central test of the adequacy of a perspective and of any work that is produced on the basis of it is how the different sets of assumptions interrelate. A further test is on the basis of expectations or predictions derived from the assumptions or from work done on the basis of them. That is, coherence and usefulness in promoting the development of the person, individually and collectively, constitute criteria for evaluating its soundness and usefulness.

That then is the basis on which this study has been undertaken. Because central significance is given to the activities of people in social arrangements and processes, the discussion has been organized in terms of participants and a central task has been to identify and include relevant interest groups. The concern with development and a sense of justice has meant going beyond obvious participants to include inarticulate, unorganized and so ineffective ones such as students as well as more powerful but relatively invisible ones such as certain sectors of government and types of corporations. Thus the discussion has been organized to proceed from more visible participants in students and teachers to less obvious groups involved in support or control activities such as curriculum development, the structuring and management of schooling, and in complex and sophisticated efforts to exercise influence upon the operation of schooling. This leads us to some of the most powerful interest groups in society but ones which have been largely neglected in educational studies, mainly due to shortcomings in the perspectives from which researchers have studied educational activity.

In setting out to consider the activities of such a range of participants, one is of course substantially dependent on available research. Generally, there is an abundance of relevant studies, and the task has been largely one of selecting those that illustrate particular points. Certain sectors have been neglected, however, and in order to discuss them it has been useful to draw upon a wider range of research than that done in respect of schooling. By such means it has been possible to put together a coherent account of the operation of schooling and identify and portray the dynamic forces that act in relation to it.

As a preliminary, however, it is useful to examine schooling in the commonly used structuralist terms to identify the main social entities wherein and between which educational and other activity occurs. That serves to provide an introductory overview and first approximation of the social reality of schooling as a system of institutions, social practices and activities, and incidentally make a number of general points about the operation of school systems. It is also useful in serving as a basis from which to move to examine schooling activity in the more dynamic terms of participants, priorities and strategies.

Chapter 2

Schooling as a System of Activity

Social reality is constituted of people with their values, orientations, beliefs, priorities, resources and strategies, acting individually and collectively in the pursuit of personal, community, organizational and other interests. The collectivities, reflecting particular values, orientations, interests and so on, arise in relation to class, race, gender, religion, location and other characteristics, situations and circumstances. As such, they invariably involve dynamic interactions within themselves and in relation to others, and so constitute major social groups operating separately and within larger and more complex social entities.

The regularities of expectations, activity and interaction vary in their degree of formalization so that groups range from some that are casually related and meet and act spontaneously to others that are formally established and organized to operate in particular kinds of ways. These latter include the more powerful and formidable organizations such as government departments and private corporations. They also develop considerable complexity and diversity, and undertake many and sometimes incompatible activities, with diverse consequences for different sectors of a society. Systems of schooling are one such type of organization, performing important and basic tasks of influencing the development of the young, but doing it in different ways for different groups of students who subsequently participate in different ways in different sectors of a society.

Formidable though these organizations are, however, they remain social constructions that are sustained or transformed by the actions of people acting through or upon them. Crucial in that process are understandings, interests, strategies, competencies and other resources relevant to the exercise of influence. Because people vary greatly in their capacity to exercise influence, some readily take existing social arrangements as constituting immutable forms of reality and accommodate their action and strategies to them. At the same time, an important few master the operation of social arrangements and manage them as instruments or agencies in the pursuit of interests. That is most evident in the entrepreneurial activities of business managers but is also common although less visible in public sector organizations. But it is evident too, from the everyday activities of less significant participants, that many can be effective in modifying, exploiting, subverting and sometimes even transforming the situations of which they are part.

Schools and the systems they comprise constitute a distinctive and significant type of organizational arrangement. They are established and operated by a variety of public and private sponsors to influence the development of the young. Their diverse concerns and priorities are reflected in their different structuring, staffing, resourcing and programming as well as in their day-to-day operation and management. As such they constitute forms of social reality to which students and staff accommodate, to be processed by the operation of the system. Yet students and staff also have some impact upon them and the more so to the extent that they realize the dependence of managers on their compliance. So while they commonly limit their efforts to achieve more congenial situations, circumstances and prospects, in reality they have considerable scope to shape organizational arrangements and procedures.

In seeking to establish a better understanding of schooling we can usefully explore several aspects of its operation. One is the sponsorship of schools which entails the provision of resources and the setting out of purposes and guidelines by which to steer their operation. A second is the organization and operation of students, facilities, programs, staff and other resources, for it is by those means that associations and experiences are determined and outcomes influenced. A third is its management which entails efforts and strategies to influence the ongoing activities of participants and ensure that intended outcomes are achieved or at least approximated. Finally, it is useful to consider briefly some outcomes of schooling for the insights they provide into its operation. They directly reflect the dynamics of schooling and give significance to the subsequent detailed examination of it as a system of social activity, comprised of many groups of participants in contestations within and between groups.

Sponsorship

The establishment and operation of schools is an attractive course of action for several reasons and correspondingly attracts a variety of sponsors. A concern to provide developmental experiences and opportunities for one's own children or for those of one's group or community constitutes a common justification that in itself is met in a variety of ways, including self-serving groups and more inclusive communal and societal arrangements. These latter vary in the emphasis given to compassion or altruism, and where those attributes are weak or absent then the arrangements may approximate a second set of concerns where provision for others is more utilitarian and undertaken for the opportunity to control and direct the experience of other children, and sometimes in ways that ensure their economic, political or other usefulness to the sponsors. In addition, a third concern to operate schooling as a commercial, profit-making process is of long-standing in certain forms but being substantially extended at the present time. In all of these arrangements, children from more affluent families are obviously at a considerable advantage in being able to determine which options they select, while those from poorer families are invariably greatly dependent on the efforts and dispositions of other people.

The provision of schooling involves no insuperable problems for wealthier people. They can act collectively by living in wealthier communities as is a practice in the relatively localized system of operating schools in the USA, or by enrolling their children in expensive elite schools that serve a select clientele drawn from a scattered population. However, even when wealthier parents are members of a more heterogeneous community or a society that provides a system of schooling for all children, they can readily provide additional resources to ensure their children experience superior facilities and are advantaged relative to the mass of children.

People with considerable resources are likely to be most satisfied with a market system. Having the resources to expend and being more experienced in market-type negotiations, they are generally well placed to extract favourable services from the suppliers of goods and services. The appeal of that form of arrangement is indicated by the regular evolution of church and community sponsored schools into market-oriented institutions.

Community sponsorship of schooling reflects ethnic, religious, locational and other bases of community. Schooling in the USA was initially essentially a community undertaking and that remains a widespread pattern even though consolidation, particularly in larger cities, means the local community has often lost much of its significance. Religious groups constitute another form of community that sponsors schools to ensure the perpetuation of the community, although again these can be very large as with the Roman Catholic Church and mean schooling is organized into substantial systems with a local community again having little significance. Ethnic groups can also see value in operating schools as a means of perpetuating the community and its way of life, although this usually has more significance when the group has minority status within a society. Ideology forms still another basis for community as is evident in the establishment and operation of progressive, traditional and other distinctive types of secular schools.

In these types of arrangements, general secular community orientations are usually a fragile concern. The larger the community the more likely it is to develop subcommunities, reflecting class, ideology and other interests that often derive from the more extensive society. Thus Lynd and Lynd (1929, 1937), Hollingshead (1949) and others in early community studies in the USA illustrated the preoccupation of groups with sectionalist interests, and so the tenuousness of any community orientation except in distinctive types of smaller and relatively classless communities such as are found among the Amish in the USA or in kibbutzim in Israel and where all students are provided for comparably.

Again, Catholic schools, even though sharing religious commitments, are also particularly prone to differ according to the social circumstances of community members. Indeed, religious orders often direct their efforts to specific sections of the general Catholic population, serving wealthier or poorer categories of children. A degree of concern for children of less affluent parents and of otherwise limited circumstances may continue to operate but usually is a distant second to self-concern and efforts to obtain advantageous facilities and programs for one's own children. Thus provision is likely to vary and be accompanied by different types of arrangements such as we will consider presently.

Societal sponsorship, while having parallels with community efforts and activities, invariably involves even larger entities and correspondingly is characterized by further differentiation in provision and practices. Indeed, it has been argued (e.g. Ramirez and Boli, 1987) that a major purpose in establishing national systems of education was to mobilize children in support of established agencies by teaching them relevant competencies as with literacy and numeracy and inculcating political attitudes of compliance. The primacy of concern with instrumental or utilitarian purposes has generally been continued as children have stayed longer at school, and institutional provision been extended with differentiation after a few years of primary schooling into essentially career-oriented middle and secondary schooling. In addition, the discriminatory process has been emphasized by such arrangements as increasing public support at higher levels of schooling which, in the main, benefits students from already more affluent families. As a consequence, those students who stay to complete a degree have several times as much public funds spent on their education as is spent on a student who meets only the minimum requirements. In such ways schooling has been established and operated to differentiate between students, essentially reinforcing the consequences arising from their different social circumstances.

Similarly, poorer students are again at a disadvantage in any market-type situation, simply because they have fewer resources with which to bargain. The chances are, too, that their parents have less expertise and confidence in the bargaining process, and so are disadvantaged in that process. Correspondingly, a feature of the centrally administered system is that it constitutes a mechanism for achieving more equitable support for schooling for all children, thereby offsetting the circumstances of more affluent families, as Ramsey and others (1983) illustrated in their New Zealand study and in contrast with the situation of stratification by local district portrayed of US schools by Anyon (1981). Even so, such interventions are unlikely to do more than reduce the more gross inequalities because wealthier parents can always find ways of offering more or better facilities, providing better staffing and ensuring other advantages.

Schooling has also long been a venue for private investment and entrepreneurial effort. In earlier times these often entailed menial and even squalid enterprises, reflecting the poverty of the times. In some cases, they have been marginal or specialized undertakings such as developing particular skills for office work. In contrast, contemporary initiatives reflect relative prosperity and affluence, and focus on areas such as business management, information sciences, biotechnology and other areas that offer prospects of considerable economic returns. Again, some corporations are exploring mainstream primary and secondary schooling, establishing the comparative and competitive appeal of commercially sponsored programs (Eurich, 1985). Commonly, too, some governments as in England are fostering commercially-oriented approaches from more conventional providers of schooling. It is possible that rising standards of affluence, or perhaps just the prospects of such a development, attract parents and students to enterprises that offer such returns and away from more service-based institutions and programs. In any case, schooling is experiencing a new phase in the processes of sponsorship and operation.

Organization and Operation

The organization and operation of schooling can be analyzed into several distinct and complementary parts such as teaching, curriculum, organizational structure, assessment and so on. However, while for some purposes it is useful to consider these as separate elements, they are also interrelated and for other purposes usefully seen in their totality. For one thing, they are invariably integral parts of a general strategy for undertaking schooling and so have a unity for providers. Again, they constitute a unity which students experience and interpret and from which they derive learnings and outcomes. Still again, the separable elements often share features that reflect the influence of other factors such as characteristics of students, the operation of the productive and other systems of social activity, or their convenience to staff as feasible modes of operating in the situation that schooling has been constituted to be. For such reasons, it can be useful to take these aspects collectively and discuss them in terms of the organization and operation of schooling. The appropriateness of this strategy is illustrated with the use of the term 'hidden curriculum' to denote the relevance to the school experience of arrangements other than the explicit curriculum. It is in that way then that I propose to consider schooling, identifying the various ways in which schooling is undertaken and experienced.

As structured and sustained social arrangements, schools reflect the influence of many forces. Some can be seen as historical, although that is probably an unsound and misleading interpretation because not all phenomena persist over time and reasons for persistence and disappearance have to do with factors operating in a particular present. Nonetheless, to take account of the historical experience can be helpful in identifying factors that are relevant to the persistence of particular school institutions. But it is also important to consider recent events and developments and identify forces operating in current situations. It can be helpful too to examine situations in several societies because that can facilitate the identification of different and possibly more general patterns and factors associated with schooling.

Historically, schools have been established in many situations and used in many ways. In much of Europe schooling was associated with religion, as with cathedral schools in medieval times, religious order schools for particular categories as with Jesuit schools for prospective leaders, or schooling for literacy in some reformation societies. Members of aristocracies and bourgeoisies also established and sustained schools for the preservation and advancement of their privileges and achievements, and sometimes, too, a church or other organization established institutions for children of the poor. A major transformation occurred from the late eighteenth century with the establishment of nation-states and the development of national systems of schools very likely, as Ramirez and Boli (1987) argued, to promote a national polity together with the provision of a workforce and to reduce the prospects of subversive political activity. Meanwhile, more affluent and privileged groups persisted with separate schools, thereby maintaining dual systems throughout much of Europe. Elsewhere colonizing societies developed schools that reflected their priorities, establishing schooling for only a proportion of the local society in order to provide administrative and other kinds of services. Only in the US was a more open ladder-type system of schools developed although the comparability of comprehensive schools was substantially limited by variations among the communities sponsoring school systems, and by tracking within schools. That is, differentiation was less visible.

The history of national systems of education for a century or more has been of expansion and extension through both secondary and tertiary levels, together with improvements to the quality of staff, programs, buildings and other resources. That growth and improvement were particularly substantial in the prosperous decades following World War II, not only in the older industrialized societies, but also in many developing societies. Often the increases in proportions of age groups staying on at secondary and even tertiary institutions were quite remarkable. There was also considerable optimism that such expansion in educational provision would mean a reduction in the differentiating activity of educational institutions as most youth stayed longer at schools and achieved higher levels of qualifications. But, as we shall see presently, those expectations were unrealistic.

The more obvious structuring of schooling is into levels as by primary and secondary types of schools. These have evolved largely out of elementary schooling established for the 'masses' and from private schools established for particular elites or communities and so initially constituting dual systems. As universal schooling has been extended, so elementary or primary and secondary have been brought into an alignment with each other to form something of a ladder of institutions. Even so, points of transfer from primary to secondary still vary greatly with some European societies transferring students to some type of secondary at 10 or 11 years of age and children in Sweden attending the compulsory school from 7 to 15, and then going on to a senior secondary school. In some societies the primary schools are continued until 14, once a common point of termination, and secondary runs for some four years after that. Some, such as England and the US, have introduced intermediate or junior high schools that overlap the upper grade or two of primary and the lower years of secondary schooling. Again, the early years of primary schooling have sometimes been separated out to junior or nursery schools, while the later years of secondary schooling are sometimes organized into senior high schools or colleges. The particular patterns to be found usually reflect the influence of factors operating in a particular society and which can also be expected to constitute obstacles to change.

Classes or grades within schooling receive some support from knowledge of the development of children by stages, with its implications that schoolwork can be graded and related to children's developing abilities. It has also been given legitimacy and meaning by the factory model of staged production, with children moving along as on a conveyor belt. The adoption of grades and forms is also related to the necessity for teachers, working with large numbers of students and limited resources, to limit heterogeneity in the range of the stages of development at which those children are taught. At the same time, to limit all contacts to children of a particular age, as in a class or form, is a limiting process, neglecting family-type, across-age groupings. Probably the best arrangements in schooling would be a flexibility that allows a mixing of patterns with some parts of a program taken with a very homogeneous group of students in terms of ages and abilities and stages of development, and others in a variety of heterogeneous groups through to involving all ages and all levels of ability and competence.

Setting, streaming and tracking involve further degrees of differentiation of students of a given class or form by some conception of ability. Setting is the more limited practice with students constantly regrouping from one set of activities to another. Streaming or tracking is more extreme, involving the complete segregation of students into virtually different types of programs, often on the basis of performance in a few areas such a language and mathematics, and some ability tests. The argument that it enables teachers to work with relatively homogeneous groups and so be more effective is a plausible one, but account has to be taken of social practices and activities associated with such groupings, and these invariably damage many children and, at most, are of advantage to only some. There is probably no satisfactory justification for streaming or tracking, but a case can be made for a degree of setting when the activity involves sequential steps and development. But even then it is contingent upon resources; with smaller classes and adequate and appropriate teaching and learning resources, teachers can handle a diverse range of students within a group.

A more substantial method of grouping and segregating students is by establishing different types of schools and of these there are many, and a long history of such practices. Religious, ethnic and some secular ideological groups operate schools to teach elements of a way of life and so to perpetuate the group or community. With the rise of the state and the establishment of public systems of schooling, such communal schools have sometimes been accommodated within the public sector, sometimes continued as private institutions, and sometimes been prohibited. Nonetheless, they can be readily understood as schools of commitment. And while they can have serious limitations as in the extent to which they limit the experiences and opportunities of children to those compatible with life in that group or community, they have advantages in preparing students for life in an often welcoming and supporting community.

Much less justifiable are schools which, purportedly at least, operate for children of different levels or types of ability, such as the selective grammar and the residual modern schools of England in the 1950s to the 1970s. They are less acceptable because the basis of differentiating children is usually dubious if not specious, and they operate to advantage some and disadvantage others in relation to opportunities to enter economic, political and other areas of social activity. Sometimes, as in West Germany, where different types of schools lead to definite and usable qualifications, they are more defensible. But even then, the basis of differentiation is usually arbitrary and closely related to social background circumstances and experiences and so clearly limiting, stereotyping and ultimately reproductive of social classes. It also means losses in that a society does not receive the benefits from some students' talents, through the sifting and sorting processes employed.

Least defensible are the selective schools that operate in relation to the upper end of the social and economic spectrum. Many of those identify as elite schools and offer justifications in terms of preparing for elite eccupations and activities or leadership. However, their availability only to people with considerable resources means that they come to constitute concentrations of advantage, while their unavailability to many who might be more effective in those positions means that they also act as exclusionary mechanisms and do not provide a society with the best leaders that could be available. And that comment can be made simply within their own framework of values and priorities. If one goes further and rejects the processes of separating prospective leaders out from prospective followers and argues the desirability of all-inclusive or comprehensive schools for organization and community building, then they are found to be even less satisfactory.

Another basis for grouping and segregating is by gender. These schools too have been established for many reasons, ranging from providing an 'appropriate' education for each sex, to keeping them apart as a way of avoiding social problems. Coeducational schools came to be promoted as beneficial to both boys and girls, being more 'natural' situations. Close study has revealed however that typically they are operated to provide benefits to males with females induced into different and even

The Social Dynamics of Schooling

lesser roles. They well illustrate, as with studies of comprehensive schools more generally, that it is just not sufficient to group students in a particular way; the pressures of forces for differentiation and stratification are far wider and more pervasive than the institutions of schooling, and if these processes are to be checked or overcome, then powerful counteractive efforts are required from those operating schools.

Before leaving this brief profiling of different types of schools, it is useful to note the relevance of social and particularly economic circumstances. Certainly there was some reduction in the incidence of structuring by the introduction of comprehensive in place of differentiated schools and deferral of the points at which differentiations were made in the life of students during the prosperous and relatively stable period of the 1950s to the early 1970s, as the account by Bellaby (1977) of the extension of comprehensive schools in England during that period illustrates. It is also clear, as Levin (1978) indicated, that differentiation was essentially deferred, and became much more extensively established in tertiary institutions. The general thesis of the relevance of economic circumstances is further supported by the lessening of commitment to comprehensivization and the growth of interest in differentiation in the late 1970s and through the 1980s. However, as the 1980s have passed by, it is apparent that prosperity is enjoyed by many and what is different is the prospects opening up with the restructuring of productive systems. It is these prospects of personal, group and organizational aggrandisement which could be reviving interest in the usefulness of schooling to differentiate and stratify its students. It is now more relevant than it has been to be 'getting ahead'.

The significance of aspirations, achievements and prospects directs attention to social and cultural elements that have been largely neglected in this discussion of structures in schooling. However, a fundamental aspect of the situation is that staff and students interact and produce subcultures and these relate to the particular types of structures whether a streamed class or a particular type of school. Parts of the subculture involve self-concepts, levels and kinds of aspirations, perceptions of others, modes of operating and so on. These are important elements in the forming of identities, including how other groups are perceived and treated, and come to regard themselves. In consequence, they are important aspects arising with the process of structuring schooling and we will consider them more closely in a later section.

Portrayal of a system of schools by type is only a first step, however. Typically, types of schools vary by resources, either by what the state supplies or by what parents and others contribute. Such factors bear upon the staff employed, their stability or transitoriness, the resources in a school, the kinds of programs they offer, the aspirations and expectations of students, the subcultures that develop, patterns of achievements, the reputations and traditions that schools develop and which their students experience, and in relation to which they develop personal qualities and characteristics. It is in relation to those aspects that elite private schools work hard in carefully selecting principals, staff and students, and marshalling resources to maximize achievements and reputations, while disadvantaged schools are likely to accept what is available to them, however inadequate and unsatisfactory that may be.

A consideration of the structuring of schools cannot be complete without examining linkages between schools and other sectors of society, and notably tertiary education and the labour force. Some such as the elite schools studied by Cookson and Persell (1985) devote considerable effort and other resources to maintaining relationships with elite tertiary institutions to ensure acceptance of their graduates. In extreme contrast are schools serving impoverished and disadvantaged families which have no definite linkages or connections and simply release their students, often ill-equipped to deal with social arrangements and processes and so virtually predestined for the least attractive sectors of employment and other areas of activity. Thus a parallel can be traced between the structuring of society and particular sectors such as the workforce, and the structuring and operation of schools. However, it is unsound to attribute the relationship to the operation of schools; the situation is far more complex and sometimes works in these ways despite the best efforts of staff and others operating in and through schools. In addition, the mass of schools is in the middle of this hierarchical ordering, not so clearly stratified, and associated with degrees of upward and downward mobility. At the same time, such mobility does not necessarily weaken the overall structuring of society but can actually serve to strengthen it by promoting more effective and easing out less effective students. In that process, schooling can also enhance its legitimacy as a sound and effective agency in the service of groups and organizational arrangements.

Management

The task of management entails the exercise of authority and the undertaking of responsibilities for the operation of schooling. The issue of authority highlights the dependent status of the manager with legal authority deriving from public or private sponsors and social authority deriving from parents, staff, students and other groups with whom managers work. In other than authoritarian situations, managers must to some extent negotiate or achieve agreement concerning what is to be done and how it is to be done. In turn, the responsibilities entail the undertaking of control and coordination, staffing and resource allocation, monitoring performance, the enhancement of the efforts of participants, and other tasks associated with the operation of schooling. Inevitably, given the complexities and uncertainties associated with schooling, the undertaking of management responsibilities may be distributed over many positions and agencies within a system, and many undertaking managerial responsibilities may usefully be identified as technical operatives.

In the study of the management of schooling it has been convenient to use two more extreme models, one centralized and the other local, and to locate individual cases in relation to them. Each particular case invariably reflects the operation of historical, ideological, economic, political and other factors, and tends to become set in its mode of operating and subject to considerable inertia, largely because those factors influence expectations and obligations of office holders and become subject to positive and negative sanctions according to how those expectations are met or the obligations undertaken.

A centralized system entails all significant decisions being made at some central or higher level point and associated with bureaucratic administrative machinery and rigidity of processes. In consequence, it is commonly seen to be somewhat stifling or inhibiting of initiative, and generative of frustration and even alienation. A positive feature is its predictability and in ensuring that the work of schooling gets done. At the same time, reasons for the employment of a centralized system of management are several. One involves a missionary zeal to establish and transmit a common set of values and beliefs, so that centralization is associated with a more dogmatic and authoritarian type of society. It can also be a means of using limited resources to produce programs, materials, teaching strategies and other facilities that enable a weak teaching force to be more effective. A third reason is to ensure that services are comparably and possibly even equitably provided to diverse groups, thereby limiting discrimination and exploitation. Again, staff initiatives for equitable treatment can generate rules and tribunals to operate over conditions of employment, and produce bureaucratic systems. An interesting feature of relatively recent times has been the increase in influence from the centre and for a number of reasons — the development of guiding principles to limit discrimination against particular groups of people, to gain access to larger pools of resources to offset the limited resources of particular communities, and as central governments and other groups have sought to transform the priorities and modes of operating schooling.

The exemplar case of decentralization, with local control of operations and activity, including the marshalling and use of resources, the appointment of staff and determination of programs, is comprised of some autonomous private schools. Such schools are usually affiliated with a particular religion or uphold a distinctive secular ideology. Generally, a necessity to obtain adequate resources means that they serve more prosperous sectors of society, while counterpart forces operate in the public sector with poorer systems under pressure to become part of a larger unit of government in order to boost their resources and so to become more bureaucratized. That is, there is a dynamic with better off sectors of society experiencing benefits by operating independently and autonomously, partly for the greater latitude they thereby achieve, but partly also by reducing obligations towards poorer sectors of society, and with poorer schools driven to dependency and bureaucratization. Those relationships are also significant to understanding the meaning of concerns about freedom of choice and the appeal of the market place; both are attractive to people with resources. However, an important exception is when a particular community expresses a strong commitment to practising and perpetuating a particular way of life and regards substantial resources as secondary to autonomy and self-determination.

While the centralized and localized conceptions of the distribution of responsibilities and authority are helpful, they are nonetheless but aids to understanding and should not be allowed to obscure or distort perceptions of social reality. As a balance, it is useful to note briefly positions in structural arrangements to which responsibilities and authority are attached; it is in relation to those that variations occur and give rise to the patterns that approximate the more polar types or some combination between them.

A first point to note is the responsibilities of the teacher to undertake classroom activities with students. There, possibly more than elsewhere, we can also note limitations of formal authority in that teachers have to obtain the acceptance or the social authority of students and colleagues if they are to act effectively. At the same time, the position also illustrates the considerable variations between teachers in the extent of formal authority with teachers in the elite schools studied by Cookson and Persell (1985) having considerable autonomy while teachers in more traditional or authoritarian societies have very restricted authority and are required to teach particular content in specific ways.

A collection of officials comprising principals and their deputies, department heads, form level coordinators, house heads, specialist counsellors and advisers and others share responsibilities and authority for the operation of schools. Their number and diversity relate to the size, level and other characteristics of schools, while the extent of their authority relates more to the degree of centralization or localization in a system of schooling. Thus a principal of an autonomous school has ultimate responsibility for such key areas as the appointment of staff and determination of the program. Invariably, of course their authority is devolved from a school board or council in a limited term appointment but nonetheless their situation is an extreme contrast with a principal in a highly centralized, bureaucratic system of schooling. It is at this level, too, that realities of formal and informal or social authority can also be evident with some occupants of positions operating in markedly different ways from what formal allocations of authority indicate. These divergencies may reflect the unreality of formal regulations, and constitute necessary adjustments if an institution is to operate effectively. They may also mean that supervision in a centralized system is of limited effectiveness so that occupants of positions substantially determine their modes of operating. They may mean, too, that position holders act in inappropriate and possibly inadequate ways, and that others act to compensate or offset, and to ensure that the institution operates effectively.

Beyond the level of schools, managerial positions and their responsibilities and authority vary greatly in relation to the general system of administration in a particular society. Those arrangements also invariably reflect local circumstances, an understanding of which is helpful in the understanding of the system of management operating in a particular society.

The English system of arrangements has been intermediate between the decentralized and centralized models, with responsibilities for the operation of schools devolved to local educational authorities, and substantial authority devolved to school principals and their staffs. Within those arrangements, teachers have had considerable autonomy in classrooms, while the national ministry has been supportive financially and with advisory services, although sometimes directive as in determining whether selective or comprehensive types of schools are to be used at secondary level. Such arrangements have been held to constitute a partnership and to reflect a long and complex evolution in relationships between several major churches, and between them and the state and those in conjunction with local authorities. Throughout, however, the state has steadily increased its influence and currently is involved in a substantial transformation to achieve a more centrally directed system of schools, very much abandoning the partnership model which hitherto has been a salient feature of the management of schooling in England.

Sweden is an interesting contrast in that it reflects a Lutheran reformation tradition with early attempts to educate all children to a degree of literacy. Being more homogeneous in religious commitment, Sweden established the European practice of a dual system, but departed from that in the twentieth century under the influence of cooperative and socialist concerns. Subsequently it has moved far, by European standards, in developing a centralized but also open-type system of schools. More recent initiatives have been to devolve authority to counties and schools, and operate a more participatory style of school organization and management. Even so, the national Parliament retains control and takes major initiatives, as in the reorganization of tertiary education, the devolution of responsibilities to schools and counties, or in curriculum reforms.

As societies that evolved from colonial settlement, the US and Australia present some interesting contrasts. Settlement of Europeans in the US was often to escape from oppression in the home society, and to establish and maintain a preferred way of life in the 'new world'. A rich environment facilitated the establishment of separate and autonomous communities, and the setting up of local school systems. Pressures for central state control and direction emerged after nationhood was achieved and when substantial migration of non-English-speaking people raised concerns about unity and 'Balkanization', and the development of a more productive economy. With the constitution leaving responsibility for education to the states, federal influence was exercised in specific and sometimes ad hoc ways, such as the establishment of land grant colleges, the application of federal laws to restrict discrimination, the support of vocational education, and support for disadvantaged groups and communities. To the present, however, in the smallest systems of the US, a school principal can also have superintendent responsibilities. More generally, the district superintendent is a separate office with responsibilities more like those of an autonomous school principal, and also with the constraint of a limited term appointment. Nonetheless, in such cases much of the decision-making and the initiatives for strategies employed in the operation and management of schooling will be worked out at the district level and in conjunction with a board that relates to a local community or district. Beyond such systems, state and federal or national governments contribute support, guidelines, requirements and control in certain areas, as against discrimination against minorities, or in 'standards' of performance, and again through a set of complementary agencies.

The more arid physical environment of much of Australia required central support of exploration and occupation and in the establishment of social institutions. But once established, central agencies maintained and enhanced their dominance, aided by their capacity to redistribute resources and to enable poorer districts to obtain better facilities and programs than otherwise would have been the case. Again, as with Sweden

The Social Dynamics of Schooling

and other societies, centralization has proved restrictive and, in the more prosperous 1960s and early 1970s and again in the 1980s, steps have been taken to devolve responsibilities to regions and schools.

The more extreme cases of centralization are usually found in developing societies where authority to operate the system is clearly located at the top in national administrative units where decisions are made in respect to such matters as programs, staffing, the allocation of resources, the use of examinations, and the types of schools to be used. In addition, close control is exercised to ensure compliance with requirements so that the authority of teachers, principals and others is considerably constrained with competent people frustrated and even alienated in their positions. In each case, however, problems of economic and social development, national unity, and the maintenance of a particular political regime are important factors giving significance to centralized modes of operating. Singapore is an interesting example. As a British colony until after World War II, no attempt was made to establish universal education. A few public and missionary operated schools provided an English-speaking program to prepare some students for employment in the administrative workforce, while the Chinese were allowed to operate schools for their own children. Since independence, the Singapore government has built an impressive and comprehensive school system but tightly controlled and directed it from the centre to ensure that it produces a politically loyal population and a competent and industrious workforce, and sustains Singapore's reputation as an efficient and reliable producer in its niche in the world economy.

However, while local economic, political, religious and other factors have been of critical significance, giving rise to distinctive features in educational systems and their management, some common trends are observable. One is the increased significance given to schooling and, accompanying that, the increased involvement of national governments in the operation of school systems. A central concern among many working in or with schools has been to secure greater resources and the national government, with the nation as its source of resources, is an inevitable target of appeals for support. Only it can increase the level of support available in poorer states of regions. It also exercises influence, as exemplified in the US, through national laws as in its constitution. Again, national governments can enable schools to respond to special situations as was the case in the US when, following the Russian launching of Sputnik in 1957, substantial resources were invested in curriculum development to raise the scientific and technical competence of US students. Similar national initiatives were undertaken in other societies, usually in relation to curriculum development and implementation, but sometimes in support of research and other activities.

A second trend has been to extend the use of indirect controlling mechanisms, operated through complementary rather than mainstream structures. The examination of students' work and the training and later inspection of teachers at work are long established practices. More recent developments include curriculum development and implementation sections of departments, monitoring by testing samples of students, the counselling and guidance of students, the training of specialists other than teachers, the creation of career structures and the establishment of tribunals or other means of supervising appointments, promotions and other changes in positions, and control over the undertaking of research to determine what is identified as problematic and how a problem shall be considered and responded to. By such means staff at all levels, including the managers, can be steered or influenced to act in particular ways. Thus the process of management reaches beyond positions within the system to government and operatives in the more general administrative system of a society.

But even that portrayal of the management of schooling is not adequate to catch the full array of forces and arrangements that operate and which can facilitate, constrain or in other ways influence how schooling is undertaken. One set of forces is made up of other government departments which allocate resources or exercise responsibilities in relation to health, law and order, industrial conditions and relations, buildings and facilities, or other matters that impinge on the undertaking of schooling. A second set of publicly operated organizations has been established at the supra- or international level as, for example, with the industrialized societies setting up the Organization for Economic Cooperation and Development (OECD) and including a section within it to work on educational issues and assist in policy development and implementation in the management of schooling. The World Bank is a comparable institution in some respects but used by industrially developed societies to exercise influence on poorer third and fourth world societies, and often on their educational policies. A further set of forces comprises the economy and the polity, together with cultural, religious and other systems of activity that depend on schooling for its work in economic, political, religious and other forms of socialization, and so have grounds for monitoring what goes on in schooling and even for influencing that activity to ensure that it is undertaken in ways that are compatible with their priorities and requirements. Of these, the economic sector is exceptionally significant, partly because it provides employment for school

The Social Dynamics of Schooling

leavers but partly because it involves the amassing of considerable resources that are deployed either directly through economic organizations and associations or indirectly through foundations, policy centres or 'think tanks' and other agencies, and which are the sources of insights, understandings and strategies for action that can have fundamental influences on the undertaking and management of schooling. Finally, account needs to be taken of a diverse array of academics, intellectuals, theorists, researchers, inventors, artists and others whose work can profoundly influence perceptions and interpretations, the identification of problems and the selection of courses of action, and capacities and competencies in the undertaking of tasks, and so bear upon how schooling is perceived, understood, undertaken and managed.

Collectively, these participants and arrangements involve important agents and mechanisms for the exercise of influence on the undertaking and management of schooling and need to be seen in relation to those processes. They are distinctive in that they exist and operate 'outside' the formal systems of schooling, although they are often able to obtain positions within the system by gaining appointments on curriculum or examination boards, school councils or other management agencies. In any case, their considerable resources and capacities often mean they are able to exercise substantial influence on how schooling is undertaken and so they can usefully be identified as involved in the steering of the schooling process.

Outcomes of Structuring Schooling

The pervasiveness and persistence of structuring to differentiate between students testify to the importance given it in the operation of schools. In some cases, as with schools of commitment, the situation is readily understandable as reflecting straightforward aspirations and commitments to a particular way of life. Others, such as streaming and schools differentiated on the basis of prior performance, or which make notable claims in the production of leaders, are much more socially significant issues, particularly given the possibility of damaging or negative consequences. Not surprisingly, then, they have attracted the attention of researchers who have produced a considerable literature on those topics. Although most of the research has been undertaken in only a few societies, it probably speaks for a wider range of situations. I propose to undertake this examination of the consequences of structuring by examining research on some selected issues, namely streaming or tracking within schools, and such differentiated types of schools as by commitment, selective and residual or comprehensive schools, and single sex and coeducational schools. Because of the mixed findings emerging from much of that research, attention will also be given to some studies of individual schools, elite schools and to a recently developed interest in the possibility of schools being made more effective.

Streaming attracted attention in the 1950s and 1960s in particular but continues to be the topic of an occasional study, but invariably with only modest and even mixed findings. A striking feature of the research is the variation in the significance of the findings in relation to the type of research undertaken. For example, two early ethnographic studies, one of a modern school by Hargreaves (1967) and the other of a grammar school by Lacey (1970), showed dramatic consequences and identified streaming as a major polarizing feature in the operation of each school. Lacey's findings are particularly significant in that they relate to a grammar school population where every child was successful at the 11+ examination. Four years later, however, the lower stream 4Ds were notorious for their anti-school behaviour and even rebelliousness. Again, Ball (1981) noted the different outcomes of homogeneous and heterogeneous groupings in that the former was associated with control problems but reintroduced to facilitate teaching in more structured subjects such as French and mathematics. Again, in a sophisticated and sensitive study of a variety of data from twenty-five schools Oakes (1985) reported substantial consequences with streaming disadvantaging less effective students in particular and offering only slight gains for more effective students. In contrast, in a meta-analysis of fifty-one studies, where findings were reported on measured outcomes, Kulick and Kulick (1982) found streaming was slightly more effective in thirty-six cases, and more clearly so where special programs had been taken for 'gifted and talented' students. But generally gains were slight and not by less able students.

One study that bridged the more measurement-oriented and ethnographic polarity was of primary schools by Barker Lunn (1970). She employed survey, observational and interview techniques and found important consequences followed from how teachers thought students should be organized, which could be independent of school policies. But while streaming was of negligible importance in achieving gains, it was associated with deterioration of performance among lower class children. In another wide ranging review of different kinds of research, Gregory (1984) noted the inconclusiveness of findings, observed that streaming practices had been used in harmful ways, and concluded in favour of the more flexible system of setting. Alongside those studies, one by Nachmias (1980) of streaming in a kibbutz is of particular interest in that he argued that the consequences of streaming relate to the extent of stratification in the community beyond the school; in the more egalitarian kibbutz, social effects of streaming did not emerge and may have operated more as a form of setting.

The more ethnographic studies are especially valuable in that they indicate something of the context of streaming and also of its dynamics. Thus Lacey and Hargreaves showed that being in a particular stream was also related to the qualities of teachers assigned to the class, resources available for teaching, type of program undertaken, provision for extra-curricular activities and status within the school. Thus lower stream students were treated as of lesser status and discriminated against, which gave rise to resentment and even rebellion. Their studies, together with those of Oakes (1985) and others, are also helpful in portraying the different subcultures that emerge, and in setting out the dynamics of the situations studied. One can with some confidence agree with Gregory (1984), on the basis of his review of US literature, that a form of setting would be a better type of structure if size of class and limited resources serve to make a degree of differentiation necessary. As he noted, too, one of the most disturbing findings is that teachers of lower performing students adjust their expectations, thereby setting a downwardly-oriented interaction process in motion.

Although groups have operated enculturating schools for many centuries, they have only recently been subjected to research attention. Indeed, the study by Greeley and Rossi (1965) of Catholic schooling in the US was a major development and stimulated several comparable studies. Repeated findings were that members of a particular faith did better on relatively lower level factual knowledge specific to the particular religion but were indistinguishable in terms of more general and basic political and social views and beliefs. Such findings prompted Wilson (1965) to argue that particular religious values become modified by more general social values, an interpretation that is consistent with, for example, the tendency of Catholics to employ birth control techniques to limit family size, more like Protestants, and move into a wider range of occupations, including entrepreneurial ones normally associated with Protestants. While the findings have not led to the abandonment of church sponsored schooling, they may be associated with the drift of members of religious orders out of teaching and the increasing laicization of such schools.

Casual observation has often led people to believe that attendance at particular schools is associated with differential outcomes. Certainly, numerous accounts identify the exceptional achievements of graduates of particular schools, and take them as demonstrating the effectiveness of those schools. On closer examination, however, it invariably turns out that such schools attract high performing students, have more effective teachers, and muster exceptional resources. What emerges quite clearly is that they are centres of concentrations of exceptionally favourable circumstances and of privileges. In particular, it is likely that their exceptional students would do well in most types of situations.

More systematic attempts to establish the relative effectiveness of schools have to deal with some very difficult problems. One major problem entails establishing the comparability of students at entry, so that school effects may be observed, or at least forms of statistical analysis employed that enable differences to be allowed for. Another is in establishing that differential achievements do indeed follow from the activities of the particular schools. When such issues are taken into account, studies invariably report mixed results or only slight differences between one type of school and another in their achievements with comparable students. Again findings appear to be related to the type of approach employed. More quantitative studies tend to report slight differences between different types of schools in their achievements. Thus in a major study Coleman and others (1966) found that differences between students explained the differences in outcomes. In a further analysis of data from that and other studies, Jencks and others (1972) came to similar conclusions and consolidated the belief that schools have little bearing on the achievements of students and 'do not matter' other than, perhaps, to have good students. Again, Coleman and others (1982), in a study of the performance of students in private and public schools, found the former to be more effective; however, other analyses of their data (e.g. Willms, 1987) have shown differences to be relatively minor. In addition, Coleman and his colleagues neglected to establish the comparability of their student populations. In another recent study, using data from the National Child Development study of a population born in a week in March 1958, Steedman (1983) found only slight benefits for those children who went to selective schools in comparison with children who were comparable in certain respects and went to comprehensives. But again, because the qualities of the schools attended were not examined, such differences could have followed from particular qualitative differences between schools rather than the particular type of school attended. Using data from the same study, Kerckhoff (1986) examined performance on reading and mathematics and found streaming tended to exacerbate the differences between high and low performers, and more so among boys than girls.

When we turn from these to more naturalistic studies of specific schools such as the ones by Cookson and Persell (1985) and McNeil (1986), we obtain fuller perceptions of the realities of different situations, and realize how unsound and unfair are the common comparisons. However, we can also identify distinctive contributions where they differ markedly as in creating a sense of specialness or superiority, or in establishing personal and group associations. Above all, such studies illustrate the significance of differences in resources and the operation of some schools as centres of advantage or of disadvantage. But perhaps a most significant illustration of the relevance of resources is from studies of schools in publicly operated centralized systems. While Connell and others (1982) presented a situation that was close to the stereotype for such schools, Hatton (1985) portrayed another state school where parents constituted a powerful force in determining the operation of the school. An important point is that the centralized administrative structure generated to manage schools can be countered by effective parents who then operate to influence the experiences of students in schools and become a structural factor in the operation of schooling and in determining the experiences of students.

A further type of structuring that has been closely examined is by gender. Coeducational schools have had wide and considerable appeal as more 'natural', and for providing more scope for heterosexual social development. A multiplicity of studies have shown, however, that they provide but another opportunity for dominance to be assserted (e.g. Spender and Sarah (eds), 1980; Kelly (ed.), 1981). In addition to general patterns, such as of male-oriented curricula, practices in coeducational schools that explicitly favour boys in relation to girls include teacher-student interaction, styles of acting towards students as in relation to laboratory or other equipment that perpetuate stereotypes in sex identities and roles, or by boys using situations to assert their dominance. From such examples it is evident that, as with comprehensive schools, it is just not sufficient to group students in particular ways; the pressures of forces for differentiation and stratification are far wider and more pervasive than the institutions of schooling and if they are to be checked or overcome, then powerful efforts are needed from those operating schools intended to counter those forces.

A relatively recent trend has involved studies of the dynamics of schools and of factors that may be associated with the effective operation of schools. Rutter and colleagues (1979) stimulated considerable interest by finding that the general ethos, together with specific factors such as strong leadership, positive teacher expectations and firm guidelines for student participation, were associated with differential performance. Again, Reynolds and Sullivan (1979) in a study of working-class schools in Wales found they could be distinguished according to whether they employed 'coercive' or 'incorporative' strategies; the former were more conflict-ridden and authoritarian, with antagonisms and rebelliousness and poor performances from students, while students in the latter schools were drawn into cooperative relationships, indicated more positive attitudes, and expressed those in better performances. Basic or fundamental were certain attitudes and styles of operating that could be associated with effective or ineffective schools. Most recently, in a comprehensive and detailed analysis of some London primary schools, Mortimore and others (1988) reported a further mass of factors associated with effective performance, consolidating the conclusion that certain characteristics and strategies enhance the effectiveness of schools.

In another recent study of fourteen US schools working with 'at risk' students, Wehlage and colleagues (1989) found effectiveness related to a school's success in establishing a supportive community, matching program to need, and thereby achieving student membership in the school community and engaging them in learning activity. As is often the case with studies of schools dealing with special populations, the findings identify practices that would be beneficial for all students and not only reduce the incidence of problems with the special population with which they deal.

In a recent review of a substantial body of research and other literature on effective schools, Stedman (1985) concluded that there can be no doubt concerning the capacity of schools to be effective. However, he also cautioned that that is usually within the terms of concerns with testable objectives which set a limited and restricted program as a framework. At the same time, he noted reports of schools stimulating students with broader and challenging programs, indicating that they could be effective in diverse ways. For schools to be successful in these latter ways, however, demands much more in teacher competencies, curriculum material and other resources, and appropriate styles of management.

The topic of effective schools has been complicated and vitiated by its general social and particularly political appeal. It is attractive to politicians and administrators, and has been used to justify the allocation of increased resources, particularly in the US. It is thus a convenient mechanism by which to direct schooling in that the criteria selected for identifying effectiveness are crucial to subsequent decision-making and so a mechanism for steering the efforts of teachers, students and administrators. Cases reported in the media suggest that any school can be made more effective; however, these cases usually involve a special infusion of resources of one kind or another, and particularly of staff. The requirements for achieving a more effective *system* of schools would be considerable and not within the resources, as typically deployed, of most managers or their governments. Typically, too, concentration on effective schools focuses attention on specific units and neglects alternatives such as increasing the effectiveness of students or of developing a more effective system of institutions.

One can reasonably conclude that research evidence does not give strong support to certain commonly used structural arrangements. Indeed, one can argue that it provides some very powerful arguments against them. Given that uncertainty, and even reasons for caution, an important question concerns why such arrangements are persisted with. Clearly reasons differ from case to case, but include a variety such as ideology, convenience for particular groups, and a degree of optimism that they can be made to work more effectively.

Streaming or tracking appears to be convenient for some teachers, parents and students. It is clearly attractive to more effective performers, and their parents and teachers, offering higher self-esteem and separation from disruptive students. Homogeneous groups can also be easier to teach, working more at a particular level and pace. However, such advantages relate to particular sets of circumstances such as the number of students in a class and the adequacy of resources in relation to the range of abilities; for example, multiple copies of a single text is a force for homogeneous grouping, while heterogeneity requires diverse material that students can work through, largely self-directed, as in some good reading scheme packages. That is, teachers' preferences can be related in part at least to the conditions under which they work. And if those conditions mean that children of a wide range of abilities can work effectively in a heterogeneous class, then some of the objections of some students and their parents would diminish if not disappear.

The persistence with some types of schools can also be readily understood and accepted. For example, a particular religion or denomination can plan to use its schools more effectively. It can also expect that benefits are achieved apart from those identified by researchers, such as bringing youth together and fostering intra-community relationships, including possibly the selection of marital partners at a later date. Such schools may also serve as mechanisms for promoting church programs, causes or activities, and thereby facilitate and sustain the operation of the community, at least on a day-by-day basis. There is also the possibility of unexpected benefits such as providing a network of institutions with daily contact with members of its community.

Single sex and coeducational schools are of particular interest in this respect, and a range of attitudes supports the continued operation of different types of schools. A more self-serving one is where a family sends daughters to a girls' school and sons to coeducational schools, seeking the benefits of both for themselves, but at some cost to the daughters of other families. Some continue with coeducational schools for daughters despite the costs, holding that benefits can be obtained, and the schools have to be operated more effectively as coeducational institutions.

Similar arguments are made for comprehensive schools. Research findings of differentiation and discrimination, usually on the basis of class and gender, and ethnicity where minority groups are present, are taken as indicating initial variety, and grounds for making them more effective. Thus, in both coeducational and comprehensive schools, the belief in bringing diverse children together, and the promotion of communities, is strong, and the discordant evidence can serve to increase efforts to make the experiment work more effectively.

The continuance of other types of schools, particularly those that entail some kind of arbitrary or dubious selection, is also not difficult to understand. As with streamed classes, selective schools can be more congenial for some parents, teachers and students, and give a basis for favourable self-concepts and higher status, together with separation from 'undesirable' students. But beyond that, and most important, is the prospect of attracting better staff and other resources, and so becoming advantaged relative to others, and a step ahead in the competition for personal and group advancement and aggrandisement. It can also be noted that teachers in higher status selective schools have commonly resisted incorporation into common school systems, as with comprehensivization. Only in rare cases, as in Leicester, England, where modern schools were modified to become comprehensive junior secondary schools and grammar schools to become senior secondary schools (Holmes, 1973), are reforms undertaken in ways that enable all participants to gain, and so achieve widespread support. In respect of our initial concern, it is apparent that different types of schools persist because of benefits to particular sections of a community or society and notably their teachers, students and parents who are also usually more influential than their counterparts in other types of schools.

At the same time, these types of schools cannot be justified. They draw disproportionately on resources and operate at the expense of students elsewhere. Hence they are institutions of discrimination, not simply preservers or perpetuators of a particular community, but rather marshalling resources to achieve advantages relative to others.

Even less justifiable are the elite schools operated to ensure entry of their graduates into high status tertiary institutions and occupations. With these, the rhetoric is even more misleading for they usually frame their rationale in terms of preparing for leadership positions. But it is in terms of leaders who have no experience of those who will be followers, and who become leaders by circumstances, while others with appropriate attributes and potential are excluded by circumstances. Thus such schools constitute both unjust and inefficient arrangements. The limited nature of their commitments is also illustrated by their readiness to service whoever can afford to 'shop' in their sector of the market.

But to return to a major issue concerning reasons for the persistence of these types of school, a further factor in research methodology is almost certainly important. Many studies of streaming and differentiated types of schooling have used quantitative data and so been limited to what can be measured. As such, their data are more concrete aspects of situations which are often of less important phenomena. The more subtle and sophisticated aspects of schooling and advantageous experiences, together with the dynamics of their operations, require naturalistic-type studies, and in the past it has often been difficult to gain their acceptance in such institutions. Their special power is that they approach more closely to the experiences of people and thus to the realities experienced by parents, students and teachers, the first of whom are often prepared to pay considerable amounts for the schooling of their children. That is, research findings may so often be inconclusive because the research methodologies have been inappropriate for revealing the more subtle and significant factors that operate in those situations.

Discussion

Schooling can be conceptualized, examined and acted towards as a system of structures, involving primary, secondary and tertiary institutions, and operated and managed through a variety of management agencies. Moreover, each institution and agency has a degree of separateness and even autonomy and can be regarded as a distinct entity. Closer examination invariably reveals, however, that they are situations of intense and often contestational activity and, at the same time, bases for activity in relation to other entities. Invariably, such activity reflects class, ethnic, gender and other characteristics and concerns and is related to political, economic, religious and other social and cultural activities and developments. That is, each institution and agency is both an entity in itself and part of a substantial system of social entities and of networks of actions and interactions.

Management agencies have a special significance in that they are units through which control is exercised. At the same time, their establishment and operation reflect political and other situations and circumstances, giving uniqueness to each particular system of managerial arrangements. Even so, they invariably become the sites of similar contestations as individuals and groups contest for opportunities, advantages and benefits. They are also invariably the targets for outsiders who seek to influence the operation of educational institutions so that they accord more closely with the primary concerns of those outsiders.

These structures are, then, essentially constructed and operated entities that are situations of intense, extensive and complex activity that is reflected in constant changes and even transformations with outcomes related to the relative influence of particular groups of participants. Hence to consider them simply as structures is quite inadequate; greater understanding can be achieved by identifying the participants and their interests, noting their resources and capacity to exercise influence, and studying their efforts to influence the operation of these institutions and agencies. Such an approach needs to relate activities in educational situations to other interests and situations of action, such as the economy or the polity, and to relative power and a sense of justice if activity and developments are to be comprehensively understood.

One consequence of this approach is not simply to relate educational activity to contexts but to interrelate the two as parts of a more extensive and complex social reality. It thus becomes apparent that placing educational activity as central or primary is somewhat pre-Copernican in character. Such a relationship does not exist in reality but is rather a matter of convenience to enable observers and interpreters to concentrate their attention on a particular aspect of reality. They limit themselves, however, to the extent that they lose sight of the integral relationships between educational and other areas of activity.

The position explored in the remainder of this book seeks to avoid this limitation by focusing on participants in particular spheres of activity. Initially, this leads to the selection of particular sets of highly visible participants such as teachers, students and administrators. Subsequently, however, it leads to less visible but possibly more significant participants, identifiable as steerers. But these also include participants acting in other aspects of their lives in other sectors of activity but who in those capacities can have a substantial impact on the operation of schooling. That in turn draws attention to the complexities of human behaviour which, expressed in social activity, gives rise to inconsistencies and even contradictions in social arrangements and processes.

Chapter 3

The Student Experience

Students constitute the most numerous group involved in schooling but they are also weak in the exercise of influence, and might well be neglected if significance of influence is taken as a major criterion of inclusion for consideration. Their lack of influence is almost certainly due to their general immaturity and lack of political, organizational and other skills and competencies, together with their relative transitoriness in the schooling process. Indeed, their status and influence may be substantially responsible for their long neglect by researchers, with serious attention given to students only in the last fifteen years or so; for example, when Calvert (1975) examined the role of the student she found little research or other literature on which to draw. It is now evident that many researchers had also turned their attention to the experience of being a student and a substantial literature has subsequently emerged. In addition, important developments in broadening or modifying conceptions of socialization (e.g. Wentworth, 1980; Ogbu, 1982; Henriques and others, 1984; Musgrave, 1987), and in the development and application of perspectives for the study of school experience (e.g. Woods, 1983) have enabled researchers to focus more broadly and be more perceptive. Partly as a consequence, much more can now be said about studenting, or interpreted from circumstances associated with being a student.

At the same time, there is no disputing that students share certain interests and have the potential of constituting a significant group of participants. One interest of primary significance, and which identifies them as of a common category, is their individual personal development. Every student has the potential to develop physically, socially, intellectually, morally, artistically and in other ways, acquiring or developing knowledge, skills and competencies that enable them to express themselves and their concerns and to participate effectively in social situations and activities. Because that development is crucial to later experiences and achievement, it is vitally important to them as well as to the communities, organizations and other social entities in which they participate.

Unfortunately, the social situations in which students live and develop are often not conducive to recognizing these as common interests which might be pursued collectively. Rather, social arrangements are often constructed and operated in ways that provide limited opportunities to achieve development and so induce competition between students. Indeed, so vicious can that relationship become that students and more particularly their parents can see the development of others as incompatible with their own prospects of achievement and aggrandisement, and so feel a necessity to achieve conditions which, while favouring their own advancement, are incidentally disadvantaging to others. In that context, the circumstances from which children commence as students are then further exploited with those more advantaged in family and other social circumstances being further advantaged by school arrangements that correspondingly adversely affect their disadvantaged counterparts. That is, students may be more appropriately identified as a category because conditions of restricted opportunities and a competitive ethos operate to nullify prospects of becoming a cohesive entity, other than in relatively small sectional groups.

When one examines the school experience of students it is important to recognize that what schooling does, and the extent to which it achieves outcomes with students is embodied in the knowledge, skills and other forms of competencies, in the values, attitudes and orientations, and in the styles of acting that they take with them and employ in economic, political, cultural and other areas of social activity. Of course, the school is not the only contributor to those aspects of development, and indeed its specific contributions, as distinct from those of the family, peer group or media, are difficult to establish. Nonetheless, it is contributions towards those aspects of development that are relevant and which can be appraised through examining the experience of students.

It is also important to recognize that several facets of that experience must be examined if the appraisal is to be comprehensive or even adequate. For present purposes they are grouped broadly into two areas of discussion with one drawing upon studies of direct experience, including students' perceptions and interpretations of schooling, and a second entailing data on more visible outcomes such as attendance rates, together with measures of achievement within and beyond schooling. Relevant here also are reflections upon schooling, particularly when that is in the light of subsequent experience. In addition, such sets of data need to be examined in relation to groupings by social class, ethnicity, religion, rural or urban location, and gender, which are often the bases of differentiation and discrimination. It is from studies of relationships between background and post-school experience that insights can be obtained into the more general social role of schooling, and whether it is operating to reproduce or transform status and social relationships.

It is also useful to examine the background situations and circumstances from which children come to schooling. They are not simply *tabula rasa* to be acted upon but differ greatly in their capacity to handle the schooling process. This differential capacity derives in part from parents who also vary greatly in their capacity and readiness to act in relation to teachers and administrators, and to negotiate their children's entry into and movement through the schooling process. It also derives from students' differences in forms and levels of development, in their feelings about themselves and their prospects, and in the relevance of the school experience to them. Hence it is important to examine how schools deal with different types of students, and establish how those different types fare in the schooling process, and so how it bears upon their subsequent entry into other areas of social activity.

It must be emphasized, however, that most of the data are drawn from only a few societies, and from a limited range of situations within those societies. We are far from any general picture of schooling, and even limited for the particular societies that are better understood. Data from similar studies in other types of societies would add considerable complexity to our understanding of schooling and greatly increase the difficulty of generating generalizations about what goes on in schooling.

Situations and Circumstances

Socialization theories affirm the active nature of the learner from conception as a participant in socialization processes. The child is active in the sense of affecting others, influencing their undertaking of parenting, teaching and other responsibilities, and also in examining and interpreting reality and experience, and in developing a sense of self, of others, and of the nature of social reality and relationships. From the outset, the child can be seen to be an active participant, although not always consciously, in the construction of social reality and relationships. At the same time, a lack of expertise, competencies and other resources and elements of power means that children are invariably subordinate participants in social interaction and relationships. They are essentially dependent on the consideration or sense of justice in others.

Accordingly, they are also very much dependent on the situations and circumstances in which they develop. And as will be noted in the discussion of parenting in the next chapter, families vary greatly in their situations and circumstances and modes of operating so that children develop in different ways and to different degrees. Thus at one extreme are children such as those in elite boarding schools in the USA studied by Cookson and Persell (1985) whose parents were often discerning and effective in their efforts to promote their children's development, knowledgeable about institutions and their programs and modes of operating, and with the material, social, and personal resources to manage their effective participation through schooling in the opportunities in higher level institutions or in employment and other activities available beyond schooling. Such children are most advantaged in the parenting they receive and its contributions can offset limitations of a child's inherited attributes. At a considerable distance from them are children such as those studied by Essen and Wedge (1982) whose parents were beset with such concerns as unemployment and poverty, poor housing and other handicapping material circumstances, ill-health and poor personal relationships, and often uninformed concerning facilities and institutions and their programs and operations, or put off or down by the styles of those operating them, and who lacked the personal, social and material resources to assist their children achieve benefits from participating in those institutions and their programs. At the extreme in disadvantageous situations and circumstances are the children and youth considered by Cornia, Jolly and Stewart (eds) (1987), MacPherson (1987) and others, and who constitute a major indictment of contemporary political, economic and other social arrangements.

While the studies noted above enable us to understand the situations, circumstances and experiences of children in more extreme positions, it is important to recognize that they report but a 'tip of an iceberg' phenomenon in each case, and that many more children approximate them in favourable and unfavourable circumstances and prospects. Moreover, the mass of children do not constitute some homogeneous population but also vary greatly from each other, as comes out in any community study such as those by Hollingshead (1949), Seeley, Sim and Loosley (1956), Newson and Newson (1977) and others. As a consequence, children in virtually any community vary greatly both in the types and levels of development they achieve during pre-school years, and correspondingly are differentially able to take advantage of the programs and operations of schooling. Fortunately, as we shall see more fully later, children can be assisted to offset those disadvantages so that the overall situation offers promising prospects. However, the present reality is somewhat tragic in terms of prospects and what they might have been.

It is also important to recognize that the situations of families and their children can be exacerbated by their concentration in distinctive types of locations and even communities, often as a consequence of social policies. For example, housing, social welfare and other policies can mean that income is a major determinant of where one lives and so results in affluent and advantaged communities involving concentrations of families such as those reported on by Cookson and Persell (1985), together with concentrations of impoverished people with limited social, personal and material resources, and involving a high incidence of families experiencing the disadvantages identified by Essen and Wedge (1982). Such situations can exacerbate problems experienced by particular families and yield, for example, communities characterized by high rates of delinquency, truancy, drug addiction, vandalism, and other indications of frustration and abuse. Again, children growing up in such environments develop subcultures that substantially steer their perceptions and interpretations, including of schooling, and so substantially how they will act as students well before and increasingly during their period as students.

People and their children and the communities in which they live can be further advantaged or disadvantaged by the attitudes and subcultures that develop in other communities and sectors of societies, including public and private agencies, with respect to particular types of families and communities. Thus prosperous and otherwise advantaged communities can come to believe that their favourable situations and circumstances derive from their own efforts and constitute part of their personal and group achievements. Conversely, people in disadvantaged situations and circumstances can be seen as personally and collectively deficient or at fault, and so responsible for their own situations and circumstances, and therefore warranting harsh and punitive rather than sympathetic and supportive treatment. Such views and accompanying actions from more powerful groups can then be also expressed in social welfare, housing, health, schooling, policing and other policies and programs of action, in the media and elsewhere, as well as in more widespread and pervasive interpersonal relationships, and so generate hostile and aggressive responses in the disadvantaged sectors of a society. In such ways, children growing up in particular family situations and circumstances become part of and reflect a wider community situation and circumstances.

The situations of children are further complicated by the complex and dynamic schooling arrangements that confront them. As illustrated in the last chapter, schools vary in many ways that require considerable knowledgeableness and discerning judgment, together with attributes of social confidence and social sophistication in making judgments and choosing and pursuing particular courses of actions. For example, schools vary structurally, being public or private, selective or residual, single sex or coeducational, comprehensive or sectionalist. Moreover, these may be further differentiated in critical ways internally with streaming, setting, heterogeneous classes or the clustering of classes into family or other groups and each with different types of programs. They are also likely to differ qualitatively in terms of types of teachers employed, levels and kinds of resources and facilities. Finally, for present purposes of illustration, they can vary greatly in character, from more formal and regulated, more academic as against more practical or expressive, or socially-oriented in being more cooptive than directive or coercive. Ultimately, they differ culturally and socially as well as structurally and in terms of resources and with important implications for practice as Rutter and others (1979), Reynolds, Sullivan and Murgatroyd (1987), Mortimore and others (1988) and others have shown. Thus schools can be more or less effective in general terms but also more or less appropriate for particular kinds of children.

Invariably, social factors operate to ensure that children are distributed systematically by social criteria through the different types of schools and the different sectors within them. In turn, that student population comes to constitute part of the attributes of a school and part of the culture-making process, accentuating characters and reputations, modes of operating and styles which then serve as indicators and involve patterns of practice which serve to consolidate characteristics, patterns and styles, and consolidate firm links between schools and particular communities. Studies such as those by Anyon (1981) and Ramsey and others (1983) illustrate that these variations are likely to be greater in locally operated or market-oriented situations than in centralized systems, although intervention in either mode of operating can change those practices. That is, either system can be operated to reduce or enhance advantages and disadvantages for particular groups of children; how they are operated depends very much on the strength of commitments to social justice or to the sectionalist pursuit of advantage regardless of consequences for others.

Nonetheless, the reality is that schools typically vary greatly and that those variations relate to the situations and circumstances of the parents and communities they serve. Accordingly, children's prospects are substantially determined early in their lives by the situations and circumstances they experience, and by the necessity to make meaningful responses to those situations and circumstances, and in terms of their understanding of social realities and capacities to exercise influence on their patterns and prospects of achievement. Those prospects are then exacerbated by the school conditions that they encounter, as they find their way or are steered through particular tracks or institutions within the schooling system.

It is also important to bear in mind that parenting and studenting and the operation of schooling take place within more substantial and extensive social situations. These entail the more extensive class, ethnic, religious, locational and other groupings, and the political, economic and other sectors of social activity which are major aspects of any particular situation and at the same time affected by more fundamental social realities and trends. Thus currently, for example, political and economic priorities reflect efforts to develop a world economy where major corporations in particular can operate freely and internationally and not be restricted by conditions or modes of operating established in any particular society. It is a period of a process that favours corporations in giving them considerable freedom to choose where and how they operate, and to bargain one society or its workforce against another. As many governments work with these to develop the political structures compatible or even supportive of such modes of operating, economic values are promoted vigorously so that schooling is presented increasingly in terms of its relevance to the production process. That means an emphasis is on work-related aspects while more general social, political, cultural and other aspects of development are neglected. Of course, political values, attitudes and competencies are not ignored or neglected; they are rather included covertly in what is more the hidden curriculum of schooling. Those values are, however, the differentiating of students in terms of their relevance to the productive process. Of course, as is usually the case, more affluent parents who can afford to send their children to more educationally-oriented schools are able to avoid the narrowness that is often being imposed on publicly operated schools.

The Experience of Schooling

Early efforts to portray classroom life, as by Waller (1932) and Jackson (1968), established its richness and complexities, its diversity and subtleties, and the variety of modes of acting associated with classroom activity, together with the triteness and mundaneness of so much of what goes on in classrooms. An abundance of subsequent research (e.g. Woods, 1983; Goodlad, 1983) provides considerable detail on teacher and student interactions and programs, and the rituals, strategies and other aspects of school life. Out of that abundance and diversity of information certain features emerge as of considerable significance and these are the focus of this discussion.

The Social Dynamics of Schooling

A common pattern to the experience, at least in industrialized societies, is for children and youth to spend some ten to twelve years at school, working and learning with teachers, and from associating with other children. As such, it is generally not an exciting experience although conscientious and supportive teachers and administrators can mean it is pleasant and satisfying, at least for more effective students.

Children typically begin with pre-school or primary-type classes and class teachers, and experience relative stability in relationships and patterns of activity. Indeed, junior arrangements are often especially adapted to receive children who, on entering schooling, are quite diverse and even idiosyncratic in personal styles, and begin their secondary socialization into the roles of students and the more formal and uniform relationships of schooling. This stage of schooling is a major case of organizational accommodation, undertaken to provide a more congenial inductive environment.

Thereafter, students are increasingly subject to the operation of formal organizational procedures. Located in classes, they move forward each year, with the same set of students, and taught by generalist teachers at the primary level and with transition to secondary schooling usually meaning more subject or content-oriented programs taught by specialists, each with his or her own style, often using specialized rooms and other facilities, and sometimes, as with setting, changes in class membership from one period to another. Relationships are increasingly specialized, often impersonal and even transitory, although cliques and groups emerge and endure. So, too, do routines, rules, rituals and other cultural elements of acting in ongoing situations. Teaching styles also remain stable with predominant modes involving teacher-centred transmission, and relatively passive students responding to teachers' requirements.

These observations become more meaningful when we examine school experience more closely, and it is useful to begin with the experience of commencing schooling. While studies of that aspect are few, derive from only a few societies, and deal with only a few aspects, nonetheless some noteworthy features are evident from them and, together with evidence from the subsequent experience of schooling, testify to the reality and pervasiveness of those features.

One study that is most illuminative of the commencing experience, although perceived through mothers' eyes, is the one by Newson and Newson (1977) of 7-year-olds at school. They reported that children's reactions varied greatly from enthusiastic to most reluctant attendance and were related to teachers' personalities or styles, to social characteristics of parents and their parenting styles, and often to several such factors in combination. Clearly, too, social class related to parents' willingness and capacity to negotiate with school staff concerning problems experienced by their children. The Newsons also provided evidence to indicate differences by gender, with girls more likely to like school, score higher on home-school concordance measures, be better readers, and generally cope more positively with teachers and schooling.

Working more directly, Rist (1973) observed children's experiences in a classroom in a 'deprived' and 'difficult' school in a largely Black section of a mid-west US city from their first day at school. He noted not only the differences among children in their circumstances and characteristics, but also the teacher's different reactions to them by perceived social class backgrounds; within eight days the teacher had organized the children into three groups, ostensibly on an assessed capacity to cope with schooling but incidentally in relation to social background (Ch. 2). The practice of differentiating and ranking is also documented by Sharp and Green (1975) in their observation of three progressive teachers in a progressive school where such practices would have been seen as unacceptable. It is evident again in a report by Nash (1973) that children in a grade one class knew their teacher's ranking of their work. The processes are taken further by structural arrangements involving different types of schools whereby children are segregated and concentrated by religious or secular commitments, or by socio-economic circumstances and cultural styles, and become different kinds of students.

The processes of differentiation, categorization and differential treatment emerge as fundamental features of school life. Often they are institutionalized, as with streaming and different types of schools, particularly at the secondary level. Studies of such situations also show differential evaluations of students, with those who are more successful also receiving more adequately resourced facilities and programs, more effective teachers and other more favourable treatments, and having higher self-regard and aspirations. A further consequence is the emergence of student subcultures through which they interpret their experience, generate responses, and in general achieve support systems for handling the situations they confront. Thus out of differential experiences children become different types of students, although at the same time reflect both different social background circumstances and different organizational and processual aspects of schooling.

The processes are well illustrated in a study by Anyon (1981) of five schools in New Jersey, USA. Her data showed systematic differences among schools in relation to social characteristics of students and their families with schools differing in plant and facilities, staff, programs, teaching resources and strategies, and expected learning outcomes. For example, teachers in the working-class schools emphasized the 'mechanical following of procedures' while those in a middle-class school highlighted 'right answers', those in an affluent professional school sought 'creative independent work' and those in an executive elite school aimed to develop 'analytical intellectual patterns'.

Such patterns, found in many studies (e.g. Hargreaves, 1967; Lacey, 1970; Ball, 1981; Oakes, 1985), testify to significant qualitative differences among the arrangements made for different streams, tracks or programs, and which are highlighted in studies of more extreme cases. Thus in the study by Cookson and Persell (1985) of elite boarding schools in the US, students who came from predominantly professional and executive families and well-resourced homes experienced carefully planned programs designed to maximize prospects of college entry, together with rich complementations of art, craft and other electives that prepared them socially and culturally for higher status positions. In addition, they were taught by very competent teachers, with exceptionally abundant and high quality resources. At the other extreme are inner city slum and ghetto schools, such as the working-class school studied by Anyon (1981), and some rural schools that are characterized by poor facilities and resources and ineffective teachers and administrators. Of course, such variations are likely to be greater in the 'market' style of provision in the US than in centralized systems such as New Zealand, where Ramsey and others (1983) found differences in provision and experiences among working-class schools, but related the differences to the relative effectiveness of schools. Correspondingly, the range in resources and possibly in effectiveness is likely to be much greater again when we consider a wider range of societies.

A second basis for differentiation and discriminatory treatment is gender, and Delamont (1983: Chs 2, 3, 4) is helpful in summarizing findings from many studies of ways in which girls and boys are treated differently in schools. She reported that they are often separated on the rolls, and by their seating, play and other space allocations, in the kind and even quality of facilities available to them, and in the self-concepts they are encouraged to develop through teacher practices or pedagogic examples or illustrations. She also provided an abundance of examples in which teachers used positive and negative references to attribute gender characteristics as devices for controlling children's behaviour. Not surprisingly, although not necessarily directly because of teachers' actions, girls are commonly found to behave differently in school, and to have different patterns of performance, doing better than boys in subjects such as language and life sciences, and less well in others such as the physical sciences and mathematics. Sutherland (1981) neatly extends our understanding with a discussion of the relevance of sex to the schooling process in many societies. Thus she documented the universality of differential treatment and of the social construction of gender types. Her further point that education should be of the person as an individual 'according to the abilities and interests of the individual' (p. 223), rather than by stereotype categories, is a useful one to keep in mind throughout this discussion.

Schools often differ again in the arrangements they make and the treatments they provide for children of different ethnic groups. For example, in the study by Anyon (1981), Blacks comprised a substantial proportion of the students in the working-class schools, but were not present in the elite executive school. While that may largely reflect class factors, more significance must be given to repeated observations of 'lower' levels of ability, a higher incidence of assignment to special classes for children with 'learning difficulties', and other discriminating and disadvantaging practices for ethnic minority children (e.g. Tomlinson, 1982: Ch. 7). It must also be recognized, however, as was noted earlier, that in some cases, as with East Asian children in the US and elsewhere, ethnicity is associated with high achievement. Even so, that does not disprove the practice of differentiation and discrimination; it may essentially mean that students from such societies are better able to handle such practices, or even attract positive discrimination. Again, studies of private schools illustrate that foreign and female students are welcomed when local applications decline (Cookson and Persell, 1985: 50–63; Walford, 1986: 150–6).

It is relevant to note that ethnicity is also a universal basis for differentiation and discrimination. Indeed, it is often the case that discrimination is worse, even to the extent of non-provision or exclusion, in more traditional societies, reflecting strong beliefs in differential qualities of groups of people. Again, ethnicity is often linked with class so that higher and lower status groups are different ethnically, with corresponding greater degress of discrimination and even exploitation. Or again, as Ogbu (1982) argued, ethnic groups can be established into a set of castes so that their range of responses is restricted to what is acceptable to more powerful participants from a dominant caste.

In varying systematically, and providing different experiences and prospects for different types of students, schools illustrate their power and capacity to require accommodation by students. Nonetheless, students are able to react, and a wealth of literature documents forms of reaction. Indeed, Willis (1977), Apple (1980–81), Anyon (1983) and others have found it useful to employ the concept of 'resistance' to indicate the many ways in which students express their reactions and disagreements. Even so, their reactions very much reflect the structuring and patterned operation of schools as is evident, for example, in that student subcultures take on characteristics of the arrangements into which they are steered. Thus they become the 'A' or 'D' classes as in the studies by Hargreaves (1967), Lacey (1970) and others, or 'bright' and 'thick' (Turner, 1983) so that those who reach senior classes hold perceptions, views and attitudes that substantially reflect their 'success' or 'failure' with school work, and so positive to negative views of schooling. Significantly, however, in a study of a comprehensive school, Ball (1981) found that polarization diminished with the operation of mixed ability classes where students were easier to manage, thereby highlighting the significance of structural arrangements. Resistance is also present but more subdued or perhaps more subtly expressed in privately operated schools (e.g. Walford, 1986: Ch. 3). In general, however, groups emerge within schools, with their associated subcultures and shared perceptions and interpretations that influence students' actions and reactions.

Several researchers (Gannaway, 1976; Nash, 1976; Woods, 1979) have established students' perceptions of teachers and produced substantially similar findings. Commonly, significance is given to teachers being 'human' in that they are sensitive to students' feelings and perceptions, and can vary from good humoured to more serious styles of acting. Firmness, fairness and consistency are also emphasized, illustrating that students expect to work and resent teachers who cannot teach them or who allow other students to disrupt the program of work. Werthman (1963) illustrated the importance given to firm expectations, and the emergence of working rules by which students appraise the reasonableness of teachers' expectations and evaluations. From such studies it is evident that students learn 'the ways' of schooling and then expect them to be maintained. Inconsistency in a teacher or among teachers can then be disruptive to modes of operating and so give occasion for concern and even protestations. Even though Davies (1982) showed that children have a considerable capacity to adapt to different styles and expectations among teachers, they nonetheless appreciate consistency from a particular teacher.

Students' experiences similarly influence or determine their views of other students. The more effective students become critical of those who are less effective, and often disruptive, and see them as 'thick' or 'dossers', while the former are seen by the latter as 'swots', 'creeps' or 'ear 'oles' (Woods, 1983: 81). Out of school influences, more paricularly from class and ethnic backgrounds, carry over to schools, influencing boys' perceptions of girls and sustaining sexual abuse or promoting ethnic antagonisms and conflicts. Similarly, class also links with performance, with working-class children and youth more often performing less effectively, and so coming to make up the counter-school cultural groups. Thus participation in schooling and reactions to its processes reflect the structuring of society more generally, and bear upon the prospects of different kinds of students within that society.

Woods (1983: 91) sought systematically to analyze students' perceptions and views, and produced a complex array of positions. Using an approach adapted from Merton, he posited variations in positions on the basis of attitudes of indifference, indulgence, identification and ambivalence, and rejection, with or without replacement to school ends and means. Thus indifference to both ends and means was held to be associated with retreatism, while identification with both produced compliance. Similarly, rejection of both without displacement also gave rise to retreatism, while rejection with displacement meant rebelliousness. Further, Woods (p. 92) saw these different reactions in something of an evolutionary relationship with optimistic compliance and opportunism occurring in junior secondary forms, and retreatism, intransigence, rebellion, instrumental compliance and ritualism occurring in senior forms. He associated those reactions to class and gender attributes, upholding the differentiating and even biased character of schooling (pp. 84–9).

Davies (1984), reviewing data on a group of 'difficult' fifth form girls and the school they attended, suggested that roots of the reactions lie in basic aspects of interpersonal relations and, in so doing, offered what is probably a more authentic interactionist interpretation. More specifically, she suggested that students 'who are denied dignity, humanity, a recognisable "specialness" to themselves and others, will resort to power confrontations to restore a feeling of presence and avenge indignity' (p. 127). It is noteworthy that the girls were hurt and even alienated by shortcomings and inconsistencies of some teachers, and responded positively to more sensitive and consistent teachers. Her conclusion resonates with evidence from many studies of the impersonalness and even uncaring attitudes and ethos experienced in schools. This would also seem to be more compatible with the position of Turner (1983) who critically appraised the subculture and adaptation models used by Woods and others, and argued the importance of students' goals and interests, and the contexts in which they interact. This position also holds students to be quite variable in their styles of acting. At the same time, the structuring of schooling is still seen to be a dominant force.

Finally, Woods (1983: 163–73) and others have found it useful to consider students' experiences in terms of careers. Obvious features are the transitions, as from one class to another, from primary to secondary and later to senior status and, for some, to tertiary institutions. A further

The Social Dynamics of Schooling

dimension arises with horizontal differentiation where students are grouped or streamed into different kinds of schools and so channelled to different careers and other prospects. Thus in a study of transition from a middle to a comprehensive school, Measor and Woods (1984) identified issues such as initial anxieties and subsequent settling in, and changes in identities and relationships as students were sorted out academically and socially in their first year. Other studies have documented the traumatic experience of streaming within schools (Hargreaves, 1967; Lacey, 1970; Ball, 1981; Oakes, 1985) and differentiation into types of schools (Cookson and Persell, 1985; Fox, 1985), and so demonstrated the profound and pervasive effects on careers of those organizational practices. These features illustrate the intractable realities to which students are obliged to accommodate but do not necessarily accept.

A significant contribution of the interactionist perspective with which Woods and others have worked has been to facilitate recognition of the active part played by students in classroom and school activities. Thus strategies and negotiation emerge as key concepts for comprehending the efforts of students in classrooms. Correspondingly, Woods (1983: 122) identified some dozen strategies, including working, have a laugh, making a noise, being friendly, making threats or offering bribery as techniques for dealing with classroom situations. Similarly, considerable effort is given to eliciting what teachers mean by their requirements, what they will accept as work or behaviour, and what constitutes positive and negative sanctions. A special case is their approach to new teachers who are usually given a probationary period during which they are assessed for their humaneness, competence, firmness or weakness, partly as a preliminary to contestations with them (e.g. Ball, 1980; Measor and Woods, 1984).

This discussion of findings from classroom research highlights several common themes, including a preoccupation with establishing order and control and managing classroom activity, and beyond that with establishing students as differential performers, and categorizing and treating them in terms of such categories. Practices present in all levels, types and aspects of school experience testify to the preoccupation with differentiating between students and ranking them in relation to each other. Much has been made of the differential and even discriminatory treatment of particular groups of students, as on the basis of class, ethnicity and gender, but it has been common to consider each in isolation. However, it is important to see them as parts of more extensive systems of differentiation and discrimination, operating not only within schooling but also in the workplace and in other social situations. That is, differentiation and discrimination are more extensive than sexism, racism

The Student Experience

or classism, and also operate on other bases within groups that are homogeneous in those terms. Hence, to segregate students into schools of particular types, as for single sex or a particular class or ethnic group, will not remove differentiation and discrimination but only change the basis on which they operate.

For such reasons, schools can be identified as primarily concerned with establishing status rather than achieving development. Why that is the case is the concern of much of the discussion that follows in the remainder of this book. Before moving on to that discussion, however, we will continue the examination of the experience of schooling one step further and examine outcomes of the schooling experience.

Outcomes

The second section in this examination of the experience of studenting involves the examination of outcomes, and several means can be used to assess the contributions of schooling. A straightforward one is to report on how long youth stay at school, or their attendance patterns. A second is to identify levels of performance which yield something of a qualitative indicator, although such indicators reflect the priorities of schools, and can neglect other important aspects of development or achievement. A further source is the evaluations of schooling by former students, gathered in surveys or by other means. Finally, some assessment of the social role of schooling and its implications for students is possible by identifying how its achievements with particular categories of students relate to the requirements of other sectors of society, such as the workforce. Collectively, these provide a useful basis for appraising outcomes of the student experience. It is also the case that data on participation and performance are available on regional and even world bases, and so some comments can be made about the experiences of schooling on a much wider basis than has been possible hitherto.

Probably little more than a few general comments can usefully be made about attendance patterns. One is that the proportions of age cohorts invariably reduce at higher age levels. In more industrially developed societies, compulsory attendance until early or mid-adolescence is usually a reality, but even in those societies subsequent patterns vary greatly. In the US, for example, some 60 per cent of an age cohort enter tertiary or higher education, whereas in other industrialized societies the proportion is around 20 to 30 per cent (OECD, 1985a: 17). Similarly, Coombs (1985: 100) presented data for 1980 that show that the proportion of 12 to 17 year age groups enrolled at any level in 1980 was 96 per

The Social Dynamics of Schooling

cent for North America, 79 for Europe but only 32 per cent for South Asia. These variations derive from many factors but principally from economic circumstances in particular societies.

A second observation is that attendance rates at higher levels have increased substantially in recent decades. Again, the US was relatively early in achieving high attendance patterns at the 12 to 17 age groups, with some 92 per cent in educational institutions in 1960. In contrast, at that time only 19 per cent attended in South Asia so that the modest figure of 32 per cent in 1980 is still an increase of nearly 70 per cent (Coombs, 1985: 100). Interestingly, at present attendance at higher levels is increasing rapidly as governments induce students to stay at school or as youth continue with schooling, either to improve prospects, avoid unemployment, or for other reasons.

The tapering nature of attendance patterns is an interesting phenomenon in itself, relating firstly to levels of performance at schooling, and beyond that to assumptions that programs should be of increasing difficulty so that fewer children are able to cope at higher levels, particularly within the time periods available to students. That situation contrasts markedly with more developmental orientations where progress is regarded in individual rather than comparative terms, with students working at their own rates to achieve personally meaningful goals or levels of attainment. Thus the tapered nature of attendance patterns reflects a particular ideology, expressed in a form of program where schooling is essentially a sifting and sorting process. It also gives meaning to the differentiating and ranking preoccupations evident in classroom activities.

A second indicator of schooling outcomes is in the levels of attainment achieved by students. Common measures are those used to establish secondary graduation, obtain a diploma or a degree, or more advanced qualification. Understandably, the proportion of youth obtaining higher qualifications has also risen markedly in recent decades (e.g. OECD, 1984: 134–6). Indeed, increased resources were put into the expansion and development of educational systems, largely on the basis of assumptions that more highly qualified people would contribute significantly to economic growth and productivity. More recently, policies have been changed to favour more vocational or technically-oriented education, reflecting assumptions that such programs contribute more to efficiency and productivity. Correspondingly, there is sometimes also a depressing influence being exercised at higher levels of educational systems to encourage higher achieving students to undertake lower level technical programs and also avoid social science, humanities and other less 'practical' and incidentally more socially insightful programs.

Increases in the proportion of youth achieving particular levels of qualifications somewhat parallel and indeed interact with attendance patterns. For example, levels at which qualifications are awarded can be a major determinant of attendance patterns. They also reflect uses made of qualifications which sometimes have little relationship with the uses intended for them, as when employers use a particular qualification to screen applicants and arrive at a small number from whom to search for prospective employees, thus creating what Dore (1976) identified as the 'diploma disease'. In such ways, qualifications can lose their credentialling values as they serve the sifting and sorting process in more sophisticated ways. Even so, it is evident that education systems have been substantially expanded in recent decades, and students' experiences of schooling have been substantially extended, leading many to opportunities they would not have encountered previously, largely reflecting a period of economic growth.

A third basis for appraising the school experience is from the assessments of former students. With these it is important to recognize that they will have had a variety of experiences and achieved varying degrees of success. They will also have had varying experiences in their post-school lives that in turn could have given rise to differing appraisals of schooling. Commonly expressed critical comments relate to the unfriendly and uncaring nature of schooling, and particularly of its teachers, and the inadequacies and inappropriateness of much of its curriculum (e.g. Collins and Hughes, 1982; Finn, 1984: 24–7). As so often is the case, such curricula are seen to be overly academic and biased towards the preparation of high achieving students for higher education; however, even those students saw them as instrumental rather than in satisfying terms. Given that such curricula lead to higher status opportunities, many students felt bound to pursue them but none or at most few valued them in their own right. In consequence, they were both unsatisfactory in themselves and also a major obstacle to the introduction of more satisfactory programs.

Dissatisfaction with schooling is a widespread phenomenon, and nowhere more strongly expressed than with some of the former students of elite schools, usually evident from autobiographical statements. However, while many see their school experiences as painful and even damaging, many also recall them with warmth and enthusiasm (e.g. Fraser (ed.), 1977). Again, students in the elite US boarding schools studied by Cookson and Persell (1985) varied greatly in their reactions with some becoming lifelong supporters and sending their children to them in turn, and others being painfully damaged, and ending associations (Chs 7, 8).

A fourth means of assessing the schooling experience is by examining relationships between performance in schooling and elsewhere, as on entry to workforce. As has been noted, attendance at schooling has a tapering pattern, in part reflecting forms of increasing difficulty or incompatibility of programs for some students, and also relating to differential requirements in the workforce. Thus successful completion of secondary schooling is commonly necessary for entry to tertiary education and to professional, administrative and other higher status occupations. Often, too, institutions at both secondary and tertiary levels are specialized and offer programs that relate to particular sectors of the workforce, and so form avenues for entry to those sectors. Conversely, less effective students usually find occupations at lower status levels in the workforce or, increasingly with the recent more difficult economic circumstances, become unemployed.

This overall correspondence between levels of schooling achieved and entry to the workforce and other sectors in society has been taken to indicate that schooling operates essentially as a reproductive mechanism, sifting and sorting children to produce a graded output for entry into a stratified workforce. Differential location of schools within any overall system supports a further refinement of this interpretation to establish schools as differentially related to the workforce, and society more generally, thereby supporting assumptions that certain schools are better than others as avenues of achievement and for access to opportunities to enter higher level and more attractive situations, or to exclusion from achievement and opportunity.

It is important, however, to take the discussion at least one step further and consider social background of students. Then, as has previously been noted, we see that achievements in schooling are invariably related to social background. Again, social background is also a significant factor for entry to particular types of schools so that the achievements of particular schools are not nearly so clearly related to their efforts with students as to the characteristics and circumstances of the students they enrol. Indeed, efforts to establish the significance of school attended have been notably unsuccessful, once allowance is made for type of student enrolled and the quality of staff, resources and practices available in a school (e.g., Jencks and others, 1972; Steedman, 1983; Fox, 1985: 57–60). What is much more clearly the case is that some schools are centres of advantage and privilege, while others are centres of poverty-stricken circumstances and disadvantage, so that schooling commonly exacerbates differences among children in their prospects for achievement and access to opportunity.

Taking the issue one step further, research findings show considerable stability over time between groups in their achievements and access to opportunities, which is somewhat surprising, given that economies grew and prospered greatly in the 1950s, 1960s and early 1970s, and that workforces grew, particularly in the higher level occupational categories. Nonetheless, Halsey, Heath and Ridge (1980, 1984) in a study of social background and school achievements of boys over several decades in England, and Garnier and Raffalovich (1984) in a study of social background and school certification in France, again over several decades, found little change in the relative achievements of groups. Indeed, in a further examination of the Oxford data, Heath and Ridge (1983) found that youth from the higher status service class were even more successful than working-class youth in achieving higher level statuses in the recent more prosperous times than they were during the depressed years of the 1920s and 1930s. Again, Radford (1962) and Radford and Wilkes (1975) studied relationships between social background and post-school destination in Australia and found little change in a time of considerable economic prosperity when opportunities for social mobility were considerable. Still again, Anderson and Vervoorn (1983), in a review of Australian studies at the tertiary level, found that elite groups dominated entry to universities and even to particular, more advantageous departments and faculties over the post-war years. Studies in Western Europe reveal similar patterns and even report that the slight gains achieved by poorer youth in the 1960s and 1970s are being reduced in the difficult economic circumstances of the 1980s (OECD, 1985a: 40–2). Finally, in reviews of US research Collins (1979: Ch. 2) and Hurn (1985: 96–100) found similar patterns of stability in relations among groups over time in their use of schooling in relation to social mobility.

In part, that trend may reflect greater uncertainty about the worthwhileness of investing time, energy, ability and other resources in furthering one's education but in part, too, it reflects recent changes in government policies which have sometimes reduced the support available to poorer students (Hunt, 1988: 44–5, 89). These findings also illustrate the point argued by Levin (1978) that relativities did not change but rather the sifting and sorting process occurred later in the system of education as more youth stayed on longer in educational institutions.

Thus we come to the conclusion that the general system of schooling exhibits considerable continuity in its modes of operating, despite substantial changes in opportunities and aspirations, and in structural arrangements and processes. These patterns are relevant to issues regarding schooling as an agency of reproduction or transformation, to which we will return later in this book. For the present, it is useful to review briefly some possible reasons for the character of students' experiences of schooling and the continuities in those experiences.

Discussion

Children develop along different lines or in different ways and to different extents in any particular respect, and so are characterized by diversity in their attributes and levels or degrees of development. Their experiences and prospects are complicated further by the different situations and circumstances in which they grow up which may vary from most favourable to very unfavourable for personal development. As a consequence, children arrive at school in various stages of readiness or aptitude to derive benefits from schooling and its programs and modes of operating. At the same time, schools are relatively ineffective at offsetting or compensating for limited or disadvantageous experiences and circumstances; if anything, they are structured to favour the already advantaged. In addition, by highlighting performance on particular dimensions of experience, and by giving differences precise expression, schooling can be said to translate more or less intangible forms of development into defined and comparable statements of achievement. That is, schooling is not a process of remedying situations and circumstances but more one of institutionalizing and possibly even exacerbating initial differences and relationships. As a consequence, outcomes are largely a consequence of initial circumstances and so are largely predictable from such a basis.

Given the surprising stability in patterns of achievement over time, despite changing social and economic circumstances, and despite efforts to change those patterns and achieve higher performance from disadvantaged children and youth, it is useful to consider briefly possible explanations of that outcome, although more attention will be given to that issue later in this volume.

One possibility is that society is already well 'sorted out', with people having found their appropriate 'levels', so that children simply follow their parents into comparable statuses and levels in society. While some find that an acceptable interpretation, it ignores the considerable evidence of differential and even discriminating treatment that assists in perpetuating the status quo.

These indications of discrimination have been argued to support a second conclusion that schooling is invariably conservative and even repressive as an institution, and linked with impersonal structures and mechanistic modes of operating. However, the soundness of such interpretations can be challenged for inadequate and even unsound social and psychological assumptions.

Hence we come to a third possibility, namely that parents and their children differ greatly in their capacities to obtain benefits from schooling, and that more socially astute and competent parents are more effective in managing the schooling process and steering their children through it to achieve the best results and gain access to more attractive opportunities. At the same time, less sophisticated parents and their children are not helped by the complex structuring of many school systems which makes it difficult for them and their children to make the best decisions when negotiating critical points in the schooling process.

The importance of sound interpretations is reinforced by the necessity to understand why programs such as those of the 1960s and 1970s that were designed to improve opportunities for disadvantaged children and youth have been largely ineffective. We will be able to comment on those issues more substantially later in this book but here a few points may be made.

One is to note that commitment to those policies has been questioned. Gray (1981) and Mortimore and Blackstone (1982: Ch. 6) observed that policies developed to increase opportunities and achievements for disadvantaged children and youth were not energetically or diligently pursued. That is, the rhetoric was not matched by effort and other resources, nor by commitment to ensure that resources were effectively employed.

A second possibility, following a point made earlier, is that more able parents have been successful in devising counter-strategies or in subverting such policies to ensure that their children continued to do well, and have greater access to opportunities. Thus the parents studied by Fox (1985: 141–64) were in part reacting against changes made in the public sector of schools and sought to achieve a comparative advantage by sending their children to privately operated schools.

A third possibility is that efforts have been misdirected and could have been more effectively directed at parents and children from disadvantaged circumstances from their earliest years.

We have noted in studies of children commencing schooling that those from working-class backgrounds are often seen as less effective students and so treated in ways that lead to lower level streams and earlier leaving and, these days, to unemployment. In contrast, elite occupations continue to draw their recruits from universities and other elite institutions which in turn recruit from advantageously circumstanced families. The continuity between social circumstances, performance at school, and levels of entry into the workforce and other sectors of society raises the possibility that rather than concentrate solely or even primarily on establishing the effectiveness of schools, as Rutter and others (1979), Reynolds (ed.) (1985), Mortimore and others (1988) and others have argued, effort and resources might be directed at producing more effective parents and students. Encouragingly, while efforts to influence early child development, as in the early stages of some major programs such as Headstart in the US War on Poverty in the 1960s and early 1970s, were found to be of limited value, some recent projects have found that early help for children has been effective (Consortium for Longitudinal Studies, 1983; Berrueta-Clement and others, 1984; Hechinger (ed.), 1986).

For such reasons, responses in the form of programs for unemployed youth may be largely misplaced and ineffective or at best a stop-gap policy. To the extent that there is continuity in situations and circumstances, achievements in schooling, and post-school prospects, with the problems beginning prior to entry to schooling, it is evident that responsive action should be undertaken at much earlier points in children's lives.

A major irony is that the operation of schooling is very much contrary to the often proclaimed goals for schooling. Terms such as 'development of the individual' or of the 'whole person' generally have reality or meaning for only a few students. In consequence, such terms have to be seen as part of the rhetoric associated with schooling and not to be taken literally. At the same time, they must not be treated lightly or disregarded. The probability is that they are convenient for disguising the realities of schooling. That is, the central tasks in schooling are actually quite different from what is commonly proclaimed. For such reasons it is now time to extend our examination of schooling to consider other participants and the ways in which they influence the operation of schooling. A most useful starting point is to examine more closely the activities of parents who clearly are a major influence on the ways schools operate, either because of what some do or because of what others are unable to do.

Chapter 4

Parenting

The process of parenting, whereby people produce children, assume parental responsibilities, undertake parental tasks, and experience parental fulfilment and satisfaction, is a complex one with profound ramifications at several levels of meaning. In some respects reproduction is almost an inevitable process as people follow their biological predispositions. For individual parents, reproduction can mean provision of future helpers in obtaining a livelihood or support in declining years or, with developments in technology and social arrangements, be a form of expression and realization of their own development through the creation of another life with comparable prospects. For a social entity, be that a band, tribe, community or society, a new member assures continuity of a social unit larger than one's self and family, and the preservation of the group's traditions and ways of living. Beyond that, as we have recently come more fully to realize, begetting children has meaning in terms of overall population, balance between species, demands on the environment, and prospects for the world of which we are part.

The process of parenting has given rise universally to the family as the social unit for the procreation and rearing of children. The particular forms vary and may be extended or nuclear, single parent or blended family, or even part of a communal group where parenting and other responsibilities are shared among many adults and even older children. Again, parents operate in many different situations, varying in cultural, religious, economic and other ways that bear upon the significance given to children and how parenting is undertaken. Parents vary too in their skills and competencies, in their values, aspirations and expectations, and the material and social resources they draw upon in parenting, whether the tasks are undertaken directly by parents or indirectly by managing arrangements with other agencies such as schools.

In consequence, the experiences of children vary greatly from one situation to another. Childhood, taking that to include infancy and adolescence, can vary from a relatively brief to an extended period, be limited by prescriptive requirements or challenged by open expectations and supported to achieve full and extensive personal development and achievement, take place in natural contexts where the laws of nature are dominant or in substantially humanly constructed situations that are to a considerable extent arbitrary and so changeable, fostering a sense of the power of humans acting individually or collectively. Moreover, these variations are often patterned relative to particular social, cultural, economic and other circumstances and personal attributes such as those noted above. In consequence again, children's prospects are often substantially predetermined by the situations and associated circumstances in which they grow up, as was illustrated in the last chapter.

That prospect, together with the limiting and sometimes negative effects of particular styles of parenting, are part of the justification for establishing schools and systems of education. External intervention is necessary if the limitations of particular practices are to be offset. A major problem, however, is that gains by hitherto poor performers may be at the expense of and possibly constitute threats to hitherto higher achievers. Such students and their families invariably resist changes in the patterns of benefitting from schooling and may well act to nullify efforts to transform patterns of achievement through schooling strategies. For those and other reasons schooling has not been very effective as an agency for offsetting initial disadvantages.

These concerns and issues reflect in turn another, namely that of the rights of children. The social reality of rights is reflected in their affirmation by many governments and by international agencies such as the United Nations, although their breaching in practice testifies to the hollowness of some of those affirmations. A second issue involves the subject of those rights; a common disposition is to entrust children to parents and regard them as responsible for their upbringing, including the choosing of schooling and other agencies offering developmental experiences. At the same time, it is not necessarily the case that parents have or should have the right to determine finally their children's development. Given a dynamic for development inherent to children, the right is not simply among parents, schools and other institutions and organizations; the child is also entitled to participate actively in the growing up process.

In the discussion of parenting, two aspects in particular will be attended to. First, I will consider the situations and circumstances of parents as these bear upon the rearing of children. Second, I will consider differences between parents and their strategies and practices in relation to the operation of schooling. In particular, concern is with the part of parents in relation to the schooling experiences of children. Curiously, although of fundamental importance to the operation and understanding of schooling, the contributions of parents have long been seriously neglected. Educational researchers have tended to take account of aspects of families and parenting styles, mainly as correlative factors, but ignored the dynamics of family activity in relation to the development of children and the operation of schooling. Fortunately, some recent studies and discussions (e.g. Eastman, 1989) are remedying that neglect.

The Social Production of Children

Concepts such as parenting, the social production of children, and becoming a child refer to a multitude of situations, circumstances and practices, and an extensive range of outcomes. Correspondingly, an understanding of the processes and outcomes involved requires examination of a wide range of situations, including studies of the development of children in different contemporary societies, in specific societies over time, and in different sectors of a society at a particular time. Fortunately, considerable study has been made of parenting and child development in those different situations and I have drawn upon that work elsewhere to present an overview of practices, and derive some implications (Hunt, 1979–80). Here a few points will be made essentially to indicate some of the differences in the circumstances and practices of parents and the situations from which children undertake schooling.

Differences in the circumstances and practices of parents are probably most readily evident from anthropological studies of different contemporary societies and from historical studies of particular societies over time. For example, the volume edited by Whiting (1963) brought together a set of systematically planned and undertaken studies of child upbringing in markedly different societies. Points of particular interest include similarities across societies as with periods of infancy and early childhood, together with differences such as initiation into adult status by 9 or 10 years of age in one society, and development through a several year period of adolescence in another. Another major difference is between child-centred parenting through to youth and even early adulthood in some more affluent societies, and others where an infant is given considerable attention to one point of time and largely neglected shortly later, as with the arrival of another baby in the family.

Such studies as these, however, typically focus on established and relatively stable communities which, although diverse, exclude the situations and circumstances of groups affected by special and often traumatic events that are outcomes of the workings of natural and social forces. For example, a significant and possibly increasing proportion of the world's population lives in circumstances that vary from precarious to destitute. While the worst of these are in third world societies, relative poverty is increasing in many industrialized societies with consequent influences on parenting and the prospects for children. Often these sectors of populations are not so well known so that discussion based on researched situations is inevitably partial and inadequate, neglecting the most disadvantaged groups of people and their children.

With regard to practices within particular societies, de Mause (1974) indicated marked changes over time in Western European societies with, for example, early modes involving infanticide and abandonment and a child-oriented approach being a relatively recent phenomenon. Again, Stone (1977), examining family life in England from 1500 to 1800, illustrated the diversity of practices employed by different groups of people at a particular period, ranging from 'negligent aristocracy' to 'indifferent and exploitative poor' to 'child-oriented, affectionate and permissive upper bourgeoisie and squirearchy' (Ch. 9).

Differences between classes within contemporary societies in child-rearing practices have been of considerable interest to sociologists and psychologists, although not so much of late as formerly. In a review of US research, Hess (1970) reported differences between children by social background in their self-concepts and esteem, personality and mental health, patterns of interpersonal behaviour, educational and occupational aspirations and achievement orientations, language and communication, and political learning, with middle-class children experiencing more favourable developmental treatment, at least in certain respects, than working-class children. Again, from their English research Newson and Newson (1963: 217) observed that within the first month of life babies were adapting to a climate of experience that varied according to a family's social class. In a later discussion Newson and Newson (1970: 145–50) identified middle-class parents as being more future-oriented, more protective and sheltering of their children, employing and cultivating more kinds of communicative skills, using more democratic and reasoning forms of control and being more child-centred. Those of course are general patterns and even greater variations are evident between more extreme groups such as the advantageously circumstanced children studied by Cookson and Persell (1985: Ch. 3) in US elite boarding schools and the children with multiple social disadvantages studied by Essen and Wedge (1982: Ch. 5). In the latter situation, children grew up in circumstances of poverty, poor housing and diet, ill-health and other disadvantaging conditions that meant they were ill-equipped to cope with problems and take advantage of opportunities associated with schooling. In contrast, children in the former category came from wealthy families, generally of professional and executive occupations, with considerable material and cultural resources, high expectations of their children, and considerable capacity to steer their children through complex and sophisticated educational arrangements and processes.

These differences between families translate into differences in the developmental experiences they provide for their children. Again, Newson and Newson (1976) are helpful in documenting practices of parents and illustrating differences between them by social circumstances. In general, middle-class parents have more resources, employ more developmental or educative patterns of interaction, and are more likely to extend the developmental experiences of their children by drawing upon institutions and programs offered beyond the home. In contrast, as has been noted, children from poorly resourced homes and other disadvantaging circumstances can be limited in some aspects of their development, low in self-esteem and restricted in the development of social skills and competencies.

Largely crossing class lines are variations within families in the ways they treat particular categories of children. Of these, treatment by gender has received considerable attention and in a review of British and North American studies, Delamont (1983: 12–20) offered a wealth of examples of differences in the treatment of boys and girls in the home, citing the use of names, the types of toys and games, of books and comics that they are encouraged to use, and the expectations parents have, and the responses they give to children by sex. Not surprisingly, Newson and Newson (1976) found that differences between the sexes were quite marked by 7 years of age whereas only class had been relevant earlier. At the same time, they noted that the differences may have been more apparent because of the greater autonomy or latitude that older children experienced. In any case, boys were less chaperoned, had greater freedom to go out and away from home, were less imaginative in their play, and more likely to enjoy 'rough and tumble' games. Boys were also more likely to fight with siblings and other children, and more difficult to control and discipline, and more likely to be given corporal punishment. It does not follow, however, that these derive from innate traits or dispositions; indeed, researchers have found it extremely difficult to establish such differences between boys and girls (e.g. Maccoby and Jacklin, 1974; Archer and Lloyd, 1982; Hargreaves and McColly (eds), 1986). In consequence, at least a substantial part of such differences must be attributed to child-rearing practices, and prevailing patterns of expectations and sanctions. In any case, boys and girls bring different skills, competencies and attitudes to schooling and act differently in respect of it.

Another factor of significance in parenting is ethnicity. In many respects different practices are essentially alternative ways of acting in the rearing of children and so some are neither superior nor inferior to others. In other cases, however, they may be related to the economic and other social circumstances of particular ethnic groups such as peasant or industrial communities and reflect class as much as cultural influences. In still other cases, some particular cultures are clearly discriminating in the status accorded particular categories such as women or other ethnic groups, or people of particular religious affiliations, and so more limiting in the scope they allow for personal and social development of those people.

Interesting insights into those practices are yielded by the practices of children of migrants as they take advantage of opportunities to select attractive features from the different cultures available to them. The widespreadness of concerns with human rights as in the women's movement or concerns for minority groups also generates more criticisms of styles in some cultures than others, and gives rise to concern to achieve reforms in such societies.

Religion is another force operating to influence parenting styles and children's prospects. Of course, in commenting on the implications of religious doctrines the problems of assessing the defensibility of religious beliefs and practices is at least as difficult as dealing with cultural positions. At the same time, relativism is no more defensible in respect of religion than it is with culture so that features can be appraised and commented upon. Thus it is evident that religions vary in the scope and character of development possible for particular categories of members; some, for example, are particularly restrictive on females, subordinating them to males; others are comparably restrictive on members of particular ethnic groups with colour a specific criterion for according lower status and restricted rights. Some limit the scope for development of the rationality and free enquiry that have been particularly associated with Western European societies. Accordingly, parents acting within those doctrines vary considerably in what they see as appropriate or desirable, and so in the scope they make available for their children. At the same time, some members' positions are comparably characterized with benefits and limitations involving anomie, alienation and aimlessness, and so offering little or nothing that is positive as a guide to children.

Less well explored but real too are locational differences as between families in urban and rural locations. Again, however, other factors such as class operate in those situations and complicate the identification of essentially rural as against urban characteristics. Again, too, differences may be essentially alternatives and not necessarily superior nor inferior to each other. The main advantages and disadvantages probably derive more from the greater concentration of power and opportunities in urban areas. Thus while rural communities can have more direct experience of nature, sophisticated types of cultural developments are associated with cities. Again, large organizations that are such a feature of twentieth century life are more directly experienced in urban than in rural locations. Still again, the experience of moving from one set of associations to another is much more readily available in cities than in villages where people are likely to know each other in diffuse, extensive and comprehensive rather than specific ways. So while rural locations can have many attractive features, they can be seen as having shortcomings in terms of many of the features that are salient in late twentieth century societies, with their rapidly advancing social and mechanical technology. Obviously, these differences are greater between some urban and rural localities than others, while there may also be important differences in the experiences and opportunities available to particular groups of people within each type of community.

Still another type of situation is provided by the different types of families that are increasingly common. The prototypes of extended and nuclear are complemented increasingly by single parent, blended and other family arrangements. There are no inevitable disadvantages or advantages with one or another of these types although the probabilities of difficulties tend to be greater. Thus one parent families entail division of material and other resources and so tend to be poorer and characterized by the problems associated with fewer resources. Again, blended families can require more adjustments among members and also entail obligations to members of other family units, thereby complicating patterns of relationships and responsibilities. Clearly, too, parents and children differ in how they handle these situations and achieve benefits rather than disadvantages for the children involved in social situations.

From these differing sets of parents, with their differing situations, circumstances and problems, and different social and cultural understandings and competencies, several important implications arise, but three in particular are emphasized here. One entails the sets of cultural elements available to parents; these vary from relatively simple and unsophisticated to complex and rich, from rigid to flexible, from principled to opportunistic, from compassionate and universal to sectionalist and restrictive and possibly exploitative. A second relates to the circumstances of parents and is expressed in variations in the personal, social and material resources on which they can draw in fostering the development of their children and so means differences in the capacities of parents to act on their children's behalf. As a consequence, schooling as a social process is much more manageable for some than it is for others. That is, children approach schooling from vastly different circumstances and vary greatly in their capacity to benefit from it.

At the same time, that differential capacity at least partially reflects the dominance of particular styles of operating both in everyday life and in social and mechanical technology, while qualities of the cultural styles of subordinate working-class, ethnic and other groups are not so expressed. Hence an important distinction to be made is between inadequacies of particular types of families, communities and other social entities in relation to prevailing or general styles of operating in contrast with adequacy in fostering the development of particular aspects of children's development.

Those points lead on to a further and most important observation that emerges from a wide ranging review of childhood and associated parenting and upbringing practices and relates to a question raised initially about the *reality* of childhood. It is most apparent, for example, that in many situations scope for development is severely limited. At the same time, while some situations appear to provide substantial scope, it cannot be assumed that they are adequate or appropriate for achieving full development. For example, while the work of Piaget and others encourages conceptions of stages of development, that work does not provide a basis for concluding that even in the most favourable circumstances all stages have been identified, let alone realized. More generally, it cannot be assumed that even the wide range of social circumstances that exists is adequate or appropriate to facilitate the full realization or achievement of human attributes and potentialities. In other words, children whom we encounter in schools and elsewhere, as with people generally, must be seen as related in their development to the situations and circumstances they have experienced. Correspondingly, it has also to be accepted that under other circumstances they may have developed differently, possibly substantially and fundamentally so. And, as has been argued earlier, it is that prospect which provides a basis for critically appraising the situations, arrangements and processes of families and schooling, together with the more substantial and fundamental processes of undertaking production of goods and services, and the governance of a society for their positive and negative influences on personal and societal development and achievement.

In an early interpretive review of mostly class-oriented research, Bronfenbrenner (1958) noted the many differences between middle- and working-class parents in their upbringing styles, and argued that the former 'led' the latter in being more developmental. Subsequently, Kohn

(1963, 1977) argued that parents derive their parenting styles from perceptions of their children's circumstances and prospects, and so prepare them for the 'worlds' they expect them to encounter. That is, middle-class parental styles reflect experiences of sharing responsibilities and participation in decision-making at work, and so negotiation and explanation with their children have meaning and rationality. In contrast, working-class parents, experiencing direction and subordination at work, see little point in discussion, explanation and negotiation, and so are more authoritarian in their parenting styles.

Such relationships between parenting styles and contexts were further evident in a wide ranging review of historical and contemporary studies of child upbringing (Hunt, 1979–80), giving meaning to practices generally within groups, and with different categories of children as by gender. More recently, Ogbu (1982) has generalized these observations and proposed a cultural ecological framework that posits that parents' strategies with their children relate to the social, political and economic realities in adult life. At the same time, it is important to recognize that the worlds in which people live, work, rear children and undertake other activities are not structurally or mechanistically determined and beyond influence but rather are socially constructed and can be reconstructed and need to be seen to be reconstructable if parental practices are to change. That is, if parents' actions in respect of the upbringing of their children are to be more developmental, then it appears to be necessary that the reality confronting parents be seen in such ways that opportunities and prospects for children have plausibility and feasibility. Obviously that is a very substantial undertaking and requires extended political and other action, and widespread public understanding and support. Such understanding and support are essential because the pursuit of opportunities and prospects for children occurs in something of a zero sum state, with advantages for some meaning a degree of disadvantage for others, and efforts at redistribution requiring a yielding of advantages by the advantaged. The competition becomes exaggerated when different groups of parents and children become segregated, as within different types of schools, and add institutional force to personal efforts in the pursuit of advantage and the achievement of superior opportunities and rewards.

These observations reflect the intimate link between parenting and the structuring and operation of societies. It is apparent that parenting is very much socially determined, with some parents holding substantial competencies and resources, and able to act in ways they determine, while others, with severely limited resources, are subject to forces operating upon them, including the consequences of the action of other people. Hence it follows that major changes in parenting that are to benefit all children could require changes in the structuring and operation of societies, and in the ways people act on their own behalfs, and in respect of each other. Correspondingly, efforts that involve changes in means, or which are essentially instrumental in nature, appear bound to be relatively ineffective where parents do not see such means as relevant or significant for them and their children. Similarly, where means such as systems of schooling are established for parents, it is essential, given different competencies in using institutions, that they are structured as openly and as simply as possible, both to facilitate understanding and to avoid structured obstructions to the progression of children through schooling.

Parents and Schooling

An examination of the situations in which parenting is undertaken establishes considerable differences among parents in personal, social and material resources and correspondingly in their capacities to foster the development of their children. While the differences are not inevitable, nonetheless they are largely the consequence of the economic, political, social and other circumstances and conditions which parents confront and their experiences in dealing with them. One consequence of significance here is that children at the age for attending schooling vary greatly both qualitatively or by levels, and by type of development. Thus some are well developed socially, physically and personally, in their understanding of concepts, their curiosity and ability to work cooperatively and interact with adults such as teachers, while others can be limited in all those respects or even have developed negative styles of acting. For their part, junior sections of primary schools are often operated flexibly to accommodate a diversity of individual styles and begin the process of socializing children into being students. However, there are limits to such flexibility and some children will be 'difficult' for teachers and schools. While this can still reflect on the relative rigidity or unadaptability of the school at a particular time, nonetheless schools have the superior position and the adjustment of the child to schools is required. From the outset then, teachers collectively relate to a diverse population in the children commencing schooling, some of whom are at a considerable advantage, while others are at a disadvantage due to how their parents have or have not acted in respect of them.

Beyond that point, however, parents continue to be important influences and their actions in relation to their children's schooling can take many forms. They can vary from little or none to substantial and from passive or even negative to active and determinative. Moreover, the different modes of acting relate to social class and other attributes and so to the contributions they make to children's development before and concurrently outside schooling (e.g. Brantlinger, 1985; Lareau, 1987). For such reasons, when schooling is insensitive or neutral in relation to the social circumstances of children, it operates to perpetuate and even exacerbate differences among them in their development.

In their study of Australian schools, Connell and others (1982) noted that the school experiences of some parents had been particularly painful and embarrassing. They had been poor learners and for that and other reasons harshly treated by teachers. Indeed, their experience of several types of institutions had been unpleasant so that some sought to develop a protective cocoon around their family life, shielding themselves and their children from further painful experiences. And these, in many respects, were more fortunate parents, people who had met congenial partners and been able to establish satisfying family life arrangements. Others who continued to experience unpleasant relationships within family and other situations offered little or nothing in the way of support and encouragement to their children, and may even have been counterproductive.

But even these more fortunate parents recalled schooling with pain and embarrassment, and had great difficulty in approaching or interacting with teachers, principals and others associated with the operation of schooling. They could be encouraging and supportive socially and emotionally, but sceptical and even distrustful of what school people were about. They and others also often had difficulties in understanding what schooling was about, some finding that curriculum content, particularly in certain subjects, was 'getting beyond them' so that they could not help their children through problems with school work. For them too, the system of institutional arrangements, with its complex assortment of schools, curriculum content and options, and examination hurdles, was not readily comprehensible so that they did not appreciate the implications of performances and decisions of particular points in their children's careers through schooling.

Parents vary greatly in these respects and it is useful to identify some who appear to be greatly disadvantaged in managing their children's schooling. They include the small but significant proportion of parents who remained in circumstances of deprivation, suffering unemployment and poverty, poor housing, bad health, unstable relationships and other handicapping circumstances throughout the years covered in the study by Essen and Wedge (1982) of children born in England in a week in 1958. They would appear to include, too, the families reported by Liffman (1978) in a study of people in poverty in Melbourne, Australia, and whose life styles were characterized by unemployment and poverty, frequent changes in housing, and unstable family relationships with, as one consequence, frequent changes in the schools that their children attended. Migrants such as the 'guest workers' of Europe or their equivalents in other societies, often coming from rural situations and bringing little or no understanding of urban-industrial society systems of arrangements, together with problems of language, and perhaps even being minimally literate and numerate in their own culture, could also be in this general category. Others include indigenous populations in colonized societies who have not been able to learn the ways of that society, but live as outsiders in what is essentially their own homeland.

While it is not difficult to identify disadvantaged groups, it is important to recognize important differences and special forms of disadvantage for some. Thus migrants can have the special problems arising from unfamiliarity with a culture, the major language and institutionalized ways of operating. Poorer people in rural areas can experience isolation or remoteness from facilities in addition to limited understanding of what is entailed in school work and in the operation of educational arrangements. Indigenous people can have their social arrangements and relationships as well as their cultural ways and traditions shattered and made irrelevant and lack the support of a community and the formulae of a culture for enabling them to respond to problematic situations. For one-parent families the responsibilities of managing a family can mean limited capacity to participate in schooling activities and arrangements. In addition, schooling as it has been or can be experienced, may have little relevance to the life patterns which particular groups experience. They can also have little experience or expertise with the management of organizations and so be forced to accept what schools and other organizations offer and so the decisions made by the people who operate them.

In contrast are parents such as those discussed by Cookson and Persell (1985) in their study of elite schools in the USA who were mostly professionals, business executives, senior administrators in public and private organizations, or occupied other high status, high earning and competency demanding occupations. Their own educational experiences had usually been satisfactory and they recognized the significance not simply of school credentials but of the experience of particular kinds of schools. Hence they not only sought an extensive school experience for their own children but sought it in particular elite institutions. In addition, they understood school content, the organization and operation of educational institutions, could readily discuss their children's schooling with teachers, principals and others, and could negotiate or in other ways exercise influence to achieve satisfactory and even favourable arrangements. Some had sufficient influence to ensure that serious transgressions by their children were overlooked by school administrators. To extend Bourdieu's term (Bourdieu and Passeron, 1977), they had considerable cultural, economic, political and other forms of capital and not only fostered development of their children but used their capital in dealings with schools.

Such parents are but the tip of another iceberg. They are but steps removed from the parents patronizing the schools studied by Fox (1985) in England, Hansen (1971) in Australia and their counterparts in most if not all societies. Invariably, they seek out high status schools, promote and support their children's aspirations, follow their school experience closely, and act to enhance the quality of their experiences and performances. Indeed, their attitudes can be such as to regard teachers as other servants, and closely monitor them for their effectiveness in achieving desirable outcomes. Moreover, the coming together of such parents in school communities can establish a coherent school ethos supporting and even driving school efforts and programs.

Given their considerable cultural, political, economic and other resources, they are also able to enhance a school's resources and place it in an advantageous position relative to other schools. They can readily contribute financial, business, legal, architectural, management and other forms of resources to benefit the operation of a school, sometimes drawing upon the resources of groups and organizations with which they are associated. For their part, school administrators have considerable incentives to attract such parents for the resources they bring to the school community, and which can be used in the advancement and aggrandisement of a school. At the same time, as these schools become centres of advantage, others serving less resourced parents are characterized by disadvantages, and so the role of schooling in the promotion of advantages and disadvantages proceeds.

In relation to schooling, these differences among parents are further evident in their different contributions to management activities. Parents whose cultural background is low status in commercial, industrial or other organizations and situations lack experience with management tasks and expertise in undertaking such responsibilities and may also lack the confidence publicly to articulate arguments and strategies for courses of action that might be pursued. To that extent they contrast markedly with and are disadvantaged in relation to middle- and upper-class parents who have relevant experience and expertise. Still again, Hatton (1985) showed that higher status parents can exercise considerable influence even within the relatively centralized systems of schools such as exist in the Australian states. That is, they are to the fore either in setting up private schools or in achieving managerial roles in publicly operated schools serving socially heterogeneous communities. In such positions they can exercise influence beyond what happens in the classroom or in the development and implementation of school policies. Thus in communities studied in the USA and elsewhere, parents from professional, executive and administrative backgrounds consistently achieved these more influential positions and were able to ensure schools operated in ways they understood and endorsed (e.g. Zeigler, Jennings and Peak, 1974).

The significance of these differences among parents can be seen at several further points. Parents, like other groups, invariably form associations to promote their schools' interests in political as well as in social, economic and other sectors of activity. Thus parent associations are generated in relation to the different public and private, religious, secular and other groups of schools. In the first instance they represent the general interests of the schools and more particularly the parents associated with each set of schools. Hence associations are often in conflict, competing for resources and other advantages which can also be, incidentally, to the detriment of other sets of schools, parents and children. Thus school parents are significant lobbyists in many societies, with elite school parents particularly effective, operating either formally as with committees, associations and public meetings, or informally through personal relationships and other forms of contact. Their contacts can include politicians and especially cabinet ministers and senior system administrators, together with key officials in media, finance, legal and other systems of activity.

Finally, we should note the exceptional avenues available to at least a small proportion of parents. Through their senior positions in corporations or other major organizations, they can have access to specially significant steering organizations such as foundations, policy centres, the media and others. I shall consider these in more detail in Chapter 9 but here it is relevant to note that many of the participants in those agencies are parents or associate with parents and take account of their parental concerns in their several sets of responsibilities and activities. Thus the influence which some parents can exercise is not simply upon educational experiences of their children or a particular school, but on conceptions of what constitutes schooling and how it is undertaken.

Discussion

Much of the relevance of parenting to schooling is neglected in the academic literature. Parents are most likely to be considered as an influence on their children, as when student performances are related to parental occupations, incomes and other circumstances and characteristics. It is clear, however, that parental contributions are critical to the development of the child and so to their capacity to obtain benefits from schooling, to the management of their children's schooling experiences and even to the operation of schools and even systems of schooling. Individually, and hence collectively to a much greater extent, they can bring considerable resources to the schooling process.

Probably the main point of educational significance, however, is the differences among parents in their material, social and personal resources or in their economic, political, cultural and other forms of capital. These differences are reflected in the contributions they make to their children's development from the outset, and which are a significant factor in the differential capacity of children to benefit from schooling. They are then further evident in parents' capacities to support and even enhance their children's school experience, even to the extent of influencing the operation of schooling as a social process. These differences are most clearly evident from the extreme cases of exceptionally advantaged and disadvantaged parents. They are also readily apparent, however, in any particular situation. Even relatively homogeneous communities are characterized by substantial differences among parents in resources and contributions which are reflected in both the operation of a particular school and in the experience and performance of their children. Again, the relevance of such differences is regularly caught in research by taking account of particular parental characteristics and circumstances. What is neglected is their dynamic or passive participation and hence their more complex and widely differing contributions to the schooling process.

It is also clear that schools that disregard parental characteristics and circumstances perpetuate and even exacerbate the patterns of advantages and disadvantages from which children undertake schooling. Children who benefit from able and active parents are at a considerable and continuing advantage relative to those whose parents do not help them or even act to limit or distort their development. Thus schools that take little or no account of background circumstances do nothing to offset the disadvantages from which children start, and which continue to limit their development and progress with schooling subsequently. In a wider social sense, schools that take a narrow or limited interest in their students, leaving it to the students to show interest and enterprise in school work, are particularly conservative social institutions in perpetuating and even increasing the disparities of the social status quo.

At the same time, it is evident that schools can contribute significantly to offsetting the disadvantaged circumstances from which children undertake schooling. Studies of pre-school programs in particular, but of primary and secondary school programs too, indicate that schools vary in their achievements with students and so demonstrate that some are more effective than others. Predictably, researchers are showing that there are no simple formulae for achieving effective schools as there are no simple formulae for achieving effective teaching, and that different strategies are required for effective achievements in different types of situations. Thus vastly different practices are appropriate in elite schools from what are effective in working-class, slum or ethnic schools, dealing with children who start with a plurality of disadvantages and difficulties, given the ways in which schools are normally operated.

It is also evident that school efforts can never be sufficient to achieve the most effective efforts by students. Repeatedly, researchers have shown that parents are conscious of the situations their children confront and prepare them 'realistically' for the prospects assumed to await them. Hence, for parenting styles, including efforts in terms of aspirations and expectations to change, then the realities that confront parents must be changed. That is, for parents' assessments of the relevance of schooling for their children to change requires changes in the realities that lead parents to assume that their children's prospects are not of this kind or another, and particularly are not circumscribed or limited in critical ways, but are more open and that points of options are of critical significance in the careers of their children.

Again, much has been made by reforming conservative politicians and other policy advocates on the right side of politics of the importance of opening up school management arrangements so that parents have greater choice. However, it is also clear that the parents most able to benefit from market situations are those with the personal, social and other resources, and with the understandings and expertise in the operation of educational institutions. Parents with little or no resources of those kinds and with limited understanding of the operation of schools are not in a position to make informed and sound choices. As a consequence, it is arguable that they are better served by community or other public systems of institutions. However, it is also clear that such institutions are not particularly sensitive or at least responsive to the difficulties of children from disadvantaged circumstances or have been co-opted by more effective parents and so service middle- and upper-class children more effectively.

That state of affairs suggests that a more effective strategy might be to encourage the establishment and operation of schools by organizations or agencies more sensitive and responsive to the needs of poorer and otherwise disadvantaged parents. Churches are one such possibility and the Catholic Church is notable for the number of orders that direct their efforts to servicing such children. It is also noticeable, however, that Catholic schools vary greatly in relation to the social circumstances of parents so that they too are seriously limited in redressing the imbalances and disadvantages from which children undertake schooling. Employee organizations constitute another possibility, although they have not shown much interest in undertaking such responsibilities hitherto. That may well reflect optimistic expectations of what might be achieved by public systems of schooling. It is at least conceivable that they could broaden their responsibilities to include the education of children of employees. Again, it has to be remembered that employee organizations such as trade unions have in recent years considerably broadened their constituencies by including many technical and even professional groups so that some national organizations are now heavily influenced by middle-class members and may be somewhat indifferent to the traditional working-class constituency.

In any case, regardless of how successful such strategies may be, they are nonetheless essentially patronizing and prone to sustain dependency. The more desirable strategy, as with students, has to involve the direction of effort to raising the competencies, confidence and assertiveness of parents so that they are better able to act on their own behalves. Fortunately, such strategies can be compatible with those directed to raising the effectiveness of students and so undertaken together. Given that orientation, they could be undertaken by a range of agencies and institutions — state or private, religious or secular, industrial or professional. The central task would be to identify criteria of effectiveness and sound ways of undertaking them.

Chapter 5

Teaching

Teaching is a most visible aspect of schooling, being directly experienced by children and of immediate and continuing significance to parents and others. It also stands close to parenting in its potential for exercising influence on children and youth and, through the orientations and competencies developed with them, on modes of undertaking economic, political and other social activities. Hence it has considerable personal and social significance and, in consequence, teachers, particularly those in the public sector responsible for teaching the 'masses' of children, are invariably closely monitored, either directly by inspection or other forms of surveillance or indirectly by structured arrangement and processes such as examinations. That has been particularly the case in the recent years of turbulent economic and political circumstances.

At the same time, the conception of the teacher as essentially a classroom performer is inadequate and even misleading in that important aspects of the situation are not identified. For example, location in a primary or secondary school, in a selective, residual or comprehensive type of institution, a public or private school, or a single sex or coeducational school indicates the system context of teachers and the focusing of their priorities so that they act in particular ways with particular sets of students. Further, many aspects of schooling, such as teacher and student subcultures and expectations, curriculum and test or examination requirements, the expectations and requirements of administrators, and the legal arrangements that apply to schooling, also act to structure and constrain the teacher in the classroom. Moreover, in taking up particular positions and pursuing careers through a succession of them, either as teachers or administrators or as specialists in programming or in other aspects of schooling, they act to sustain the structural arrangements and the modes of operating employed in systems of schooling.

Other less visible aspects of teaching are evident in the extensive range of activities in which they engage. In addition to classroom activities, teachers participate in the conduct of systems of examinations, in curriculum development, and in subject, industrial-professional and other associations to promote particular interests and causes. Ultimately, their concerns include personal and professional development and careers, and opportunities to achieve and prosper as members of a society. Thus their interest in exercising influence is substantially greater than as classroom participants.

Significantly, teaching has never been accorded the autonomy of full professional status even though, nominally at least, it has an appropriate responsibility in fostering the development of the young. However, while it does not have the exact knowledge and the preciseness of strategies of occupations such as engineering or medicine, possibly more important as a determinant of its status is the sensitivity of its responsibilities: the diversity in school practices possible from a fully autonomous professional group, particularly if child development and well-being were taken as central concerns, could be quite disturbing of the operation of other social arrangements and processes. At the same time, the prospect of such a development may be diminishing with the efforts being made to transform the operation of schooling, and as other established professional groups are increasingly employed within organizations.

The attacks on public schools and their teachers that have been particularly vigorous and common during the 1970s and 1980s are also of considerable significance and most illuminative of the forces at work in respect of education. Assertions have been made that public school teachers are responsible for declining standards of achievement, for the production of unemployable youth, and even for deliberately subverting core values and practices in societies. As the unsound and even irresponsible character of those assertions has been exposed, it has also become evident that the attacks, often highlighted in certain sections of the media have been not simply ideological or political in character, but calculated and even unscrupulous, and testimony to the reality of a campaign to transform the priorities of public schooling by undermining confidence in its teachers and ultimately in public school systems.

Fortunately, considerable research on relevant issues has enabled the situation to be appraised more informedly. While that research has been done in only a few societies, it is particularly significant because they are the ones where attacks on public schooling have been most vigorous and critical. Hence we can obtain a more systematically established and comprehensive view of teachers in action and also see again some of the fundamental features of schools that become evident in examining the experiences of students.

To catch the diversity of activity and concerns, recourse must again be made to many types of studies. Ethnographic research has been helpful in providing details of interpersonal interactions between teachers and students and with other teachers, parents and administrators, and in different types of class and school situations. Studies of teachers in different types of schools and in relation to different types of students illuminate practices of differential treatment and so of sifting and sorting students. Political and historical studies throw light on teacher activities in their associations and wider social and political activities and roles. Hence it is necessary, as with students and parents, to employ a comprehensive approach in examining the activities of teachers.

The Structuring of Teaching

Teachers are commonly seen and indeed often see themselves as the central figures in classrooms, acting autonomously in teaching and directing the learning of a group of students. The reality is more complex, largely reflecting the diversity and dynamic nature of the situations in which they operate. Much of this chapter will be directed to examining how teachers handle those situations but as a preliminary it is useful to indicate how those situations are structured to establish constraints that operate upon teachers. While these all operate in the present through interpersonal and situational experiences or as a result of the perceptions and understandings by which teachers act, it can be useful to explore some situations in terms of the historical and social contexts of teachers' activities.

One indication of the constraints acting upon teachers is to be found in the ways in which their responsibilities have been differentiated and arranged within a system of schooling, such as was indicated in Chapter 2. Probably the most basic variation is by level with primary teachers taking responsibility for a class for a year or more for most if not all of its programs so that teacher-student interactions and interrelationships are extensive, diffuse and continuing, while secondary teachers have more specific interactions and relationships. That basic variation is extended at the extremes where junior primary teaching can be similar to pre-school or kindergarten developmental work or comprise the wide ranging and complex responsibilities undertaken in a one-teacher primary school, while senior secondary teachers can be highly specialized and academic, approximating tertiary work in forms of specialization and styles of teaching.

The situations for teachers vary again at particular levels and much more at secondary than at primary levels. In addition to subject specialization, schools are often streamed so that teachers work with particular groups of students and with different types of schools such as selective and residual or comprehensive, or academic and practical or vocational. In other situations the structuring of teaching responsibilities and modes of acting is related to the differentiation of students by gender, ethnicity, community location, religious affiliation or social class. The last is particularly salient, giving rise to privately operated elite schools serving the children of more affluent families as well as public schools serving some middle- and most if not all working-class students, with particularly significant ramifications for teaching responsibilities and modes of acting. Invariably, their students are then seen to be qualitatively different and so to warrant different kinds and even levels of programs with profound implications for the kinds of expertise and forms of teaching employed (e.g. Anyon, 1981).

Ultimately, the diversity of schools and teaching situations reflects diversity of values and systems of beliefs, together with circumstances such as the distribution of power, involving resources and capacity to exercise influence on how schooling is undertaken. Moreover, these different types of situations have usually existed over extended periods of time and favour the development of distinct types of schools with particular kinds of student and parent expectations, teacher subcultures, school ethos and modes of operating. In consequence, teachers are considerably influenced as to how they operate from the point of taking up an appointment. That can be seen from a brief examination of modes devised to manage schools, including practices in the appointment of teachers and in structuring the career paths made available to them. For example, elite groups invariably establish relatively autonomous or 'independent' schools and assign major responsibilities for their management to principals, thereby creating situations of autocracy or at best of benevolent dictatorship. Then in the appointment of staff such principals commonly emphasize academic qualifications and allow considerable autonomy in undertaking teaching. But the teachers are nonetheless accorded a status of subordinate dependency and so precluded from working as fully autonomous professionals. In contrast, public systems of schooling are established under laws and regulations and more likely to be operated as bureaucratic organizations. In consequence, new teachers are commonly appointed by central administrators to junior positions and clearly subordinated in status and limited in their responsibilities. They are also substantially controlled or constrained by their subjection to regulations and bureaucratic checks on their performances, and a necessity to operate within a complex system of rules.

Specific types of school situations also vary greatly in the career prospects they offer. In schools which are entities in themselves, as with many private schools, promotion is likely to involve movement out to other schools. In situations characterized by commitment to a religion or an ideology, appointments can be long-term, with satisfactions coming from involvement with the organization and the community of which it is a part, and so the pursuit is of a calling or a mission. In elite institutions, as in the schools studied by Cookson and Persell (1985), careers can vary markedly but invariably entail giving greatly to the organization, and sometimes being 'let go' when effectiveness declines or behaviour or performance becomes unsatisfactory.

It is in the larger public systems that careers are more hierarchically structured, reflecting the bureaucratic nature of the system. In addition, tribunals or other agencies established to adjudicate on appointments, promotions and other aspects of conditions of employment add to the bureaucratic complexities in the operation of such a system. A point to be emphasized is that such conditions reflect concerns of both staff and management.

In addition to the differentiated circumstances associated with particular types of schools, teachers share some general characteristics and circumstances that further constrain them as an occupational group. As Lortie (1975: Ch. 4) pointed out, it is usually a flat or 'unstaged' career path, involving few promotional steps, with advancement taking teachers into administration or other specialized areas of activity. That is, teachers have little scope for achieving recognition on a hierarchical basis and are also precluded from establishing a professional reputation and developing a successful practice as in medicine, law and some other professions. As Sikes, Measor and Woods (1985: Ch. 1) illustrated, the fewness of steps is now made worse by the slowing down in movement between them as declining enrolments and contractions in educational activity reduce promotional opportunities. Under those circumstances, the appeal of teaching lies more in opportunities for personal interaction, nurturant activity, and compatibility with one's other activities, all of which have meant it has been seen as more appropriate for women, reflecting constraints operating on other aspects of their lives. That in turn has been associated with the devaluing of teaching as an occupation and so further affecting its status. Again, while teaching also appeals as a socially constructive occupation, offering opportunities to foster the development of children, its sifting and sorting and other more reproductive and conservative responsibilities, largely arising from operating with particular kinds of programs within an extensive system of schools, are not readily apparent. The growing understanding of the 'darker side' of teaching may be a factor in later experiences of stress, alienation, staff turnover and other negative reactions to teaching.

Teachers are at a disadvantage, too, as Lortie (1975: Ch. 3) again pointed out, in that a body of arcane or special knowledge and techniques has not been established to give the authority of special expertise and justify autonomy in their practices. In part that may be due to complexities and uncertainties of their responsibilities and tasks, making specific technical knowledge inappropriate. In part it may follow, as Popkewitz (1987) following Foucault argued, from the dominance of particular forms of discourse, reflecting empirical rather than interpretivist or other more sophisticated perspectives in the conceptualization and understanding of situations, and ultimately in the development of practices. But in part it derives from the organizational situations in which teachers work and where technical knowledge appears to be less relevant than relational and organizational competence (Grace, 1978: 167). It is at that point, too, that bureaucratic and commercial administrative considerations intrude to give an unreality to the pedagogical knowledge and expertise of developmental activity.

In turn, these conditions and circumstances bear upon the general standing of teaching as an occupation in society. On the basis of at least a nominal responsibility for the development of children, teachers have a reasonable claim for professional status. Such a status is also congruent with the concept of service to others commonly attributed to professionalism and used to distinguish it from bureaucratic performance (e.g. Blau and Scott, 1962: 60–74).

Nonetheless, for reasons noted above, such as conditions of employment, including limited career prospects, and lack of a particular technical competence, teaching has not been accorded such status. Now in the contemporary period degrees of autonomy previously accorded teachers are being restricted (Grace, 1985; Lawn and Ozga, 1986), and even those in elite schools may be losing some of their prestige and status as their schools change from giving primacy to inducting students into ruling-class cultures to emphasizing performance in more meritocratic approaches to the preparation of the young. Under those circumstances, as Walford (1984) and others have shown, students are more disposed to view their teachers as paid servants and expect them to 'deliver the goods', reflecting a more mercenary or commercial approach and the increased significance of productive or economic priorities in social activities. As schooling and education more generally become increasingly incorporated into the productive process, the prospects of independent and professional status appear to be lessening.

It is with the sharper distinctions of Marxist analyses that the ambiguities of the status of teachers have been highlighted. Such analyses, as by Ginsburg, Meyenn and Miller (1980), find that teachers are neither part of the capitalist nor of the working classes, but constitute part of an ambiguous zone of middle-class technocrats and contribute to the operation of the productive process by improving human capital.

Such features as the uncertain status of the teacher, being neither wholly professional nor bureaucratic, nor clearly located in a class structure, together with a lack of specific and explicit technical modes of operating as apply in medicine, engineering and some other professions, also mean vulnerability to the manipulations to which they have increasingly been subjected in recent years.

The subordinate and other status characteristics of teachers also bear upon recruitment and career experiences. Ambiguous status and other factors mean that teaching does not attract students of the calibre of those who go into the arts, sciences, medicine, law and some other specializations. Rather, as Lortie (1975: Ch. 2), Wragg (1982: 15–20) and others have noted, entering teaching often involves a step upward in social mobility, largely due to its visibility as an occupation, being part of every child's growing up experience, and also that it is a step away from the less secure and lower status occupations of may parents.

Priorities and Strategies

In examining the activities of teachers in relation to particular situations Woods (1983: 9–11), Hargreaves (1984) and others have found the concept of strategy useful for generating questions and steering observations. It acknowledges the active nature of the teacher as a participant and also accommodates the diversity of situations and conditions with which teachers have to deal. It is particularly useful here where a broad range of teacher activities and situations is examined.

If one turns first to the classroom, it is relevant to note that although teachers act in a variety of ways in different classroom situations, the common conception of a teacher directing the learning of students has some substance to it, largely because of the preoccupation with control and direction that is built into the teaching position. The extent and significance of the control imperative are evident in many features of schooling from requirements of compulsory attendance to the design of buildings and classrooms, the prescription of curricula, the operation of examinations, and in day-by-day regulatory and administrative mechanisms for influencing student and teacher activity. Indeed, such is the pervasiveness and significance of the control imperative that it is evident from the most subtle indicators; for example, in an illuminating analysis Stubbs (1976) indicated that concern with control pervades the use of language, with the teacher deciding what is a topic for discussion, what is problematic in a discussion, how a potential respondent will be recognized, and what is an acceptable answer. That is, 'talk' is an important mechanism for establishing a teacher's requirements and steering student participation and performance in classroom activities.

But perhaps the clearest indication of the preoccupation with control and direction derives from the relatively weak position of alternative approaches to schooling. On the surface, prospects for different approaches to teaching appear to be open with options offered in different conceptions of purposes. They can take many forms, but a long-standing and widely accepted dichotomy involves giving priority either to the development of the child or to the operation of society. These express progressive and traditional positions that have been discussed on many occasions, as by Evetts (1973) and Bennett (1976: 37–41), and only a few comments are necessary here to make relevant points.

The two positions embody contrasting assumptions about the nature of children, social reality and how it may be known, and the role of the teacher. Ultimately, however, they are distinguishable in one being egalitarian in respect of the development of children and the other expressing hierarchical predispositions and so being elitist in its essential priorities. The latter is also clearly widespread in practice, reflecting the distribution of power among social groups.

In taking the child's development as primary, progressive educators seek to provide experiences that promote the development of social, cognitive, physical and other competencies, the expression of personal feelings and thoughts, and the achievement of independence and even autonomy. Such priorities reflect a concern to promote the development and realization of children's diverse potentialities. In seeking those outcomes, progressivists purport to be neither differentiating nor discriminating but essentially egalitarian in seeking to achieve the full development of all children.

To give priority to society evokes a reassuring sense of community but that is misleading. In principle, an emphasis on the operation of society upholds the transmission of existing culture and modes of acting, and involves passing on the heritage of achievements of previous generations to enable children to benefit from past experience. Hence transmissive styles of teaching are appropriate and readily complemented by examinations to check on the learning of students who are thus put into positions of recipients and limited to relatively responsive roles.

However, problems arise from the diversity and differential influence of groups within a society with only some determining the operation of schooling. As a consequence, schools serve sections of society differentially with some offering distinctive programs and opportunities for prospective 'elites', while others establish 'less effective' performers, usually from disadvantaged backgrounds and circumstances, in lower level positions in society. Thus schooling operates as a sifting and sorting mechanism that stratifies school populations, treating children not simply as different but in terms of evaluated social categories or even stereotypes, and reproducing those types and relationships

Despite the congeniality of traditional schooling and teaching to established social arrangements, the incidence of progressive schooling became a major political issue in many societies from the late 1960s. In retrospect, it is now evident that in the prosperous 1950s and 1960s schooling in many societies was not only substantially expanded in its availability but also modified progressively in its operation to facilitate extended attendance and higher levels of attainment for more students. It was also widely accepted that teaching styles became increasingly progressive. Indeed, English primary schools of the late 1960s attracted international attention as embodying the progressiveness of the Plowden Report (1967), while 'progressive' innovatory schools were established in many societies. However, while the extent of progressivism in teaching styles can now be seen to have been substantially exaggerated, conservatives claimed that progressivism was rampant and launched a succession of critical attacks from the late 1960s (e.g. Cox and Dyson (eds), 1969a, 1969b). Subsequently, an assortment of critics, including some academics, some parents and members of the general public, and some business, political and other societal managers, asserted that teachers had yielded up their authority and allowed students to determine the curriculum, modes of learning and so of teaching, and even what counted as acceptable performance. They also had some useful allies in sections of the media which gave considerable publicity to their critiques, together with reports of studies held to support those interpretations, while others that did not do so were ignored. Moreover, as researchers subsequently established the falsity and even the mischievousness of many of the claims, their reports were also regularly ignored so that public impressions were not balanced by fuller and more soundly established data. Interestingly, one of the studies most highlighted by media agencies as demonstrating the effectiveness of traditional methods of teachers, namely one by Bennett (1976) on teaching styles in relation to student progress, actually found that relatively few teachers employed informal or progressive methods, and those that were so categorized could also be readily categorized as mild autocrats. In addition, one of the most effective teachers in the sample employed more informal styles of teaching. It is also particularly indicative that a re-analysis of the data which showed that differences between styles in relation to effectiveness were insignificant (Aikin, Bennett and Hesketh, 1981) was neglected by the media.

More significantly, however, Berlak and Berlak (1981) examined the progressive English primary schools of the early 1970s and found the formal-informal dichotomy to be inappropriate, and that teachers invariably closely directed and monitored their students' work. Galton, Simon and Croll (1980) also found that teaching styles in the schools they studied did not match the formal-informal dichotomy employed by Bennett, but operated in more complex patterns. If anything, however, they were more formal and traditional overall.

Similar observations emerged from an extensive study of middle schools by Delamont and Galton (1986) and in studies of teaching in the US (Goodlad, 1983; McNeil, 1986) and elsewhere (e.g. Connell, 1985). Significantly too, research attention has long moved on from styles of teaching to other aspects such as time on task and qualities of tasks (Bennett, 1987) and to effective and ineffective teachers and schools (Rutter and others, 1979; Reynolds, Sullivan and Murgatroyd, 1987).

In general, it is evident that teachers invariably seek to control their students and direct their activities, and are also substantially occupied with teaching the basics of language and mathematics, together with other conventional areas of knowledge and skills. While some employ flexible arrangements, associating students together in groups, the latter nonetheless mostly work individually. Clearly, a primary responsibility accepted by teachers is to manage the learning process and to do so by directing and encouraging children in their activities, answering their questions and checking their work. Variability among teachers is more in terms of competence so that it is ineffective rather than radical or progressive practices, and inadequate or inappropriate resources and facilities or organizational arrangements and management that are associated with poor performance or with students doing little or no work or becoming antagonistic or rebellious in schools and classrooms (McNeil, 1986; Sedlak and others, 1986). Accordingly, the issue of the progressive-traditional dichotomy has to be seen as substantially exploited as a political device for attacking public schooling, unsettling parents and students, and establishing a climate congenial for conservative and even regressive transformations in school practices. Perhaps a more useful distinction is the one between teachers and technocrats offered by Wolcott (1977) who distinguished between those oriented to the development of the child, whether by progressive or traditional methods, and others oriented to serving dominant social groups by preparing students to be effective operatives within established systems of production, government and other systems of activity.

To return to the consideration of the teachers in the classroom, however, it is important to note that while teachers are in a strong position legally to enforce requirements, they also have to gain the compliance and even active cooperation of students. Indeed, such is the degree of interdependence that Delamont (1976) insightfully titled a concluding chapter of her discussion of teacher-student interaction as 'Let the battle commence'. It is out of such circumstances that teachers develop strategies to establish social as well as legal authority in order to be effective with students.

In a review of research on teaching, Woods (1983) identified a variety of strategies such as domination, negotiation, fraternization and even absence for coping with difficult situations (p. 110) but gave emphasis to negotiation (Ch. 7). Denscombe (1985: Ch. 4) offered a more comprehensive and concise conceptualization in characterizing strategies as emphasizing domination, cooperation and classroom management. Clearly, domination has a long tradition and continues to be widely used. However, social changes have given rise to a readiness to discuss and negotiate and obtain the cooperation of students, and establish mutually acceptable actions and sanctions. More sophisticated and probably more effective for managing students, however, are classroom management strategies that entail the organization of work into tasks and requirements, and the gaining of acceptance of them by students. When they are developed in more substantial classroom projects, then students can experience a sense of substantial and meaningful achievement. In turn, such agreements become binding on teachers as well as students and establish a stable system of relationships and modes of acting.

It is also important to recognize that control is significant for much more than to ensure that students undertake classroom work. For example, Pollard (1980) observed that control enables teachers to pursue and achieve personal interests, including limit demands made by students and avoid situations damaging to reputations and self-esteem. Again, in a perceptive discussion of teaching in a small rural school in the US, McPherson (1972: 32) noted the use of indicators of control as a basis for mutual assessments; thus, for example, leaving one's door open was a device for communicating to colleagues that one was in control of a class. More recently, in an extended discussion of classroom control, Denscombe (1985: Ch. 5) gave particular attention to the significance of noise as an indicator of competence in classroom management. That is, the establishment of control is also central to how one is seen by others and so to one's reputation as a teacher.

Closely associated with control and direction are evaluation and differentiation and even discrimination. As was indicated in Chapter 3, the studies of Rist (1973), Nash (1973), Sharp and Green (1975) and others showed these latter processes to be universal, pervasive and fundamental to the teaching process. In respect of those processes, too, Barker Lunn (1970) established the significant part of teachers in that while differential evaluation and treatment occurred in all types of primary schools, including streamed and unstreamed, it was essentially a matter of whether or not teachers believed, for whatever reason, that children should be graded and treated differently. Significantly, however, students are commonly characterized not so much in academic or cognitive terms but as types of children. That is illustrated by teachers' constant recourse to such terms as 'cooperative', 'pays attention', 'works independently', is 'responsible', 'mature', 'courteous' or, on the negative side, 'lazy', 'chatterbox', 'disobedient' or 'easily distracted' (Woods, 1979: 173). Indeed, a most important and revealing finding coming out of studies of teachers' categorization systems is a preoccupation with social characteristics (e.g. Williams, 1981). Such a preoccupation suggests a close link between evaluations and teachers' responsibilities to promote learning in particular directions or on particular kinds of programs.

A further salient aspect of differential evaluation and treatment by teachers, as was indicated in Chapter 4, is that they are invariably related to the social background situations and circumstances of students, as with class, ethnicity and gender. Thus working-class children have invariably been seen as less able students and assigned to lower streams and residual schools. Ethnic students have attracted more diverse reactions with children of some ethnic groups being treated similarly to working-class children and others, notably from East Asia, attracting positive reputations as capable and industrious students. In the case of gender, earlier practices directed boys and girls to different types of programs and treatments; however, while those practices have been generally abandoned, studies reveal that teachers continue to treat students differently by gender and thereby perpetuate gender stereotypes. Thus teachers have been established as major agents of differential evaluation and discrimination, often to a greater extent than they are aware, and more than is the case in the home, school and other situations.

While the reasons for that situation are many and complex, one rather obvious set of factors is that much of teachers' patterns of actions reflects the situations in which they work and particularly inadequate or inappropriate resources. For example, if resources were adequate for teachers to be able to work with students on a one-to-one basis, then many of the differentiating aspects of current practices would be irrelevant. Again, if resources were adequate or appropriate, then teachers could readily work with heterogeneous classes, as they do in particular types of reading and other programs. That is, the practice of homogeneous groupings rests substantially on inadequacies of time, material and other resources with which to work with students.

It is that set of circumstances, too, that makes competition relevant as a classroom strategy to generate interest and motivate the work of students. In that context, examinations are valuable, as Scarth (1983) noted, because they constitute an impersonal, often external force against which students can be pitted in competition with each other. The salience of that press can often be seen too in teachers' recourse to admonitions to perform better than others by use of such categories as girls versus boys in classroom activities.

That is, a necessity to achieve high level effort and performance from students serves as an incentive to pit them against each other individually and by groups, and to express approval and disapproval in social terms. Under those circumstances, class, ethnicity, gender and other characteristics are readily available as bases for differentiation, identification and discrimination.

The strategies considered so far are essentially to do with classroom management. However, teachers also have to deal with the requirements of principals and other administrators and with policy-makers and implementers as they impinge upon school and classroom activity. For those they employ additional strategies and move from individual to collective or social strategies. For example, in an analysis of teacher programs, Lacey (1977) found students adapted to supervisors and administrators by using strategic compliance, internalized adjustment or strategic redefinition as means of handling difficult situations. In their later study, Sikes, Measor and Woods (1985) found teachers used those strategies extensively throughout their careers, together with some of those noted by Woods (1983: 110) such as fraternization and absence, together with some more recent options such as early retirement. Indeed, the pursuit of careers, whether to find more congenial situations, as with particular kinds of classes or in particular types of schools, or to achieve advancement or aggrandisement through promotion, is in itself another form of strategy.

Collective or social strategies arise in relation to shared concerns when concerted action is relevant, and are commonly expressed through associations or other forms of organized groups. Thus cooperation is a central feature but often in response to a prospect of rivalry, competition and even conflict with others.

One major basis for collective action is specialization. The need to specialize arises substantially from the growth in knowledge and difficulties of establishing competence. It is substantially driven by the practices of researchers in the production and dissemination of knowledge but also related to the increased competence and complexity of interest of students. At the same time, specialization is advantageous to teachers in that it enables them to pursue areas of interest, limit obligations to particular areas of expertise and so protect themselves from being called upon to teach in areas where they do not have expertise. Such differentiation of tasks and responsibilities into positions and their arrangement into career structures can also be convenient for administrators as means for providing satisfaction for staff and achieving more manageable and effective forms of organization.

Specialization commonly gives rise to the formation of departments and so to political activity to maintain or extend personal and departmental scope through interdepartmental contests for students, resources, achievements and status. A study by Ball and Lacey (1980) and a review of research by Ball (1987: Ch. 9) illustrate that such political activity is a substantial part of school politics. Sometimes, too, departments are the basis for different ideological positions within a school and beyond; for example, as Ball (1981) illustrated, the structuring of teaching and the streaming or other forms of stratifying students are more likely to be favoured by science, mathematics and foreign language teachers and to be opposed by humanities and social studies teachers. More generally, traditional or conservative as against progressive ideologies are likely to be linked with one sector of teachers rather than another.

Related to specialization and departments are associations that can be important mechanisms for support and reinforcement of identity and improvement of expertise, and for undertaking defensive or offensive campaigns on behalf of a teaching responsibility. Through such associations teachers can argue the importance of their areas of expertise in the undertaking of schooling and seek support for projects as they did in research and curriculum development in the prosperous period of the 1960s and early 1970s. Subject associations have also been crucial in the operation of examinations, including for the support or exclusion of particular subjects (Goodson, 1987), and to limit and structure schooling for which there is more scope in periods of economic constraint.

Teachers have developed a further set of organizations to pursue more general industrial interests such as conditions of work, together with education issues, including the operation of sound systems of education (e.g. Johnson, 1984; Spaull and others, 1986). Commonly these organizations relate to particular groups of teachers such as those working in public or private schools, in primary or secondary schools, or as teachers as distinct from administrators, including school principals. In doing that, such organizations reflect and even amplify differences among teachers and are mechanisms for sectional group advancement and intergroup conflict. Thus they can also be limiting or weakening agencies, particularly in times of adversity when sectors of education come under attack and even restriction. Even so, the plurality and diversity of teacher associations are sustained by particular sectors believing they can achieve more than others, which provides incentives for remaining sectionalist and competitive. A contrasting tendency in some societies, such as Australia and England, has been for teacher associations to affiliate with other employee organizations in trade union movements in the pursuit of greater strength and bargaining power. Meanwhile, however, divisions between teachers persist, reflecting the salience of sectional interests and the perceived advantages of competition and conflict.

Such organizations are also major mechanisms by which teachers resist policies, and their resistance can reflect conservative concerns. Thus teachers in selective academic schools have resisted the opening up of schools into more comprehensive-type institutions. Similarly, teacher subject associations have resisted the introduction of more flexible forms of curriculum and sometimes sought to retain 'obsolete' subjects. Still again, teacher organizations have acted to establish hierarchically structured and overly regulated institutions as situations for career opportunities.

At the same time, these organizational efforts do not exhaust the range of social strategies employed by teachers. Many see their developmental concerns as linked to the necessity of a congenial social and physical environment for children and youth to grow up in and pursue those priorities by joining civic, environmental, humanitarian, animal rights and other types of causes and organizations. That is, there is no substantive break or incongruity between involvement in such organizations or in relation to such causes and activities as teachers; rather, they can represent a further expression of a developmental concern. That is, a developmental concern has very wide ramifications that can include concerns about the quality of a society, including its productive and other sectors of activity, and implications of their modes of operating for the quality of life, together with concern about the environment, the treatment of minorities in one's own society or others, and even about the treatment of other species. At its widest, this concern can be to promote what Husén (1974) termed the 'educative' society. As noted in Chapter 1, that concern can mean an interest in the fundamental character of a society, and particularly in the practice of democratic ways of acting. Accordingly, it is not surprising that teachers frequently engage in activities associated with those concerns, for in doing so they express concerns that are in harmony with developmental and educational priorities in their widest sense.

The concern with a context consistent with and supportive of developmental-educative activity can be identified as altruistic rather than self-interested in character. However, such concerns are rarely altogether one or another; they can also be seen in personal terms as instrumentally useful if one's work in the classroom is to be effective, and desirable that those efforts be sustained by reinforcement in the wider society. Similarly, while a concern with a career can be seen as a personal concern, it can also be seen to bear upon the calibre of people who are attracted to teaching, and so on the general quality of the schooling process.

In drawing attention to the range of strategies that teachers employ, it is also relevant to note the increased significance of social strategies in more recent times. Studies of two or three decades ago, and possibly in some societies at present, showed teachers as responsible in their classrooms and shielded from parents and others by 'gate-keeping' principals. That situation has changed, requiring teachers to be able to articulate their concerns and requirements, and to deal with other groups who also have legitimate interests in what goes on in schooling.

Discussion

The position of teacher, with its responsibilities to influence the development of the young and, in doing so, to reproduce or transform social processes and relationships, is of major significance for both individuals and social entities such as communities, organizations and societies. Largely as a consequence, it is invariably closely controlled or at least monitored although allowed more latitude in times of prosperity and stability when dominant groups feel more secure or are at least less threatened. Again, because of the diversity of courses of actions with profound political ramifications that teachers can pursue, it is situated in complex and even contradictory arrangements with which to work and confronted by diverse and even conflicting expectations. In practice, however, these problems are substantially resolved by differentiating teaching into different types of situations where some at least confront less complexity and incongruity. Even so, all teachers continue to experience the troublesome dilemmas identified by Berlak and Berlak (1981) to do with control, curriculum and society, and which derive from fundamental questions concerning basic assumptions and priorities regarding desirable forms of social arrangements and processes.

The difficult position of teachers is further complicated by their ambiguous social position and the circumstances under which they work. Although having a social responsibility of major significance, they have not been allowed to operate and develop as independent and responsible professionals. Although having some elements of specialized knowledge and skills, they are required to operate in structured situations and perform by relational and organizational criteria. Thus they are neither professionals nor bureaucrats but blend elements in a form of middle-class technocrat and increasingly are required to employ their expertise by contributing to the development of human capital. While societies express a commitment to the education of all by legislating to compel attendance, thereby confronting teachers with a conscripted clientele, they do not provide the resources to educate all fully and effectively. Ultimately, provision reflects social circumstances rather than personal or social requirements so that schooling operates as a sifting and sorting mechanism.

Conditions associated with schooling and teaching bear upon the status accorded the position and contribute to the perpetuation of a quasi-professional status. Public perceptions and circumstances of constraint and even direction, together with inadequacy of resources, mean that many talented, imaginative and enterprising students are attracted to other occupations, leaving teaching to be, often, a step upward in social mobility and encouraging a sense of personal achievement and a disposition to be satisfied with the social status quo, and amenable to continued control and direction.

The situation thus is a most unfortunate and frustrating one, particularly for developmentally-oriented teachers. On the one hand, the responsibilities are of the greatest significance and it is a responsibility that requires special knowledge and expertise. But for teachers to operate developmentally requires a fundamental transformation in the structuring and operation of society and has profound implications for beneficiaries of existing arrangements and processes. Hence efforts by teachers to promote developmental priorities and strategies are likely to be vigorously and even ruthlessly resisted.

At the same time, it is unlikely that the situation confronting teachers will change to any substantial extent. In addition to the problems to be confronted in the social arrangements external to schooling, some teachers enjoy an unequal distribution of benefits and resist changes in those patterns, as they have done in the past. Thus a substantial proportion can be expected to continue to support differentiation and differential treatment that ultimately involves preparing children for accommodating to prevailing social arrangements. Hence teachers can be expected to remain divided into sectors pursuing sectional priorities and advantages, even if that is to the disadvantage of some other teachers and many students, mostly from poorer circumstances. That is particularly unfortunate when there are good grounds for teachers finding common cause in a professional position that adopts a form of Hippocratic oath that commits all teachers to promote the well-being, development and education of all children.

Finally, the growing commercialization of schooling is likely to mean substantial changes to the tasks of teaching and to the conditions under which teachers operate, while ensuring the continuance of teaching as an occupation undertaken within larger but, in this prospect, profit-oriented organizations. At the same time, the probability that teaching will be increasingly undertaken as entrepreneurial 'for profit' activity has some ominous consequences, particularly for certain aspects of school programs and for certain categories of children.

Again, because technology and programs relevant to education are proliferating and becoming available for use in homes and elsewhere apart from schools, there is scope for the expert specialist, more perhaps as a consultant to parents and groups. But again, given the general reluctance to support substantial educational efforts for *all* children, that is likely to mean opportunitites will be limited to servicing the more affluent, leaving the masses with impoverished public sector services and so the continuance of dual systems of services in education as in health, legal services and elsewhere.

Chapter 6

Programming

The central point of concern in this chapter is the determination and undertaking of activities in schools to influence the development of students. The term 'curriculum' is commonly used to denote the programs of activities designed and offered to students or, as Skilbeck (1984: 21) more flexibly and inclusively put it, their learning experiences in relation to school goals and objectives. The use here of the term 'programming' is to go beyond curriculum, even as it is more inclusively defined, so that attention is also given to development and implementation activities, including the initiatives of teachers and students as they take advantage of opportunities that arise during the teaching and learning process. Indeed, there is justification for a still more inclusive concept such as 'schooling in action' to include teaching strategies and styles, organizational forms and administrative practices and strategies as integral parts of the situations which students experience, and from which they learn. Sometimes, too, such elements are sounder indicators of school values and priorities than the more explicit curriculum. However, because some of these are also substantial elements in themselves and considered in separate chapters for their effects on students' experiences, 'programming' is used here in a limited sense, but to include the social activities associated with development and implementation.

In turning to examine programming, a first observation is that programs invariably include subject or other forms of content as central elements, but differ in relation to groups of students, not simply in terms of knowledge or skills that they may need in the workforce or elsewhere, but also in relation to ways in which they have been identified and categorized. The predetermined and differentiated character of programs means that they generally serve as vehicles of transmission to produce different types of students, usually in accordance with their perceived circumstances. That is, programs are invariably conservative in content

The Social Dynamics of Schooling

and style, and those characteristics persist despite considerable efforts to establish alternatives, testifying to the influence of powerful forces on school programs.

A second observation is of the extensiveness, complexity and dynamic nature of the activity associated with the production and implementation of programs, and of the diversity of participants involved in it. One sector entails political, business, administrative and other societal managers who seek to determine program content and organization, largely by managerial or bureaucratic means. A second involves academics, including both general theorists and discipline specialists who seek to establish what might be included in programs. Still another involves teachers and principals, and curriculum and other specialists who operate at more practical levels to influence what happens in schools, together with examination and test specialists who translate goals into objectives and devise instruments to measure students' performances. Involved, too, are tertiary administrators who rely on schooling to provide bases for tertiary studies and for selecting students for admission. Ironically, the students who are most directly affected by programs, together with their parents, have limited scope for exercising influence, other than by the former reacting in classes or by 'voting with their feet' in accepting or rejecting particular subjects or programs. That is, we can expect to find many if not all the other groups associated with schooling striving to exercise influence, notably on or through more specific control or steering mechanisms such as examination authorities, particularly in more turbulent times when conditions and prospects are uncertain and such groups find it prudent to consolidate support and facilitate the success of their activities by marshalling the activities of social institutions such as schooling.

In the discussion that follows these two aspects are considered in turn. The first is used to indicate how conceptions of program content have been developed into major contemporary forms. In the second, attention is given to the dynamic behaviour of participants in the formation or social construction of programs. Of course, what is said here has to be taken in relation to what is said in other chapters in order to represent a more comprehensive concept of schooling in action.

Content and Organization

The program is a central feature of schooling, and a sound understanding of what it entails is of critical importance. For example, it is tempting to think in terms of a single program and ignore the variety that are formally devised and undertaken with different groups of students. It is also tempting to think in terms of the prepared or intended program and ignore the realitites of what occurs in classrooms which is what children actually experience. Again, following Jackson (1968: 33), thinking and acting in terms of the explicit program and neglecting the hidden program can mean both are undertaken ineffectively. That aspect takes us into a wealth of elements such as buildings and facilities, styles of undertaking schooling, and the ethos established in a school, all of which can be crucial elements of a student's experiences.

Conceptions of school programs usually recognize variations between primary and secondary schooling but acknowledge that all entail some combination of subjects and activities, with the emphasis on subjects increasing as students progress through secondary schooling. That is, while primary schooling usually has recognizable subjects, programs entail considerable activity, justified on the basis of the developing nature of the young student and facilitated by the one teacher to the class form of organization which, among other things, permits more flexible scheduling of the daily program and the use of longer or shorter periods for different types of activities. In contrast, secondary programs typically involve specialist teachers teaching their particular subjects. It is at that level, too, that there is considerable horizontal diversity, reflecting ways in which secondary schooling has been differentiated with different programs generated for different categories of students. Thus abstract and theoretical academic subjects have a long history, employed when schooling was for a limited and usually elite group of students and now invariably offered to students aspiring to enter elite institutions, such as universities, and higher status careers. The establishment of mass education, following from the Reformation in some societies and the development of nation-states with national systems of schooling in others, usually saw the establishment of a second set of schools to serve the 'masses' with distinctive programs that gave emphasis to literacy and numeracy, together with certain social, political and religious attitudes and competencies.

As mass schooling has been extended to serve larger proportions of students staying longer at school, program offerings have been further modified to offer content and experiences that relate more closely to the attributed interests and needs of those students. A major strategy in that process has been to develop several secondary programs for use in streamed classes or differentiated schools as means by which students can obtain 'practical' qualifications and move into trade and other types of occupations. Invariably, such programs are taken by working-class students thereby illustrating the class-related, stratifying nature of schooling.

Other forms of differentiation, with programs to accompany them, have been developed for students categorized on bases other than class. Gender has involved greater complexity, giving rise to different programs for boys and girls by class background. That is, not only has the education of boys and girls been different, it has also differed according to class with, for example, upper-class girls experiencing finishing schools and working-class girls learning useful domestic skills (Arnott, 1983). Ethnicity has also been relevant and again often related to class or caste with different ethnic groups constituting dominant and subordinate groups. Different types of programs have also been devised for students in rural areas and from different religious groups.

However, while these illustrate the existence of a diversity of programs, they are at the same time variations within a range that serve to perpetuate existing social arrangements and processes. That is, despite their diversity they have in common a relevance for preparing people to occupy positions in existing or emerging arrangements and processes, and assume that students will accommodate to or comply with those requirements. Thus they are essentially conservative or reproductive in character.

Fundamentally different conceptions of programs have been developed in the last century or so, although they exist more as conceptions than as developed practices. Their distinctive character is in giving emphasis to the development of attributes of the person such as curiosity, creativity, expressiveness, constructiveness and intellectuality. They are progressive or radical in emphasizing the development of attributes and potentialities of the person independently of their relevance to existing social arrangements and processes. That is, such approaches are centred on the child or person rather than on society and in that way are radical or progressive.

Progressive education has had considerable appeal and attracted considerable attention but not been widely adopted outright. It has been most fully employed in a few 'light house' schools (Connell, 1980a: Ch. 5), and is most widely adopted in pre-school agencies such as kindergartens and the junior levels of primary schooling. In the twentieth century the primary school has often been the site of tension reflecting the efforts of advocates to extend developmentalism to higher grade levels and into new areas of the curriculum, and the defensive activities of traditionalists seeking to maintain the standing of traditional subjects and approaches. The outcome has often been a blending of approaches and methods by individual teachers, as indicated in the previous chapter, thus giving rise to a blending of activities in school programs. If progressive educational programs gained any ground at the secondary level, it was in classes for less able or lower achieving students with whom activities and learning by doing were thought to be of greater interest. Correspondingly, the type of program also acquired a lesser status than the academic program of traditional subjects. In addition, teaching in such programs was accorded lower status and so often assigned to less qualified, less experienced and less effective teachers, and used as a basis for a rationale that justifies less vigorous teaching and lower expectations of students. Ironically, when good quality, integrated, activity-based developmental programs such as *Man: A Course of Study* (M:ACOS) have been devised, and demonstrated that such units can provide demanding and educative experiences for students, they have also been vigorously attacked by fundamentalist and conservative critics who can tolerate quite unsound and immoral content in traditional subjects. It is unfortunate that more such challenging and demanding units have not been developed and taken by competent teachers.

At the same time, it is important to recognize that content does not have to be integrated from different subjects to be usable in developmental and progressive ways. It is more a case of how material is used and that in turn can reflect conceptions of subjects or disciplines. For example, the practice of drawing solely upon information from a discipline is a common one; however, that represents the use of only the findings of such a mode of enquiry and ignores the processes of how those findings were generated. The school experience becomes a more developmental one when a subject is treated as a mode of enquiry and students use its contributions in conceptualizing situations and processes and in forming questions and responding to them. As Apple (1979: Ch. 5) and others have pointed out, to do that is to employ subjects authentically and incidentally developmentally.

Developmental programs are valuable both in themselves as a type of program and also for exemplifying particular sets of assumptions and beliefs or ideological positions in practice, in contrast with the positions underpinning traditional subjects or content-oriented approaches. However, it is also important to establish that the dichotomy of progressive and traditional programs is at the same time an example of explicit programs which are complemented by what Jackson (1968: 33) identified as the *hidden* curriculum.

A major value of the concept of hidden curriculum is that it directs attention to organizational features and processes that accompany the explicit content, and constitute part of the situations that influence children's learning. The hidden curriculum has many features and only some examples will be used here to illustrate its significance. They include, for example, styles of operating such as teaching and administering, ways in which situations are structured as with class and school organization or in which activities are undertaken as by authoritarian or participatory processes. They also include the physical plant and equipment as they are used in school programs. Probably the most systematic and effective use of the hidden curriculum is achieved in some elite schools where use is made of specific facilities to establish a particular ethos that will have an impact on students. Thus facilities such as school chapel can be made central to a school's life, both physically and socially, in an effort to establish its significance in students' ways of thinking, feeling and responding. Again, ceremonies and rituals, together with forms of dress and personal styles, are often employed in the construction of a school's character and to establish a social impact on students. Effort has also been put into the construction of traditions in order to develop a particular kind of reputation and assist in achieving particular kinds of effects.

Such efforts illustrate the concept of the program as involving schooling in action and mean the comprehensive use of content, arrangements, facilities and processes to achieve effects upon students. Indeed, there is probably no limit to what can be used by ingenious staff in creating situations and environments with which students interact and from which they learn. Consideration of these possibilities also highlights the aridity or inadequacy of many conceptions of curriculum or even programs that do not take such elements into account. Attention must also be drawn to the limitations and inadequacies of testing or assessment practices that are indifferent to those aspects of school programs. As a consequence, they can only very partially test a school's efforts and equally partially monitor the learnings of students in relation to their school experiences.

Consideration of the hidden curriculum also directs attention to the relevance of ways in which programs are developed and implemented for it is in those processes that the explicit and the implicit sectors of the program are produced.

Development and Implementation

While sound conceptions are important, being fundamental to sound program development and implementation, ultimately the critical factor is power and who has the expertise and other resources to establish particular conceptions. Hence in this section I turn to the dynamics of program development and implementation to explore the activities of participants and their influence on those processes. As previously indicated, that entails examining a variety of situations involving participants from teachers and their students through an array of specialists to theorists and administrators, politicians and other societal managers, together with the processes and mechanisms they employ. Because those situations are so diverse, complex and dynamic they are difficult to study and interpret adequately. In consequence, there is much that has not been researched and with so many parts to be understood and interrelated, one must repeatedly 'make do' with available material and work towards tentative interpretations and conclusions. I have found it convenient to begin by briefly reviewing the centralized and local modes of operating that constitute polar types, then examine developments in the 1950s, 1960s and early 1970s when the processes of curriculum development and implementation became even more complex and dynamic with even more participants, and finally examine developments in the 1980s when considerable effort has been put into transforming the priorities of schooling and to influencing the development and implementation of programs.

The oldest and formerly most common mode of developing and implementing programs has been for teachers to act individually or collectively in a school. Indeed, it was the widespreadness of those practices that gave significance to the efforts of the Jesuits in the seventeenth century in establishing a common program for all their schools. The pattern of central development and direction of implementation of programs was then taken up in the emerging nation-states of Western Europe in the eighteenth and nineteenth centuries as means of universalizing literacy and numeracy and mobilizing support through developing religious and political commitments. Concurrently, practices such as teacher inspection with payment by results, the use of systems of examinations, and centrally controlled teacher education programs that socialized prospective teachers into system priorities and practices were commonly adopted to extend central control by indirect mechanisms. These have subsequently been developed in more sophisticated and subtle forms of ensuring compliance so that in many societies teacher and school responsibility for programming is limited in scope.

Largely reflecting its particular historical experience, substantially different modes of operating were established in the USA, with schooling and programs growing out of local support and control, and so initially characterized by a diversity of practices. Partly in consequence, it was an initiator of the use of more 'useful' subjects such as modern as against classical languages, and the establishment of a more open ladder-type system of schools in contrast with the dual or multiple systems employed elsewhere. In addition, Dewey provided a powerful rationale for more developmentally-oriented programs that had substantial impact in the twentieth century (e.g. Cremin, 1961). Even so, such indications of openness and of common programs are deceptive in that schools in the US were clearly differentiated qualitatively by type of community, and so provided different kinds of experiences for different groups of students as Lynd and Lynd (1929, 1937), Hollingshead (1949) and others demonstrated in early community studies.

In contrast, England constituted an intermediate case which included both central and local responsibility at different times and for different sections of schools. Thus religious pluralism was early associated with a diversity of practices and substantial teacher and school autonomy. As the public system of control developed during the nineteenth century, diverse mass programs were initially controlled by teacher inspection and payment by results, and then increasingly by the establishment of systems of examinations and teacher training programs. In the 1920s central control was relaxed, possibly as a conservative government device for preventing a future socialist government from establishing national control over school programs (Grace, 1985; Lawn and Ozga, 1986). Since the 1970s, however, the trend has been towards increased central control of programming as another conservative government has set about transforming the modes of operating of not simply English schools but the society of which they are part.

The basic polar situations have been widely employed and are useful examples in illustrating features of each type of approach. Thus in more centralized systems, program development and implementation have commonly entailed the establishment of specialist sections that work within the bureaucratic modes of operating and the career structures of large-scale systems of schooling, with direct consequences for the modes of operating. For example, the centralizing of responsibility can be valuable when teacher and other resources in schools are limited or when a change of direction is required and existing teacher and other resources are inappropriate. However, central control is also a convenient means for imposing a particular ideology and its associated practices or for establishing and maintaining the dominance of particular groups within a system. In either case, it can be restrictive and frustrating for teachers. Indeed, its usefulness diminishes as teacher and other resources improve and provide a more adequate basis for local initiatives.

For their part, local responsibility and control of curriculum development and implementation are valuable for the greater flexibility they allow in responding to the interests and requirements of particular groups of children and communities. However, because of the crucial nature of adequate resources, they have serious detrimental consequences for poorer communities and their schools.

Partly because of shortcomings with these more conventional modes of undertaking curriculum development and implementation, it is useful to examine developments during the 1960s and early 1970s when considerable resources were available. This was also a period that saw a considerable increase in the range of participants and in the complexity and sophistication of curriculum development and implementation work.

The period following World War II initially entailed considerable expansion, partly to establish schooling for populations hitherto not served, as in third world societies, and partly to provide secondary schooling for hitherto neglected sectors of populations in more industrialized societies. Concern with content and quality was stimulated by the significance given in the 1950s and 1960s to economic growth, including imperatives for third world societies to develop industrially, and by the 'cold war' relationships between the West and Eastern Europe. These concerns were then given additional priority in the West with Russia's launching of Sputnik in 1957 which was taken as demonstrating its considerable technical competence and even superiority, and used, particularly in the US, to make a case for greater resources for education.

The 1960s saw a virtual explosion of program developmental activity, initially in the US but soon emerging in other societies. Largely under the umbrella of a National Defence Education Act and a later 'War on Poverty' in the US, a nationally established Schools Council in England, and counterpart organizations in some other societies, substantial resources were invested in curriculum projects. Thus post-Sputnik fears in the US about scientific and technological competence led to the undertaking of many national projects, involving academics and teachers in particular disciplinary fields, together with curriculum development, evaluation and other specialists, to produce programs that drew on recent developments in disciplines. Indeed, the concern with special expertise was sometimes taken to such an extent that attempts were made to devise 'teacher proof' programs. A similar approach was employed in some Schools Council projects in England, although teacher influence there was greater, partly because of the high proportion of representatives from teacher organizations on critical committees, and partly through their influential involvement in project activities. Interestingly, teacher adoption of the programs devised was usually limited, and probably the most significant outcome was through the experiences of participation with teachers carrying over insights and increased competencies into their classroom practices.

In an informative 'insider' study of one such project, Shipman (1974) illuminated the experiences of participation and the problems encountered in an integrated studies project. Working on a 'one-off' type of project, team members had to learn as they worked, and work in too short a time period, with schools participating for many reasons, often related to circumstances associated with their particular situations and priorities. All too soon, too, team members became concerned with their own career prospects. So while it may have been a useful step in a process of developing theories of program development and implementation, the project led to uncertainty concerning outcomes and influences on school practices or on theoretical developments.

Other national projects have been undertaken under different conditions that offset some of the problems reported by Shipman. For example, the Australian federal and state governments set up an Australian Science Education Project (ASEP) in the late 1960s and a Social Education Materials Project (SEMP) in the early 1970s which were undertaken by seconding specialists from school systems and by working with schools from within the public and private systems. But they, like the operation of state departmental curriculum and research sections, have not been studied and so their dynamics have not been reported on. Some obvious limitations derived from their location in bureaucratic or systems contexts where initiatives and activities were constrained by career and organizational priorities.

The Australian experience also illustrated sensitivity of centrally operated projects and programs to the concerns of particular interests. For example, state and federal ministers of education intervened following expressions of concern by community groups about ways in which human sexual activities and relationships were presented in materials. More conservative groups were able to gain high level political support in Queensland and have the M:ACOS program and a SEMP unit withdrawn from use in schools (Smith and Knight, 1978).

The period of heightened interest in curriculum development also generated considerable academic interest in establishing 'sound' educational bases for curriculum decisions. For example, Phenix (1964) in the US sought to identify a basic set of 'realms of meaning' and Hirst (1965, 1974) in England developed an analysis in terms of fundamental and distinctive forms of knowledge that could constitute sound bases for school program activity. However, while their analyses and arguments generated considerable debate, and were useful to proponents of particular specializations, they exercised little influence on overall program planning in schools, other than some official statements in England in the late 1970s and early 1980s. Reservations about them related to a preoccupation with 'knowing that' rather than 'knowing how' and a neglect of children's knowledge (Pring, 1976), and more generally with their overall rational emphases (Griffiths, 1986; Schilling, 1986).

These rational analyses were also countered by other developments.

The 1960s was a period of heightened concern about human rights and opportunities to develop and participate in political and other social activities. Those concerns were associated with the development and articulation of minority points of view and favoured the emergence of interpretivist positions that gave legitimacy to the alternative perceptions and interpretations that sustained minority movements. This trend was assisted by developments in general social theory (e.g. Berger and Luckmann, 1966) and the emergence of the 'new' sociology of education (Young (ed.), 1971) which emphasized the socially constructed nature of reality. Bernstein (1971) provided a framework for examining those trends with his characterizing concepts of classification and framing and his identification of collection and integrated types of curriculum. In particular, he highlighted the significance of power and of efforts to exercise influence through the work of curriculum development and implementation. Bourdieu and Passeron (1977) highlighted the cultural character of knowledge generally, and of school knowledge in particular and the role of elite knowledge in the reproductive role of schooling, while Foucault (1972) established the concept domains of discourse to identify groups and their socially constructed forms of communication. Thus the political character of disciplines and school subjects and curricula was established so that disciplines could be seen as social communities employing power and other resources to establish and maintain areas of academic and school activity, and the efforts of Hirst and others looked very much like efforts to give traditional subjects a legitimacy that masked their conservative character.

The prosperous times also facilitated the development of interest in more open arrangements. An articulate counter-cultural movement generated critiques of the rigidities and repressiveness of schooling in many societies (e.g. Holt, 1965), while openness was articulated and encouraged in England in the Plowden Report (1967) on primary schooling and found expression, albeit in closely controlled ways, in 'open day' schools in the late 1960s and early 1970s (Berlak and Berlak, 1981), and in Schools Council and other projects that explored integrated types of curriculum projects. It is important to recognize, however, that these developments did not necessarily become widely established; as indicated in the previous chapter on teaching styles, teachers remained predominantly conventional. Innovation in curriculum development was more in the visible projects and not necessarily in the ongoing day-by-day teaching undertaken in schools.

The obvious limitation of national projects, together with sentiments upholding the importance of teacher participation, generated efforts to establish curriculum development and implementation as a school-based activity. For example, Stenhouse (1975) argued that teachers should have a more substantial role and undertake research and development responsibilities. More recently, Skilbeck (1984) has argued the case for curriculum development and implementation being undertaken in schools and, in an accompanying volume (Skilbeck (ed.), 1984), provided numerous examples of competent contributions from people working in or associated with schools. Seen in the general context of the literature on classroom practices, together with those reported by Berlak and Berlak (1981) or the classroom work reported by Armstrong (1980) where the teacher operated an open, participatory type of relationships and employed art, space and literary art, and fostered creativity, imaginativeness, expressiveness, curiosity and exploration in learning activities, school-based curriculum developments emerge as exceptional examples, often occurring in exceptional circumstances in terms of resources and other conditions. As we saw in Chapter 5, the more usual preoccupations of teachers are with formally organized areas of knowledge, control and direction, and evaluation, differentiation and differential treatment. We also find substantial differences among teachers so that, for example, even within the same subject, as in the social studies studied by McNeil (1986), some teachers taught 'defensively', minimizing interaction, discouraging curiosity and questioning by students, and routinizing the teaching and learning processes, while others achieved more dynamic interactions.

It is in classroom studies, too, where observers have noted the interactions and negotiations between teachers and students, with students checking and testing norms, and establishing the extent to which the intended program can be modified or subverted. Classroom observations also enable observers to discern the selective and limited nature of what is checked on by monitoring tests, examinations or other forms of surveillance, and arrive at a sounder appraisal of the kinds and levels of student performance and achievements, as Stenhouse (1975) and others illustrated.

It is also in classroom studies that differentiation and discrimination have been recognized to be so prevalent. Thus Delamont (1983) and others have documented the variety of forms and the extent of gender differentiating practices, while Oakes (1985) reported strategies that result in ethnically differentiated groups, and Hargreaves (1967), Lacey (1970) and others have shown how streaming or tracking differentiates working- and middle-class students into different programs. Finally, Keddie (1971), McNeil (1986) and others have shown that 'bright' and 'dull' students can have quite different programs even where formal arrangements indicate programs are to be comparable.

Such situations and observations also remind us that for quality work to be done at the school level, however, poses substantial problems in the availability of time, expertise and other resources. Indeed, it is clear that when the operation of schooling is thoroughly decentralized, including access to financial and other resources, then schools can vary dramatically in capacity to mount and undertake programs. That certainly has been the case in the US with considerable variations in resources from one system to another, as well as from one state to another. Such differences are illustrated in the study by Anyon (1981) of five schools which varied markedly in resources and in the programs available to students and in how those programs were undertaken. Indeed, it is such variations in the situations and circumstances of schools that have generated efforts to combine the resources of communities into larger systems of administration to give access to more substantial state, regional or even national pools of resources, and thereby establish a prospect of raising the level of resources available to schools in poorer districts. The study by Ramsey and others (1983) of working-class schools in New Zealand illustrated that working-class districts in centralized systems can experience good schools and teaching so that children are not penalized by the disadvantages of low incomes and other inadequate resources experienced by their parents. Desirable, then, is a form of partnership with appropriate kinds of contributions made by the different sets of participants.

These studies of teacher situations in schools also remind us of the efforts of teachers to influence program development and implementation within and beyond the classroom and through their departments and subject associations. As Ball and Lacey (1980), St John-Brookes (1983), Ball (1987) and others have illustrated, secondary school departments constitute crucial units in the processes of developing and implementing programs as they attempt to increase resources and status, and to obtain better performing students, usually at the expense of other departments, thus generating interdepartmental contestations. They are also important units in networks that reach beyond schools to subject and other associations which can be important in the process of establishing, maintaining or enhancing a subject's identity or status, and thereby its significance in schools as well as the prospects of its teachers.

Goodson (1987) illuminated aspects of the role of such associations in studies of the emergence and development of geography, biology and environmental science in England, and illustrated the dynamic interaction that can occur between teachers, academics and others, and the significance of academic acceptance in the process of becoming 'established' as a school subject and as a university discipline. Again, Goodson (1987) showed how geographers and biologists who experienced marginality in their own subjects or disciplines took up environmental studies as an alternative domain of activity, while other, more mainstream specialists acted to inhibit the achievement of status by new subjects. Richardson (1973) reported similar efforts by history and geography teachers to block the establishment of social studies and humanities courses in their schools. At the same time, limits to possible achievements are evident as with the decline of classical languages which occurred despite the best efforts of teachers and departments to maintain their significance. A further interesting observation arising out of Goodson's study is that in the course of becoming academically acceptable, a subject is transformed, yielding pedagogic and utilitarian concerns, and becoming more appropriate for elite purposes such as the entry of higher performing students to tertiary educational institutions, and increasingly irrelevant to the majority of students. Goodson (1987: 10) cited Layton's analysis of the development of science in the nineteenth century in England which involved moving from justification in terms of its relevance to the needs and interests of students, to a reputation and growing status as a subject, and finally to initiation into a tradition, with established rules and values, with students' attitudes 'approaching passivity and resignation, a prelude to disenchantment'.

The discussion of social education subjects in England in the 1970s by Gilbert (1984) suggests some qualifications to this point. That is, legitimization of a subject at tertiary level and acceptance in university departments do not necessarily influence the content as taught in secondary schools. Rather, a modified version can occur so that content is fitted into an organizational or perhaps consensual functionalist framework, thereby presenting a content that legitimates existing social arrangements.

This may well occur at the tertiary level, too, but conditions and circumstances in secondary schools facilitate the dominance of such approaches. From there it is but a step to the defensive or routinized teaching reported by McNeil (1986). Goodson's study also identified sources and points of substantial influence within a system of schooling and which operated to sustain particular traditions such as the academic, and oppose or subvert other forces such as the requirements of the productive system. Therein incidentally lies a central dilemma for teachers, students and others involved in schooling, namely a tension between doing what is interesting and educative, and obtaining a credential that may be useful in furthering a career, whether for the teacher or the student.

Finally, in relation to the general situation, attention needs to be given to participants from outside the system who have had considerable impact on curriculum development and implementation. Altbach and Rathgeber (1980) indicated the considerable significance that major publishers have had on the production of books and other material, particularly in third world societies, while Mattelart (1979) indicated the emergence of huge conglomerates in media activity by the mid-1970s and their very considerable power arising from their control over media production. Since then, of course, the concentration of control over media resources has evolved much further with some now being media operators on a world scale, and able to influence the development of culture, the selection and presentation of knowledge, and the general content and identity of consciousness of populations (Hammer, 1989). By comparison, underresourced schools are rather minor participants in the task of establishing understanding and cultivating bases for social, political and other forms of action.

We must also note in passing some other agencies that contribute to the program development and implementation processes, and have critical influences. Publishers of material can be critical in the supply of material generally but they take on additional significance when particular interest groups emerge and actively pursue policies. Then publishers may act cautiously so as not to offend religious, business or other groups, or emphasize commercial considerations, which was a factor in the production of materials in the project studied by Shipman (1974).

Finally, in this consideration of a diverse range of participants, situations and activities that have been involved in programming, it is useful to note briefly some recent developments in the 1980s. To a degree they follow from development since the late 1960s with the emergence of a conservative reaction to alleged progressivism in many societies. But they also substantially reflect the turbulent economic circumstances of the 1980s and in relation to which governments in many societies have taken initiatives with profound implications for programming activities.

The ever-present tension regarding schooling, reflecting different ideologies and conceptions of what schooling should be used to do, and how it should be operated, re-emerged in the late 1960s with the conservative criticisms as in the Black Papers in England (Cox and Dyson (eds), 1969a, 1969b). Moreover, they were particularly astutely targetted with claims that standards of performance were declining and responsibility attributed to progressive program, pedagogic, organizational and other practices (e.g. Ball, 1985).

The concerns and anxieties that such attacks stimulated were exacerbated by the onset of difficult economic circumstances in the mid-1970s. Problems of inflation and recession, the dislocation of production and supply, the rapid increase in unemployment, particularly among youth, generated frustration and anxiety among students and their parents. At the same time, some politicians, employers and other social managers held schooling to be largely responsible for the economic malaise and often used it as a convenient scapegoat. Thus a period emerged of considerable criticisms of the effectiveness of schooling that were held to justify a wide array of efforts to establish greater control over its operations. In England, for example, an extensive battery of techniques and mechanisms has been employed to transform the priorities and modes of operating schooling, including the reorganization of examinations and teacher education, the support or sponsorship of vocational education through the Department of Employment's Manpower Services Commission, and more recently a major Bill that involves such requirements as a national curriculum and the periodic testing of students.

The trends are familiar to educators in many societies, although a point of interest is in the diversity of techniques employed to achieve similar outcomes. A conservative US national government has operated by reducing support for education, while states have resorted to objective tests that can limit the aspirations of teachers and students. Similarly, an illuminative development in Australia is the federal Labor government's placement of education in a 'mega-department' of employment, education and training, with a concurrent expression of considerable commitment to subordinating education to productive activity, particularly in tertiary institutions, where the federal government has more influence. At the same time, development in the mid-1980s typically involves recognition of high level technical competence so that the process is one of limiting in type rather than by level.

One can also speculate, with reasonable grounds for doing so, about power struggles within public bureaucracies as particular sectors of civil servants seek to take over other areas of activity. Again, long-standing patterns of activity are being overturned in tertiary institutions with, sometimes, entrepreneurial initiatives that relate clearly to economic prospects, but sometimes, too, to a new breed of academic 'predators' scourging the academic scene.

These larger-scale movements also enable us to identify some of the more substantial although often less directly involved participants in program development. Thus we have noted, for example, ideologues such as the Black Paper protagonists. We should also take account of those involved in producing such reports as *A Nation at Risk* in the US which, although a somewhat specious document, was significant in generating discussion and stimulating action to undertake 'rescue' operations in respect of schooling, and possibly neglect action in other more significant areas. Such contributions in turn direct attention to the media which usually highlight reports critical of schooling and consistently ignore supportive reports. Such highlighting and anxiety-producing activity in turn affects parents, politicians and others, and may also induce employers and others indirectly associated with schooling to add their comments, and so worsen the situation regarding schooling.

The turbulent and difficult times also encouraged or challenged some educators to reassert educational priorities in programs and, in particular, to attempt to achieve the establishment of a more comprehensive core in school programs. While in some respects their efforts have continuity with the work of Phenix, Hirst and others, they have usually extended their efforts beyond the rational elements to include expressive, creative and other types of activities. For example, in a discussion of core curriculum, Skilbeck (1984) offered the proposal of the Australian Curriculum Development Centre (CDC, 1980) as an example. It involved such areas of knowledge and experience as arts and crafts, social, cultural and civic studies, health education, scientific and technological ways of learning and their social application, communication, moral reasoning and action, values and belief systems, and work, leisure and life styles.

Such proposals have had little impact, however. As the period of economic turbulence has continued and even intensified within an increasingly integrated and competitive world economy, together with considerable developments in technology and so in processes of production, the prospects of particular societies have changed and governments have been increasingly disposed to harness education to operate more effectively in relation to their production systems. Political managers have been disposed to require more traditional subject areas that lend themselves to transmissive teaching but in the process subvert the essential character of specialized enquiry approaches. Those requirements have been complemented by recourse to testing programs that emphasize the teaching of relatively trivial factual information rather than the use of more complex processes. Schooling for personal development and for political, cultural and other forms of development has received little attention or support and is commonly being reduced or made an optional extra.

At the same time, managers of government, business and other major areas of activity do not have total control over school programming. As noted previously, the efforts of educational theorists to assert a broad, more educational core program would give schools considerable scope for developmental activity. We must also note developments in social theory where perspectives other than the traditional scientific, positivistic, behaviouristic positions that sustain transmissive teaching have yielded considerable benefits to research and theory development, and have profound implications for teaching. Again, developments in technology and modes of production, and the competitiveness of the world economy, may sustain and even require more dynamic and creative school programs and teaching styles. But perhaps most important in this is for students hitherto differentiated and discriminated out of opportunities to be assisted in ways that enable them to see themselves as having more realistic opportunities in the world that is emerging.

Before we conclude this section on influences on program development and implementation, it is important to return to the topic of examination authorities. They are the formal mechanisms instituted to control the certification process and in doing so largely determine the character of senior school curriculum. In addition, their preferences for particular forms of knowledge exercise a broader influence on schooling more generally. Again, because of their significance they attract groups interested in exercising influence on senior secondary schooling and so become key political managerial agencies. For that reason we will consider them further in the next chapter. We should also keep in mind that examination authorities are a particular kind of body and in other societies that do not have them, other kinds of structures and mechanisms are necessary.

The discussion in this section has identified some of the participants in programming and related their activities to more general social situations and circumstances. Typically, both such participants and circumstances are seen as parts of the context in which curriculum development and implementation are undertaken, giving central significance to specialists in that area of activity. Such a view is clearly misleading; all are major participants and the former appear to be influential in fundamental ways, creating the possibilities and options from which curriculum development and implementation specialists work often as technocrats in severely constrained situations and circumstances. It is on that basis that we now turn to consider the major modes of operating, namely at national system and at a local and even school-based level.

Discussion

This chapter has examined programs experienced by students and activities associated with their development and implementation. The broad conceptualization takes in aspects of topics discussed earlier in the context of studenting and teaching, and could well include issues discussed later under servicing and managing. All are elements of the situations directly experienced by students and from which they learn, and arrive at conclusions relating to the school experience.

It is also clear from this view of the situation how complex and dynamic the programming process is. Hence, for example, conventional conceptions of centralized or school-based approaches identify only parts of the activity and some of the points of action associated with program development and implementation. Studies reveal the intense political activity that goes on within schools and through subject associations, examination agencies and other organizations to determine characteristics of particular subjects or what constitutes a program, or what place a particular element will have in a program.

In seeking to establish patterns or forms in program development and implementation, it is helpful to analyze schooling by levels. Thus it can be said that at junior levels teachers can be taken to have considerable authority and even autonomy to determine what shall be undertaken. Clearly, there are very strong expectations that children attain competency in literacy and numeracy but often, beyond that, teachers can work from very general principles in the activities and content they employ. It is here, too, that the developmentalist position has more scope.

The more extreme contrast with that is at the senior secondary level, with its specialist subjects, departmentalized structuring of schooling and links beyond the school with teacher, subject and academic associations, with examination agencies and tertiary institutions, employer and other special interest groups. The variety of groups reflects the more immediate social significance of the work done at that level, and the concerns of many groups to exercise influence on what is done. Correspondingly, the stakes and pressures for teachers are greater.

It is also tempting to interpret this situation as revolving very much about concerns with status. Certainly that is an important element but much more is involved. For the student, success at established requirements means entry to tertiary studies or more directly into higher levels of the workforce, and the opportunities for more interesting, congenial and rewarding employment. For the teacher, senior secondary teaching can be more interesting and rewarding, and possibly closer to one's own academic interests. Good performances at examinations are also tangible rewards for administrators and evidence that they are managing an effective school. Successful performance by children can also mean that parents' efforts and expectations have been satisfied. The returns to tertiary institutions, employers and other managers are probably more of convenience. Successful performance on appropriate programs provides a sound basis for selection or recruitment, and thereby the satisfactory operation of one's institution or organization into the future.

At the same time, this examination of the program development and implementation process has also indicated that many steps and situations are involved and many points at which activity occurs that are relevant to the ultimate experiences of children in classrooms. But this type of situation is not a mechanical one and so not simply as strong as the weakest unit, as in, say, a sound system. If there is a crucial unit in the process, it is almost certainly the teacher in the classroom. Well developed and produced program material is only valuable if it is used effectively by classroom teachers and richly experienced by students. But while good program material does not ensure effective teaching, good teachers can be effective with limited resources. Hence, if any single step is to be taken to improve the quality of schooling, it is almost certainly to be taken in respect of raising the quality of school staff. That point is probably the reason why administrators of leading schools pay close attention to the staff they recruit and do not give comparable priority to curriculum projects. That is not to suggest that the latter are of little significance, but simply to acknowledge that the latter are of limited value without good teachers.

A third theme that emerges from this examination of programs is of differentiation among program elements and their differential relevance to particular categories of students. While the rankings appear to be similar from one society to another, with high status given to more abstract, theoretical and academic subjects, it is not clear how the rankings are established. The analysis by Goodson (1987) is probably indicative of more than just the English situation; in that case acceptance of a subject depended on the response of the examination authority and in which tertiary discipline specialists constituted influential members. Their influence related in turn to their status within the tertiary sector; thus the academic status of biology and geography improved greatly when their subjects were more readily accepted in universities, and departments were more readily allowed or accepted. Thus criteria follow from the research or knowledge production status of a subject, and efforts by tertiary academics to align secondary teachers to their priorities are supported by secondary teachers who benefit from the alignment in terms of their own standing, access to resources, appeal to students and in the value of their subject in the sifting and sorting process. One can assume that similar processes operate in other societies, although the main mechanisms may be different.

For other students who are not disposed to abstract, theoretical academic subjects or find them difficult, then lower status, more practical programs and identities await them. In some societies, such as Germany, the status differences appear to be not so marked, and success at practical courses can lead to high status occupations and careers. But generally students are distributed across different kinds of curricula, given different levels of status, and other characterizations, and move along in a process of occupying different kinds of positions in society.

Unfortunately for students, these tendencies relate not only to the program aspect of schooling but to the allocation of resources more generally. As we have seen from the study by Goodson (1987), the subject base is an important point in the process of maximizing status, resources and opportunities to attract good students, and so obtain good results. Those efforts impinge on or interact with other areas of activity within a school, such as the servicing and management of schooling activity. Hence it is convenient to turn our attention to those other processes.

Chapter 7

Servicing

While programming is a major process employed in schooling, it is far from the only one. The assessment and evaluation of the performances of students and staff, the pre- and in-service education of teachers, the counselling and guidance of students together with social welfare work with students and staff, the undertaking of research, and policy analysis and planning constitute other tasks that have been differentiated out and undertaken as specialist activities, either taken up by or assigned to particular kinds of specialists. All constitute services of one kind or another, although it is not always clear whom they are servicing. While on the one hand they are often tasks or responsibilities relevant to the undertaking of teaching and studenting, teachers and students rarely if ever have responsibility for or control over them. Typically they are established and operated to facilitate the management of a system of schools. At the same time, these activities are of interest in themselves and attract participants who develop expertise and pursue achievement, aggrandisement and careers, and possibly in ways that are not compatible with the priorities of teachers or managers. That is, servicing involves a set of activities and an array of participants who constitute dynamic elements in the schooling process.

Although some services such as the examination and assessment of students have a long history, most are of relatively recent origin. At the same time, all have developed greatly in recent times and now entail extensive and complex operations and involve specialists, often organized into specialist units, and thereby generate further requirements in the management and operation of schooling.

A multitude of factors are associated with their emergence as specialized practices. A major one is the growth of knowledge that encourages differentiation and specialization and the development of particular kinds of expertise. Those processes are assisted by the varied interests and

The Social Dynamics of Schooling

competencies of participants who find opportunities and satisfaction through specializing, and further their prospects by developing programs, careers and organizational arrangements. At the same time, sponsors and managers also find these specializations useful both in the general undertaking of schooling which has become so much more complex a process, and as agents whom they can influence or steer by setting up particular kinds of projects, or by offering support, careers or other incentives. By such means, sponsors and managers mobilize expertise and effort onto particular tasks and even to work along particular lines, thereby influencing the ways in which schooling is undertaken. Of course, those specializing in these complementary tasks, like teachers, are not necessarily passively compliant so that although many may operate as mercenaries and do what they are directed to do, some act from theoretically developed positions and maintain integrity and diversity in the undertaking of schooling.

These activities and agencies attract not only specialists but also participants from other situations who find the tasks relevant and significant and seek to contribute in one way or another. Thus teachers often work with specialist agencies to gain additional experiences and contribute from their expertise as classroom practitioners. Academics see scope for applying their theoretical and technical expertise, exercising influence and possibly enhancing their reputations as educationists. But managers and others operating from outside schooling also see these agencies as avenues for exercising influence and so as mechanisms for steering the undertaking of schooling. More fundamentally, those with considerable resources can establish special agencies and structure them to operate on particular issues and in particular ways and so influence the identification of problems and the selection of means of studying and responding to them.

Unfortunately, the array of specialists and the varied ways in which they undertake their tasks have received little attention from researchers. As we have seen, programming is a notable exception. Significantly, each of the processes considered here has been the subject of extensive technical discussions which incidentally neglect social issues and implications and, in taking social aspects of situations as given, are essentially conservative and fail to make critical contributions. Such limited technicist perceptions encourage viewing these specializations as forms of technocracy, undertaken by mercenaries who hire their skills and expertise to available sponsors. However, as noted, some specialists are socially sensitive and perceptive so that at least some few qualify as professional specialists who act independently and responsibly.

In the absence of research studies of these servicing specialists in action, however, discussion must be largely speculative and particularly tentative in any conclusions drawn. Nonetheless, many points can be made that bear upon the operation of schooling and so the discussion of specialists has relevance not simply in itself but also in directing attention to an important aspect of the operation of schooling.

Assessment and Evaluation

Closely complementing programming in the operation and undertaking of schooling are the assessment and evaluation of the performances of students, staff and institutions. These entail the monitoring of performance by a multitude of means, in part to facilitate the improvement of performance but also to enable influence to be exercised in the control and direction of schooling. That is, while assessment and evaluation constitute key processes in the tasks of learning and teaching, and are of relevance to students, teachers and parents, they are also of considerable relevance to prospective employers and managers of tertiary institutions in their selection and excluding processes, and to system and society managers for their usefulness in controlling and steering a system of schools. By such means, priorities can be established, including definitions of what counts as knowledge and what constitutes meritorious or other performance. They exemplify the process of management by determining objectives and judging the efforts of respondents to those requirements. At the same time, they are not simply nor solely imposed processes in that teachers and others cooperate for such reasons as commitment to the worthwhileness or importance of the processes, to obtain opportunities to exercise influence, or to gain personal and collective status and other benefits. Ultimately, some of these become the specialists who undertake assessment and evaluation work, and so make 'the system' work.

It is incidentally interesting that although these activities have been the subject of extensive discussion in the literature, the vast bulk of that discussion is technical and neglects the social and political character of assessment and evaluation. Occasionally historians such as Roach (1971) and Montgomery (1978) have examined developments and related them to social circumstances, but the study of their contemporary use as social processes and in relation to contemporary social circumstances was long neglected. Accordingly, the slight volume by Broadfoot (1979), contributed to a series prepared primarily for students of education, constituted a landmark discussion in highlighting social features of assessment and evaluation activities. To her further credit, she wrote at a time of dramatically changing economic circumstances and identified connections between regressive trends in these practices and deteriorating economic circumstances.

Historically and contemporarily, assessment and evaluation procedures have entailed an extensive array of techniques. At one time or another they have involved individual or class testing and the more systematic examination of students, sometimes in a context of paying teachers in accordance with the results obtained with students. They have also entailed the inspection and assessment of teachers and the appraisal of schools. Contemporarily, they entail system-wide internal or external examinations, testing programs for all students or for selected samples in special monitoring programs, the testing of teachers and the credentialling of all at one point or another.

Partly reflecting developments in theory and practice and in the mechanical technology available, and partly reflecting an increase in the significance of schooling in selection and recruitment processes, the use of assessment and evaluation has been greatly extended in recent years. One such extension, reflecting also the emergence of more competitive and uncertain political and economic situations, has been the development of national programs such as the National Assessment of Educational Performance in the USA and the Assessment of Performance Unit in England to monitor school systems. A second has been the assessment and comparative evaluation of the performances of students across societies as with the International Association for the Evaluation of Educational Achievement (IEA) project with results then used to rank nations and sustain enquiries into how systems of schools may be operated more effectively (e.g. Husén (ed.), 1967). Partly as a consequence of the establishment and operation of such specialist agencies, measurement theory and practice are seen to be experiencing considerable development with profound implications for the undertaking of schooling. For example, Masters (1988), working with one such organization in the Australian Council for Educational Research (ACER), enthused about possibilities for assessment, diagnoses and credentialling through developments in standards referencing and item response theory, particularly when use is made of modern computer technology. Reassuringly, there was a recognition of the arbitrariness of what is selected as 'right' and 'wrong' answers, although cause for concern in the neglect of issues such as how students have 'gone wrong' as in their individual styles of thinking (p. 31). At the same time, such developments illustrate how educational developments are generated in that they opportunistically exploit developments elsewhere, as in technology for production and management, rather than obtain the development of technology that directly serves educational purposes. They are generated, too, by the adoption by system managers of styles of operating such as corporate management strategies with their proclivity to individualize and minutely specify task requirements and then establish performance indicators as bases for increasing achievement. In such ways, educational innovation can be steered by developments in other major areas of activity such as the economy.

Inevitably, practices diverge, reflecting different values, purposes, interests, ideological positions and other factors. A major basis for difference concerns whether the use of assessment and evaluation is for grading and credentialling or for diagnosing and treating learning difficulties. A concern with normative assessment is long established and of considerable significance to employers, managers of tertiary institutions and others who select from among sifted and sorted school leavers. It has been significantly modified in recent years by recourse to criterion referenced testing and its modern expression in standard referencing which are more explicit regarding what students can do; nonetheless, they remain means of portraying students' achievements and for the operation of the selective process. Diagnostic testing, reflecting concerns to promote the development and achievement of individual students, is more highly valued by educators but of little significance to selectors of higher performing students. Quite clearly, however, the dominance of particular interest groups such as employers and managers of tertiary institutions with their preoccupations with selection has sustained the preoccupation with psychometric approaches and techniques and the measurement of selected individual attributes. Meanwhile, teachers support diagnostic testing on which to base their teaching and developmental work. But more imaginative and creative approaches such as connoisseurship (Eisner, 1985) fare poorly in school assessment and evaluation.

Such developments have also been substantially assisted by managers with problems in monitoring, controlling and directing what is occurring in schools and by the efforts of steering organizations such as foundations, together with agencies they have sponsored such as the Educational Testing Service in the USA, the National Foundation for Educational Research in the UK, and educational research organizations in several other societies. In brief, a combination of forces, involving people working through organizations or less formally structured groups, has promoted the development of assessment and evaluation as another specialist area. We shall return to this point in Chapter 9.

As a consequence, assessment and evaluation are increasingly undertaken in specialized units. It is convenient for managers to establish sections or agencies as parts of the administrative apparatus for managing systems of schools, and which are directly under their control. Private sector steerers, particularly in the USA, have promoted formally independent organizations that nonetheless are dependent on systems and other patrons for support and contracts and which can significantly limit their autonomy and independence. Concurrently, specialists have promoted their expertise and sought to establish specializations within more autonomous and independent institutions such as universities. But other interested groups such as teachers whose activities are constrained and even directed by assessment and evaluation, together with employers and managers of tertiary institutions who are dependent upon assessed and evaluated school leavers, find it useful to exercise influence by joining the organizational agencies established to undertake assessment and evaluation.

The work of Goodson (1987) illustrates that credentialling bodies are subjected to considerable efforts by teachers in schools and tertiary academics who see acceptance of their subjects in the credentialling process as critical to achieving, maintaining and even extending status and prospects, while a contrary strategy can be to oppose the participation of rival subjects and their associated protagonists. Sometimes, too, these efforts derive from factions within a subject or discipline who use the credentialling process to establish dominance and reduce the influence of opponents. In such situations protagonists of a discipline in tertiary institutions, with their superior status and influence in disciplinary affairs, can be especially relevant and influential. Such contestants also illustrate the plurality of forms of knowledge and the political character of the activities entailed in determining what is taught in schools and thereby the educational experiences of students.

Less obvious and not well understood contributions are made by sponsoring organizations and agencies. For example, the Carnegie Foundation has been a major supporter of educational measurement and test development work, both supporting projects to develop expertise in and techniques for the measurement of individual attributes and performance, and establishing educational research and testing centres for the undertaking of assessment and evaluation activity (e.g. Lagemann, 1983).

Other participants in the assessment and evaluation processes are invariably drawn from employers and other economic managers. Their interest in the quality and employability of school graduates sustains their interest in credentialling not necessarily so much for ensuring particular kinds of knowledge or skills, as for ensuring that assessment and evaluation yield comparable measures which enable them to select the more talented in their recruiting.

The diversity of participants and their priorities and interests mean not simply a complex political situation in assessment and evaluation units but also trying times for the specialist operatives. In particular, specialists with more restricted technocratic perspectives can experience considerable frustration, seeing the situations as involving misuse of their expertise. Their real problem is in their political naivety, often following from more traditional and limited 'scientific' perspectives which assume that particular 'educational' aspects of issues can be abstracted from 'real' situations and treated in isolation, a situation that can be achieved only conceptually and has limited usefulness. In consequence, if specialists in assessment and evaluation are even moderately socially perceptive, then inevitably they recognize that they are participants in a socially and politically important activity, and thereby heighten the dynamic nature and tension of assessment and evaluation activity.

Teacher Education

Although a commonly used term, teacher education is at least partly euphemistic due to the exceptionally social and political nature and significance of the work of teachers and, correspondingly, of the work entailed in their preparation. Preparatory programs usually comprise several elements, some of which emphasize technical competence, including pedagogical techniques and strategies, while others emphasize social understanding and competence and bear upon what tasks are undertaken and how they are undertaken (e.g. Alexander, 1984; Schneider, 1987). Accordingly, the social aspect of their preparation is of particular interest to system and other societal managers, and invariably more closely and critically monitored than other aspects of their courses or the courses of other professionals. Indeed, this prospect for teacher education courses to be closely monitored and the subject of directive government action has been a reason for university managers to be reluctant to accept them into their institutions (Patrick, 1986).

At the same time, the preparation of teachers has been and continues to be undertaken in quite diverse ways, both generally as well as between types of teachers. Thus those who undertake more senior teaching, as at the upper levels of secondary schooling or for other higher status, more academic programs, are invariably prepared through more academic institutions such as universities, and sometimes without a specific educational component. In contrast, those prepared for junior pre-school to primary and even junior and lower status secondary teaching have varied from few if any requirements to apprenticeship training to more fully developed theoretical and practical programs. Similarly, once specific preparation has been accepted, then institutions have varied, substantially in an evolutionary process, developing from normal schools to teachers' colleges to state or other forms of sub-university institutions. An important feature of the development, incidentally, has been a succession of strategies for ensuring that teacher education was undertaken within institutions that were operated as part of a system of schools rather than as separate autonomous institutions. Only relatively recently, and then often as a consequence of politically required reorganization of institutions, have courses for lower level teachers been incorporated into universities.

Factors associated with their different practices are also many and diverse. In part they derive from the aspirations associated with particular kinds of schools. Thus the families and managers associated with elite schools such as those reported on by Cookson and Persell (1985) seek to maintain their status by recruiting from higher status tertiary institutions and programs, giving significance to candidates who themselves attended such schools. Correspondingly, lower status schools, often at a disadvantage in terms of resources and other conditions of operating, are obliged to be less selective and accept from a wider range of less well qualified although not necessarily less competent candidates, judged in terms of other priorities and styles of operating. A second factor is a concern for managers to control and direct and ensure that teaching is undertaken in 'safe' ways often, as has been noted, in institutions operated within the general system of schools. Prospective teachers constitute a further force in that, by pursuing particular programs and career paths, they endorse not only the particular forms of structuring schooling but also of teacher education and the diverse arrangements and programs that are operated. Finally, for present illustrative purposes, institutions and their programs are determined in part, too, by the priorities, orientations, commitments and other characteristics of their staff. These vary on such dimensions as the theoretical and the practical, the teaching of specializations or the development of the child, the transformation of society or reproduction of the status quo in important respects. At the same time, certain of these elements relate to levels of teaching with transmission and incidentally reproductive modes driving senior secondary teaching and progressive or developmental and incidentally transformative modes influencing the education of teachers of younger students at pre-school and junior primary levels. Interacting with those situations and teacher education, and influencing the significance of particular factors, are more general economic and political circumstances with developmentalism more favoured in prosperous times, and transmission, differentiation and stratification more strongly promoted in times of recession and greater competitiveness and uncertainty.

In the contemporary period the main undertakers of teacher education are the professional and academic specialists who staff the colleges and university departments involved. These comprise a diverse array, varying from more technical specialists in 'how to' competencies such as teaching at primary or pre-school level or in the specializations involved at secondary level, to foundation and other specialists whose work relates more to the 'contexts' in which teaching and learning are undertaken. The former practical concerns have a long history of inclusion whether in apprenticeship-type situations or in more abstract, academic and theoretical forms of pedagogy. However, while they have an obvious relevance, they are too readily limited by a narrow focus on the more visible aspects of teaching and a neglect of less obvious factors that nonetheless substantially influence the activities of teachers and students.

Early additions to these more practical specialists comprised those who provided a social or moral framework and content for teaching and socialized prospective teachers into particular orientations and modes of operating. These were seen as important elements because of concern among some political, religious and other societal managers that schooling might raise aspirations among lower-class people and thereby generate social unrest. Their activities progressively evolved into work by historians and philosophers and, as more authentic and competent specialists such as Durkheim and Dewey developed their teaching responsibilities, made important contributions both to enriching the experiences and development of students, and to promoting the more comprehensive understanding and effective practice and operation of schooling.

A further addition to those types of expertise emerged with recognition of the significance of an understanding of children and so the appointment of psychologists to teacher education institutions. They in turn have reflected trends in the source discipline of psychology and often expressed more scientific orientations and approaches that have little to do with the development of children and their background circumstances and experiences and ongoing development. Also, reflecting common preoccupations with control and management, their psychological and more particularly psychometric orientations and approaches have appealed to managers and assisted their rise as a dominant group within teacher education. At the same time, reflecting the contributions of some notable psychologists such as Piaget, they have made valuable contributions to teacher education and consolidated their positions on educational grounds.

The more prosperous economic circumstances of the 1950s to the early 1970s were associated with expanding conceptions of relevant factors in understanding and undertaking schooling. The stimulants to those developments derived partly from more generous and altruistic dispositions from those enjoying greater prosperity, and also from the aspirations of hitherto substantially excluded or discriminated against socio-economic, gender and ethnic minority groups. Their experiences and circumstances and increased assertiveness influenced developments across the social sciences and incidentally the study and practice of schooling and teaching. Hence sociologists, anthropologists, economists, political scientists, demographers and other specialists found important problematic issues in the general operation of schooling, and explored its operation in relation to the operation of the state, the economy and other systems of activity. They also indicated connections between more specific aspects of schooling such as the curriculum, the teaching of particular subjects and topics, and school organization and system management, and so exposed systemic features, including processes such as differentiation and discrimination in the undertaking of schooling.

The relationship of the development of these approaches to the more prosperous times of the 1950s, 1960s and early 1970s is further testified to by the discouragement of them by political and other societal managers in the economically turbulent late 1970s and 1980s. Political direction of researchers has substantially reduced activity in the 'foundation' studies in a number of societies but notably in retrogressive Thatcherite England, and fostered restricted, more 'practical' conceptions of what is entailed in schooling (e.g. Woods and Pollard (eds), 1988). Such restricted views also favour simplistic conceptions that interpret situations in terms of individual behaviour and give little or no credence to the capacity of people to organize and act collectively and through structures in imposing arrangements that constrain and even direct the activities of others. More seriously, it is highly probable that the managers do not see any advantage or useful purpose in these situations being examined and analyzed but are content with a jungle-type situation of competition and struggle. The limitation to that interpretation, however, is that such managers readily favour more established and successful participants through manipulating both the collection and the distribution of public resources in schooling and in other systems of activity. Invariably, they are far from impartial as managers but rather concerned to preserve particular privileged modes of operating.

It is also evident that many other than professional specialists participate in teacher education programs. There is considerable reliance on classroom teachers who demonstrate practices and supervise students at practice, together with school administrators who organize and manage aspects of the practice situations. Less obvious but of greater significance in important respects are the system managers, politicians and others who establish structures and generally control teacher education institutions and arrangements. In many societies teacher education is carried out within institutions that are part of the overall system of schools, and mechanisms are employed to ensure harmonious relationships with considerable socialization of prospective teachers to maximize their accommodation to the operation of schools. In less regulated societies such as the USA, teacher education is much more subject to 'market forces' and major operators such as the business sector ensure their priorities are considered and compatible structures and strategies employed, largely by working through sponsorship arrangements. Thus foundations, for example, have expended considerable resources in working on identifying and examining problems, devising policy recommendations and providing inducements for particular policy initiatives to be promoted and implemented (e.g. Carnegie Council on Policy in Higher Education, 1979; Buss, 1980; Carnegie Forum on Education and the Economy, 1986).

Others influence the teacher education process incidentally rather than directly. Significant among these are theorists and researchers such as Marx, Durkheim, Freud and Dewey, Piaget, Bourdieu and others who have provided insights and understandings that sustain particular modes of operating schooling and undertaking teaching and learning. Teacher education is not a discrete activity but interactive with developments in other aspects of social activity upon which teacher educators draw in their examination and interpretation of schooling activity and in undertaking practical activities from teaching to the establishment, operation and management of schools.

So, while seemingly undertaken in discrete institutions and in distinctive ways, teacher education is of considerable significance to a wide range of people from those working in schools and the parents of children who attend, through to the political, business, religious and other managers of society. At the same time, the specialists involved in teacher education find it useful to draw on the resources and contributions of other agencies and specialists in order to enhance their own activities, achievements and contributions. Thus it is a complex system of activities, no less diverse in its range of participants than schooling itself. Teacher education has been preponderantly oriented along particular lines, varying over time, but reflecting the priorities of dominant groups in those times, and so particular kinds of influence on how teaching is perceived, interpreted and practised. And that is no chance event, but reflects the definite efforts of particular managers or steerers of schooling activity. This is again being borne out in the present when, in the name of economic crisis, teaching and teacher education are being steered to operate as more narrowly conceived and thereby conservatively undertaken modes of operating.

Research

The process of research involves the development and use of systematic approaches to the identification of problematic issues, the formulation of questions and the examination of situations and experience. Of itself, it is a straightforward enough process, widely undertaken in one form or another and to some extent or another. However, it is also a remarkably complex activity, involving not simply technical diversity and complexity in the methods and strategies employed, but also different perspectives, derived from different ontological, epistemological and moral assumptions, as was indicated in Chapter 1, and which sustain alternative approaches to research. In consequence, researchers constitute a set of diverse and dynamic social communities and often compete and contest in the undertaking of research and in the examination, analysis and portrayal of reality.

Partly reflecting those conditions, researchers exhibit considerable diversity in their situations and circumstances and in the work they do. Although curiosity is an individual characteristic, and much good and even exceptional research is done by individuals operating alone and even idiosyncratically, a widespread tendency is to organize researchers into teams to work on assigned problems. In organized and institutionalized activity, research assumes much greater significance, being the process by which the problematic, modes of undertaking enquiry, and forms of responses are determined. In a fundamental sense, it is a major instrument for determining concerns and agendas and the modes of operating of participants in both organized and unorganized forms of social activity. That is, it can be used as a central political process, and the object of control and direction, as with other parts of system activity. Thus system managers establish and operate sections or departments, while public and private sponsors establish units to which they direct resources and substantially determine their agendas and modes of operating. Indeed, as we shall see more fully in Chapter 9, sponsors can substantially determine who undertakes research and how it is undertaken, and thereby substantially predetermine outcomes and responses to particular issues and problems. Less formal negotiations occur between researchers and sponsors and between researchers and managers of schools and systems and the students and staff who are active within them.

Universities in some societies have sought to retain academic freedom and the control over resources that that requires, but government, business and other managers have used relevance, the 'needs of society' and the purported economic crisis to assert their influence on the basis of their control over resources. Hence a widespread trend is for system managers to nominate what they regard as problematic and call for expressions of interest from researchers ready to work on those problems, often in ways acceptable to the sponsors (e.g. Nisbet, 1985).

Such modes of operating have a surface legitimacy in terms of the apparent appropriateness of the manager's position for identifying problems. At the same time, an abundance of research illustrates the bias of such preoccupations and the partiality and inadequacy of their perceptions. Indeed, the emergence of interpretivist positions in the 1960s reflected the activism of minority groups and their assertion of different perceptions and interpretations. Clearly, the assertion of managerial priorities is more for control and direction purposes than for increasing understanding and achieving better performance. Examples of that priority occur all the way from managers of small-scale systems to the more substantial societal managers who operate through corporations, government departments, foundations and other major organizations.

Concern for control and direction of the research process as an aspect of management, together with concern for the assertion of minority and subordinates' concerns, are reflected in issues to do with research perspectives. In particular, management has found the functionalist concept of organism convenient as a metaphor for the organizations they manage. They have also found the behaviouristic concern with observable and measurable data convenient as a basis for impersonalism and apparent objectivity in the bureaucratic styles of operating employed in managing situations. A serious limitation is that it disguises the point that only their subjective choices and concerns are taken into account. At the same time, its usefulness to managers has incidentally been helpful to specialists whose careers and organizations are advanced by the attractiveness of their modes of operation to those managers. However, by excluding the subjective concerns of subordinate and minority groups, such processes are inherently discriminating.

Alternative interpretivist, conflict and other perspectives thus have theoretical and practical justification and appeal in that they are more illuminative and useful, particularly for minority groups and subordinate sections of a population. Thus in schooling, for example, interactionist perspectives have provided a means for catching students' perceptions and interpretations (e.g. Woods, 1983), while conflict perspectives have highlighted differences in power and the conflicts among groups in the assertion of priorities and the achievement and maintenance of dominance (e.g. Collins, 1979). These features initially encouraged interpretations that ethnographic perspectives were inherently conducive to democratic research but it is evident that managers can use them to ascertain what troublesome subordinates are concerned about. Thus research perspectives are not inherently instruments of domination or participation but can be used for a multitude of purposes. Hence a critical issue is the control of resources to enable the research process to be used in one way or another.

The differences in perspectives and approaches also have implications for those who participate in the research process. Some more established positions such as behaviourism, with their conceptions of impersonality and objectivity and a high emphasis on technical competence of rather limited kinds, are most exclusive, justifying the researcher's right to make decisions on all major aspects of a research project while assigning passive and compliant roles to subjects and others. In contrast, a service approach seeks to ascertain the problems of others as those to be researched and involves those others in the research process, as in some forms of action research. Again, authentic enquiry-style social science education in schools can involve students as enquirers or researchers, learning their social science by 'doing it'. In these cases the specialist shares responsibility with others in more participatory or democratic forms of behaviour.

Such modes of operating are relatively rare, however, and normally sponsors and specialists control and direct research activity. The considerable incidence of such modes of operating at least partially testifies to the social and political significance of the research process as the mechanism in controlling and directing schooling and other activities.

Policy Development and Planning

These two sets of activities are integral parts of all aspects of undertaking and operating schooling. They are also undertaken by all involved in schooling in that parents, students and teachers as well as administrators appraise situations and devise policies and plan their strategies and, in doing so, undertake forms of research and other activities. As is often the case, however, the activities of developing policies and undertaking planning are preempted by system managers so that only their activities in these areas are formally recognized and given significance. By such means, the concerns and activities of other participants are effectively disestablished.

Formerly, as with assessment and evaluation and other activities, policy and planning activities for systems of schooling were formally undertaken by managers incidentally in the course of undertaking management tasks. More recently, reflecting growth in the complexities of systems and in the knowledge and other resources necessary for examining and interpreting situations, specialization has evolved and resulted in the appointment of specialists and in the establishment of special policy and planning units. These now exist as sections within departments and systems of schooling, or in organizations such as parent, teacher and other associations, or in 'think tank' policy centres in academic or other specially established institutions. As academics have become involved, then further specializations such as policy analysis, involving the analysis and appraisal of proposals from public departments and private organizations, have become important activities.

As with research and other activities, policy development and planning are important aspects of managing organizations and systems of activities. It is through policy development that options are identified and strategies developed, thereby determining how problematic situations will be responded to while, incidentally, other possible courses of action are excluded from consideration. For such reasons, control of policy development and planning is of critical significance, thereby explaining the practice of establishing and operating specialist sections within public departments and private organizations.

It is also the justification for corporations, foundations, governments and other holders of considerable resources to establish or support policy centres and 'think tanks' as well as particular projects to undertake studies on specific issues and develop policy proposals and strategies. Private sector operations are particularly common in the USA, and have been especially prominent in developing strategies in relation to education issues, thereby helping to set the courses of action which public authorities are likely to pursue. As such, operating from 'outside' systems of schooling, they qualify as steering agencies and will be considered further in Chapter 9.

An important issue associated with the appointment of specialists in policy development and planning concerns the kinds of expertise relevant to their work. Because they deal with the 'real' world in all its complexity and volatility, no specific academic specialization is adequate to enable them to operate soundly and effectively. For their part, social scientists seeking to understand the 'real' world find it useful to draw upon particular forms of expertise such as those of sociologists, economists, political scientists, and other specialists. On the other hand, a temptation in policy work is to employ people with particular techniques such as those of the econometrician, or draw upon someone who has achieved a reputation in discussions of a particular issue such a gender discrimination in education. However, if they lack the sound and extensive cultural capital of particular social sciences, then they are notably inadequately equipped for understanding the totality of social reality to be confronted in policy and planning work. Hence, although inconvenient, a sound approach to policy development and planning involves a team of complementary specialists, with anything less likely to be inadequate and unsound.

The significance of policy development and planning means that it attracts considerable attention, and efforts to participate or exercise influence in other ways. The specialists are the obvious leading participants but they invariably work in situations, steered or monitored by committees, task forces or other collections of representatives of managers or steerers. In addition, an extensive range of parents, teachers, employers, concerned citizens and other groups is interested in any issue given attention for policy and planning purposes. Moreover, these groups can be expected to have different views from each other in their concerns and priorities and also to comprise differing sections within each group. Ultimately, decision-making reflects relative power and goes beyond technocratic procedures and entails political activity, both among the specialists and their managers and steerers.

Steerers also include researchers and theorists who contribute to the policy and planning processes. Researchers such as economists, sociologists and other social scientists portray the social reality to which policy and planning relate, and the data that they take into account. In addition, philosophers and social and other theorists elucidate what is involved in policy and planning processes, and so give legitimacy to their modes of operating. Such expert contributions are not sufficient, however, to ensure the acceptability of practices; power is a major consideration so that present and future reality can be constructed and sustained coercively to meet the requirements of managers and others with exceptional resources. For example, in a study of educational planning in a third world society, Jones (1989) illustrated the significance of intra- and international political and military relationships for the undertaking of educational planning, resulting in ritualistic rather than realistic activities. In such situations, policy and planning specialists, wittingly or unwittingly, are often the tools of major operators in the operation of systems of schooling. Gaining their cooperation entails the provision of rewards in the form of income, status and influence, and sometimes the opportunities to do work of interest to them. That is, as with other activities, policy and planning activities involve many types of participants with considerable incentive for specialists to collaborate or be coopted to work on the projects of those with resources. Conversely, scope for those with independent or alternative views and strategies is severely limited.

Psychological and Social Services

The appointment of specialists to undertake psychological and social services is a relatively recent development, and one that reflects a growing recognition of personal and social problems of students and staff in schools and school systems. Provision of the services also represents a shedding of responsibilities by managers and their assistants as they recognize that they are unable because of the pressure of other demands, inadequacy of appropriate expertise or other reasons to deal adequately with these problematic conditions and circumstances. The provision of the services also reflects an evolutionary development in comprehending issues involved, moving from initial perceptions of problems as being those of individuals to later perceptions of the relevance of social arrangements and processes as contributing circumstances.

The provision of such services was initially in response to problems in dealing with students. The development of psychology as a specialization also produced specialists seeking employment and opportunities to undertake psychological work and develop career opportunities. Concurrently, managers have found it useful to employ specialists who explain students' performances in such terms as intelligence, motivation or other personal factors. Subsequently, sociological and other research revealed that students' performances reflect more complex situations, including family and community situations and circumstances, and factors to do with the operation of schools. However, psychologists have remained attractive to school managers and other staff because of their disposition to modify students rather than require modification of organizations, and thereby support the entrenched positions of more powerful participants in schooling.

A more recent development has been to recognize personal and relational or social problems among staff. These involve states of morale and mental health and stress, and can often be related to dramatic and substantial changes in the operation of schools and the systems of which they are part. The individualist interpretations favoured by psychologists are less tenable in this area, possibly because staff can be more articulate and assertive regarding their concerns about situations, and make claims about conditions and circumstances in schools and systems such as rates and extent of change, limited career prospects, and other constraining and damaging circumstances.

While comprehension has extended the range of identified problems and their incidence among staff as well as students, and established the relevance of organizational as well as family and community factors, it has not been straightforward for specialists to act effectively in response to them. That they are employed by and responsible to school and system managers and achieve somewhat bureaucratic career structures within systems of schools predisposes them to serve the organization rather than the students or staff clients, as Cicourel and Kitsuse (1963) noted many years ago. Correspondingly, they are substantially neutered as professionals and have to be seen more as technocratic specialists operating in accommodation with management requirements to run a smoothly functioning system of institutions.

Better prospects for professionals may arise from employment within teacher, parent and other associations or in private practice. Such circumstances do not compromise them against personal clients, although at the same time they do limit their capacity to act in relation to the organization and the system in that they are now outsiders. In that respect they can be helped, however, by involvement with an association that can act in relation to the organization or the system.

Even so, these specialists constitute but a small proportion of participants in these services. Counselling and advising are activities undertaken by most participants in schooling — teachers of students and their colleagues, students of each other, principals and other administrators of staff and students, parents of their children and other parents and so on. Indeed, it is the widespreadness of advising and counselling that enables systems of activities to persist.

In that context the formal undertaking of counselling and advising assumes a more particular responsibility such as to deal with more critical or significant situations and experiences or when they become of a level of incidence that overloads informal arrangements. The appointment of specialists also offers the bypass of what could be confrontational situations for students and teachers or for either of those and administrators. And although specialists may be seen as separate from management, their appointments and prospects nonetheless indicate a dependence on management patronage and support and encourage a compliant and supportive approach that dissipates problems in the operation of schooling. Nonetheless, alternative rationales emerge and can sustain more independent and even assertive servicing strategies which can be inconvenient for managers. Generally, however, counselling and advising specialists are not ready or common sources of critical let alone subversive action but operate to facilitate the operation of organizations and the work of managers.

Consultants

The emergence of consultants is a relatively recent development, and a most interesting one to appraise. Clearly, it is related to the times which are congenial for entrepreneurialism and the restriction of the public provision of services. At the same time, it is a development that favours those with resources and leaves poorer people relatively unserviced. It reflects heightened self-centred individualism and lessened concern for economically, politically and otherwise disadvantaged people.

The novelty of consultants is that it involves different ways of providing services. Systems of schooling have hitherto mainly employed specialists to contribute expertise to particular tasks, as we have seen in discussing programming, assessment and evaluation, and other services. But although the 'in-house' provision of services is convenient, it is also an onerous undertaking involving long-term commitments in the provision of careers and associated benefits, and restrictions in that services are supplied only by employed specialists. Consultancy means that the client can 'shop around' and so select and negotiate services. By holding the resources, they can still control the conditions for the provision of services, while having greater flexibility in selecting specialists and not being locked into long-term commitments to employees as with the provision of career structures.

On the surface at least the specialist also experiences some advantages. For example, they can now operate as autonomous specialists, develop a practice and a clientele, and achieve increasing professional autonomy as they gain a reputation. At the same time, however, they remain dependent on patronage and so can find it necessary to provide satisfactory services. At that point, educational consultants may have some difficulty in that they do not operate in such clearcut situations as medical, engineering and other professionals who have greater recourse to objective criteria of effectiveness. To the extent that their effectiveness cannot be so effectively established, then there is scope to compromise integrity and provide a dubious service.

At the same time, it is useful to take account of developments in other professions and recognize possible prospects for education. One very real prospect on that basis is for the collectivization of consultants into organizations. Just as medical, accountancy, legal and other specialists

143

have found it convenient to join together in clinics and partnerships to provide a wider range of services, reduce overheads, obtain other benefits and possibly provide better services, so the prospect must be attractive to educators. But that again can be but an intermediate step with subsequent developments being for such groups of specialists to be incorporated into larger conglomerates. Thus an educational consultancy might be a useful section within a larger media group moving into the general field of educational services and complementing other sections of a media empire. In those contexts preoccupations can readily become with growth, market share, profit and other commercial priorities, while professional integrity can become dysfunctional and vitiated by commercial and other priorities and practices.

Such trends and potentialities have to be seen as very real at this time of rampant entrepreneurialism. At the same time, it is important to recognize that fashions change and so the priorities of clients and specialists can also change. While such a change is not seemingly imminent at present, it has to be recognized as a possibility. For the present, however, the trend seems to be clearly towards entrepreneurialism, initially in terms of individual specialists but ultimately as specialist units within conglomerates, and reflected in strategies for marketing a range of products and services, and oriented towards growth and profit rather than service.

Discussion

Schooling, like other systems of organized activity, has become increasingly complex and differentiated in the nineteenth and twentieth centuries, and given rise to increased specialization in the undertaking of responsibilities. In part this stems from increases in the scale of activities, with both a growth in population, at least until relatively recently, and increased participation as students stay longer at school. In part, too, it stems from growth in knowledge and its application in technology and other ways. One consequence is that particular operations such as assessing and evaluating or research have become more complex, adding to the complexities and difficulties of managerial activities, requiring the establishment and operation of specialist units, and also providing opportunities for staff to specialize and develop careers. However, it also creates a complex set of relationships, involving managers and technical specialists with concerns for the effective operation of systems of schools but also having sectionalist and even individual priorities and concerns. For such reasons the undertaking of specialist activities and their management involve a dynamic set of relationships that bear substantially on the operation of schooling.

For one thing, they contribute to the construction of perceptions of schooling. Theorists and researchers define and portray schooling either on their own conceptions of what is problematic or in response to managerial directives. Again, evaluation and assessment specialists establish conceptions of competence and inadequacy and so structure educational perceptions of students' performance in such terms as satisfactory or otherwise. Still again, tertiary academics and teacher educators establish conceptions of knowledge, including modes of organizing it, which can in turn structure curriculum and determine teaching styles and strategies and conceptions of achievement and performance. Thus in a multitude of ways specialists determine the operation of schooling and the undertaking of teaching and learning.

To argue in those terms is not to suggest that teachers are passive and accommodating to the initiatives and strategies of others, but it is to recognize and assert the considerable influence of others and thereby the interdependent if not dependent position of teachers. For while the teacher has a sobering contact with the realities of schooling to influence perceptions and interpretations, specialists operating within administrative frameworks are also sustained by the power of managers who can structure the situations in which teachers and others operate. In addition, and possibly more significant as an influence, are participants with exceptional resources from outside systems of schooling who offer powerful inducements to specialists and have them produce studies, reports and other material that contribute to the production of perceptions and interpretations, and to the determination of responses to events and situations. Accordingly, teachers and specialists may have to accept and act in relation to reality as defined, and even structured, regardless of its relationships to reality as they perceive and interpret it.

In undertaking their work and pursuing careers, specialists in conjunction with managers contribute substantially to structuring how schooling is undertaken. For example, they can constitute the centralized apparatus of systems and so limit the scope and autonomy of teachers. At worst, they can use excess proportions of social, economic and other resources so that work in schools is undertaken on substantially restricted bases. Such circumstances can in turn lead teachers to conclude that opportunities outside the classroom are more attractive than those inside, thus setting up a process that draws staff away from primary responsibilities.

At the same time, specialists and managers can move into tensions and contestations. Their priorities and concerns, reflecting managerial and specialist technical concerns, are inherently different and readily incompatible. In addition, of course, they experience common individualistic priorities and concerns that can generate tensions and contestations within sectionalist groups. These add to the complexities of priorities and activities, and to the difficulties and constraints under which teachers work.

Finally, given the intensely political character of schooling, these specialists are all deeply involved in the political activity of which schooling is part. Curiously, however, many exclude perceptions of the political character of their activities, largely by taking the system and particular situations such as schools as givens, and then seeing problems and issues as essentially technical matters. That that, incidentally, is a less stressful position from which to operate is a major factor influencing many specialist staff, and the perceptions and interpretations from which they operate and which in turn help to structure perceptions of schooling as essentially a technical operation. It can also mean that technically-oriented specialists are disturbed by more socially aware and questioning participants who do not take such situations as givens but question the status quo and recognize political realities. Nonetheless, by such means technocrats sustain the managerial positions and established modes of undertaking schooling.

Chapter 8

Managing

The management of schooling is virtually required by increases in scale and complexity of operations. These generate such imperatives as to direct and coordinate the activities to staff, use resources effectively, pursue certain priorities rather than others, and deal with external groups and issues. Indeed, conventional styles of management, with the appointment of a principal, superintendent or director, usually mean that these become the most visible, high status and possibly influential officials within the unit of activity. Not so evident but of considerable significance, too, is an array of associates, sometimes holding bureaucratic or political positions as with the management of finance and other resources or with responsibilities that bear upon policies and practices in schooling. In addition, as we saw in the last chapter, specialists work either within the system or in organizations that operate in close association with the system, and their efforts bear upon managerial activities and responsibilities. Influencing and possibly directing the operation of them, then, is a further management responsibility that grows increasingly complex in the contemporary period.

Invariably, management structural mechanisms take many forms with their number and diversity increasing with growth in the scale and complexity of school systems and in efforts to exert greater influence. A basic distinction, as indicated in Chapter 2, is between centralized and localized forms of control relating to whether authority is exercised substantially from the centre or the top in an hierarchical and bureaucratic system of structures or dispersed to schools or local districts as has been and still is substantially the case in the USA and in autonomous private schools. At the same time, this distinction can be more apparent than real, varying according to the degree of significance given to particular complementary mechanisms where control is exercised through the allocation of resources, the setting of objectives, the use of guidelines or other means. The nation-state commonly holds the legal authority in respect of schooling but that authority may be devolved although, even then, it is usually latent and can be reasserted. At the same time, groups beyond the formal school system have substantial influence and so also have to be taken into account in any consideration of control and management arrangements.

A second important aspect of management is how it is achieved. The more readily apparent strategies are where authority is centralized and control is exercised through the formal structures and involves directions, demands, requirements and other communications and actions. Less obvious is the use of sanctions as with control over conditions of employment, including promotions, salary increments, leave arrangements and other perquisites or incentives for cooperation and compliance. Less obvious again are the arrangements that are used in decentralized situations where accord has to be negotiated, and informal techniques of personal interaction, especially talk, together with gestures expressing cultural styles, reputation including charisma and the use of socialization are employed. Finally, account must be taken of basic modes of undertaking the operation of schooling, involving business management modes and sometimes factory styles of undertaking schooling 'production' processes.

Management is a central and pervasive process. In the discussion that follows, I will consider two aspects largely as they have been introduced here: first, the forms in which management is undertaken; and second, the dynamics of management processes. They are also especially difficult to study and are less well understood than other processes such as teaching. For one thing, they have less obvious relevance to understanding the school experience of students, and so have been relatively neglected. Again, managers are better able to limit observation or prevent studies from being undertaken. Still again, as with studies of the operation of power generally, it is one thing to observe managers at work but quite another to determine how much influence they exercise relative to other participants, and whether they or others are the main decision-makers on a particular issue. Further, the process of managing is undertaken at many points and includes students and teachers in classrooms in certain respects, and ministers in government in other respects, and perhaps others beyond them, as having a part in the management of a system of schools. Thus here more than elsewhere, conclusions have to be tentative. In addition, situations and circumstances, and the ways in which tasks are undertaken, can quickly change.

At the same time, limitations of research on management can be offset to some extent by turning to historical, comparative and other studies and sources. While they also have limitations, they nonetheless offer useful insights and clearly extend the understanding possible from contemporary social research on a particular system of schooling. Thus collectively it is possible to provide a substantial picture of managers at work, and of the dynamics of management.

The Structuring of Management

Despite ready use of the term 'manager', characterization and identification are not straightforward processes. By definition, managers are responsible for such tasks as direction and coordination, determination of priorities and strategies, allocation and use of resources, and reviews of practices and achievements. However, they are not 'owners' or in other ways the ultimate controllers of educational activity; rather, their authority and responsibilities are delegated and so may be changed and even withdrawn. Again, as has been noted, there can be an array of managers such as political ministers or board members, professional directors, superintendents or principals, and bureaucratic managers. Still again, professional managers of schools and other educational units also delegate authority and responsibilities to deputies and other subordinates, including teachers and specialists so that managerial authority and responsibilities can be widely shared. It is also the case that a particular unit manager or even director of a system of schooling, with considerable authority and extensive responsibilities, can be a technical operative for the political minister or board that appoints him or her and so subject to direction, restraint and even dismissal, as has happened more commonly in recent difficult economic and political times. However, while these conditions mean that it can be difficult to distinguish managers in all cases and circumstances, nonetheless they are usually readily identifiable and so can usefully be considered as a specific category of participants. In particular, their identification is assisted by giving consideration to the unit of interest so that managers of systems and schools, together with particular sections or other complementary agencies of management, are identified in those situations.

Making the distinction has to be related then to the system or unit under consideration. Increases in size and scale of operation are associated with complexity, specialization and often delegation of responsibilities and authority. Nonetheless, delegation is central so that subordinates are accountable to superiors and subject to direction and constraint. The incidence of managers and specialists is also related to economic, political and other circumstances in that more are likely to be employed during prosperous times. Educational systems are notable for their capacity to generate higher level administration positions, as was evident during the prosperous 1960s and for most of the 1970s, and comparably to be subjected to rationalization and the production of redundancies during the 1980s when political intervention has been a common feature of the operation of school systems in many societies. During such periods, major areas of decision-making that were formerly the responsibilities of professionals have been taken over by political managers who act with limited theoretical expertise and sophistication. Such actions, together with an unusual readiness by alternative governments to discharge and replace senior executives, testify to the delegated nature of authority and responsibilities. In those situations, it is arguable that even the most senior professional and bureaucratic managers are rather operatives responsive to political managers; they act on the basis of delegation and tolerance, but without ultimate authority for determining how systems and institutions will be operated. Such situations also testify to the reality of Marxist distinctions as between ruling and ruled classes, and highlight the usefulness of professionals, bureaucrats and other service personnel in the operation of systems of activity (e.g. Ginsburg and others, 1980).

The many positions of managers, together with the diverse responsibilities assigned to them, and the varied circumstances under which they operate, illustrate ways in which their situations and responsibilities are structured and to an extent controlled. Something of this structuring was indicated in Chapter 2 where school management was shown to vary between small- and large-scale systems, with authority concentrated at the centre or dispersed to local units as in US public schools or in many private schools. Again, principals can operate primary or secondary schools or, more commonly at the secondary level, particular types of schools such as selective and residual or comprehensive, single sex or coeducational, public or private, religious or secular, middle- or working-class, ethnic communal or integrated and so on. As with teachers, their responsibilities vary but more particularly they deal with different kinds of parents and students, often employ different kinds of staff, and develop different orientations, priorities, traditions and modes of operating Collectively then they are principal agents in sustaining and even reproducing systems of schooling in relation to prevailing social arrangements.

The discussion so far has been primarily of those directly responsible for the operation of educational institutions such as schools and the systems of which they are part. As illustrated in the previous chapter, however, the management process has become remarkably more complex in the last century or so with the establishment and operation of specialized agencies to undertake responsibility for particular tasks such as programming, assessment and evaluation, teacher education, research and so on. The operation of these entails not simply their management as sections or departments within a system but in such ways as to exercise particular kinds of influence on the undertaking of schooling and so to direct its functioning. Of these, assessment and evaluation are probably the most crucial as the means for managing schooling by determining the objectives towards which staff and students must work. Altogether, however, management through the operation of complementary agencies entails a more sophisticated mode of operating by comparison with management in straightforward hierarchical or even collegiate forms.

The position of manager reflects not only the deliberate structuring of social arrangements, with their assigned authority and responsibilities, varied according to location within a larger system, but also the more general and fundamental ethos and styles of a society. Thus English arrangements have reflected the gradual joining together of diverse elements into a national system comprised of local and national authorities working in partnership, with considerable responsibility devolved to the principal and the school. US practices have reflected the early enterprise of local communities and the persistence of considerable control at the local level. In contrast, France, the Australian states and some other societies reflect the establishment of large-scale, centrally controlled systems, with managers assigned more particular and often specialized responsibilities within those systems. Elsewhere, relative poverty, as in some third world societies, or religious or political authoritarianism have resulted in highly centralized control and direction with managers accountable and closely minitored by central bureaucratic and professional staff. But by and large, the salient unit has been the national system.

In the dramatically changing times of the present, however, the usefulness of the nation as a unit is being substantially challenged, not simply in education but across a range of social activities. Business, for example, has long operated beyond such boundaries with multinational corporations and even mega-coalitions of such corporations involving production, finance, transportation, media, research, entertainment and other activities as portrayed, for example, by Ohmae (1985: Ch. 9), constituting major forces in the contemporary world. As such, they can dominate the small societies who depend on such corporations and coalitions of corporations for investment, the establishment of productive and other activities and thus the operation of their economies. These and other developments have induced governments to act cooperatively, either through the establishment and operation of particular agencies such as UNESCO, OECD and ASEAN, or the World bank, or by setting up supranational arrangements such as the European Commission whose laws can restrain the governments of member states. With movement towards a single economy in 1992, Western Europe is setting in motion a fundamental and complex process that can be expected to have profound implications for the operation of schooling and, in particular, for its managers in the undertaking of their responsibilities. In several respects, however, Western Europe constitutes a particularly interesting case; while a number of factors such as the development of a single economy and increased geographical movement among members of the workforce are likely to constitute forces for integration and uniform practices, other factors and notably cultural pluralism could well foster greater diversity. It is conceivable, for example, that national governments could continue to concede power to a central management but that concurrently particular populations such as the Welsh, the Irish, the Scottish and the Bretons, or collectively the Celts, together with the Basques, the Catalans and others could assert their identities to establish a far more diverse set of European communities. In Eastern Europe, Africa and Asia, ethnicity, tribalism and other factors have the most profound significance for future possible rearrangements of political entities.

In other parts of the world, however, some societies face more difficult situations if larger units and even forms of integration are an advantage. Korea, for example, located amongst Japan, China and the USSR is unlikely to elect to be an integral part of any of those societies and a regional grouping is an unlikely event. Singapore, with its population predominantly of Chinese origins, would not meld readily with its Malaysian, Indonesian or other neighbours. Again, Sweden, although historically an integral part of Europe, has long maintained an independent status and may seek to retain its autonomy and distinctive identity. Still again, Australia and New Zealand constitute two small Europe-type societies off the southeast tip of Asia and can be expected to seek to preserve a distinctive social identity. Israel is still another case of a society that is unlikely to join readily with its neighbours.

What is clear is that substantial changes are occurring that bear upon the organization and operation of societies, and in particular upon their education systems. While these changes are clearly affecting the operation of schools and the priorities of managers, they are also impinging on the societal units that constitute the basic systems of activity.

Dynamics of Management

Given the diversity of situations in which managers operate, the tasks of managing entail almost infinite activities and strategies. Accordingly, this discussion can be little more than illustrative and examples have been selected to represent a diversity of situations and practices. Unfortunately, such a task is hindered by an absence of studies of many areas and aspects of managing. Sometimes, however, something can be derived from studies that were not primarily directed at the management process. Again, by drawing on studies that are either historical in themselves or now largely of historical interest, the range and diversity can be extended. Despite these limitations, they show collectively how complex and dynamic a process managing schooling is, and how it is an essential part of the more general political process of managing a society.

The critical part of teachers in the management of schooling is evidenced in their preoccupation with control and direction in classrooms. As was illustrated in Chapter 5, teachers maintain organized programs of work and use talk, negotiation and other techniques to achieve control of students and obtain work and learning from them. Indeed, it is a constant process of contestation, with dire consequences for the teacher who is ineffective in handling students. But part of their tasks, too, is to manage the perceptions of responses of other teachers and of school administrators as means of ensuring the congeniality of their situations. Studies of teachers also indicate, as again we have noted, their varying responsibilities according to system and situations. Thus the teachers in England studied by Berlak and Berlak (1981) had considerable authority in determining the operation of the classroom, while those in more authoritarian schools and systems can be restricted to operating prescriptively or by formulae. Variations also occur within the same system as when junior primary teachers have more authority and latitude than senior secondary teachers who are constrained by organizational requirements, external examinations and other arrangements.

Management responsibilities within the school can be distributed to a number of positions, but invariably entail considerable devolution, with the school principal exercising overall responsibility. Elite school principals such as those studied by Cookson and Persell (1985) exercise substantial and pervasive influence while devolving considerable responsibility to staff. The extreme contrast is in authoritarian systems where principals can be little more than executors of system managers' decisions or, in the words of one such principal, 'The Ministry is very kind; they make all the decisions for me.' In contrast with those, Richardson (1973) portrayed the complexities and uncertainties for all when a principal encourages staff participation in decision-making. Such studies also illustrate that the relevance of particular strategies is dependent on the situation: for example, when power is concentrated at the top of the hierarchy, then direction can be readily resorted to; however, in more participatory situations, principals need skills of crystallization and articulation to capture and portray the orientations and sentiments of participants. In such situations, talk is a particularly important means for exercising influence during interaction with deputies and other staff (e.g. Gronn, 1983).

Studies of participatory schools (e.g. Ball, 1987) also illustrate the extensiveness and complexities of activities directed towards influencing the management of a school. Thus individuals and groups of staff can be significant participants if they have established a special standing with the principal or have other bases for asserting their priorities. For example, apochryphal accounts are of particular individuals — teachers, secretaries or maintenance staff — who have built up special knowledge or undertaken particular responsibilities such as timetabling or school security that are helpful in promoting particular concerns. In more complexly organized secondary schools, departments commonly constitute significant units, deriving their significance from the nature and status of their subject, including its appeal to students, the competence and effectiveness of a departmental head, or the significance of the department in the overall operation of the school. Indeed, much of the activity in a school derives from the efforts of particular sections or departments to influence the allocation of resources and facilities and of students and staff in order to improve their conditions and standing, and thereby the satisfactoriness of their work life. In turn principals need to be adroit in the handling of staff if they are to maintain respect and operate a smoothly functioning school.

Other important devices in the operation of schools include ceremonies, rituals, assemblies and other means for celebrating social occasions and processes. Kapferer (1981) perceptively portrayed opening and closing occasions in a school year, and indicated ways in which they bonded students and parents to the school. Fostering the notion of a particular and even special community can be used to enhance that effect. Again, more affluent institutions invest substantial resources in impressive grounds, buildings and other facilities such as chapels that foster a reputation of specialness, and a sense of privilege with involvement in such a community. Because these devices are available to more affluent and exclusive schools, their significance relates to their scarcity. At the same time, Outward Bound and other types of schools find other bases for specialness, and establish comparable bonds with specific but clearly different communities. Still another case is offered by the small rural school where the intimacy of such communities as much as the school itself is responsible for the considerable bonding that is often associated with such schools and their communities and with former students. This suggests a range of possibilities that are contingent upon sensitive and resourceful leaders and staff identifying, establishing and celebrating features that distinguish a particular community.

In a study of a school board in the US, Kerr (1964) illuminated some aspects of the operation of such a unit of governance. Although legally schools are operated through school boards, citizens find it difficult to identify issues on which to stand for election and are even further handicapped by ignorance as to how the school board operates. In actuality, school superintendents effectively manage board members and limit their opportunities to form troublesome cliques. In the case studied by Kerr, an interdependent relationship had been established whereby board members supported the professionals in their management of the school system and in the event of some serious mismanagement could terminate a superintendent's appointment and appoint a more effective successor. The situation of the superintendent was further illuminated by Gross, Mason and McEachern (1957) who identified the complex and often incompatible responsibilities they have to undertake, from keeping costs down while ensuring adequate salaries for staff, to satisfying different ideological expectations in staff and community regarding the programs offered by schools. Superintendents could resolve some problems by ensuring particular groups were aware of each other's views and expectations, and seek accommodation and compromises. In other situations they managed by controlling the flow of information and limiting awareness of what was happening elsewhere in the situation. Like their counterparts, the principals of autonomous schools, they tread a precarious path and rely substantially on overall satisfactory performance, including an ability to handle particularly contentious or explosive situations and to establish a competent team of assistants from teachers through to deputies.

Bush and Kogan (1982) give some understanding of the work of a counterpart official in the director of an English local education authority (LEA). Working essentially from interview material, they portrayed the many groups these officials work with, and the often time-taking discussions and negotiations that are necessary if administration and particularly changes are to be undertaken effectively. Again, delicate balances and complementation emerge, with key members of local authority committees sometimes making crucial contributions to the management processes. They also face complex sets of expectations, varying according to whether these emanate from school staff and parents, local or national authorities, national parent and teacher associations and employer or other special interest groups who take an interest in what goes on in schooling.

The difficulties of establishing how managing is undertaken typically increase as one ascends the management structure to national and interna-

The Social Dynamics of Schooling

tional levels. Nonetheless, some useful insights are available. In a study of policy-making in England in the 1960s and 1970s, Kogan (1975) identified major participants as involving parliament, the minister and the Department of Education and Science (DES) with its bureaucratic administrators and professional inspectors, local government authorities, teachers and parent associations, and some other special interest groups. Among those, some individuals were of special significance because of their general competence, understanding of situations and issues, and standing with their constituencies. In other aspects that situation contrasted markedly with those in the US where senior administrators are part of a presidential team and at most last no longer than the president and usually much less. Thus the account by Dershimer (1976) of educational politics in Washington in the 1960s is of a much more fluid situation with people and policies changing in rapid succession. In contrast again are situations in more authoritarian societies where stable elites and subservient bureaucrats and professionals generally ensure stability and the perpetuation of the status quo.

It is also difficult to assess the implications of such different situations for staff in schools and elsewhere in a system. Inevitably authoritarianism is associated with stability of a stultifying kind. The situation in the US could mean considerable scope for autonomy, including manipulation and exploitation of opportunities at particular points because of the exceptionally 'loose coupling' at higher levels of the system. The situation in England would appear to give a more congenial stability and hopefully establish a more constructive and productive national climate. Certainly it was in the late 1960s and early 1970s that primary schooling in England attracted international attention and repute, and comprehensiveness replaced the exclusionary process in schools, at least to a modest degree. While these developments were associated with more prosperous times, they may also have reflected a stable and enlightened system of management.

The activities and strategies discussed so far are those employed in the management of units located in the mainstream of the operation of an education system. In addition to those, however, as was indicated in the previous chapter, are complementary specialist agencies that bear directly on the operation of schooling and which can therefore be identified as management agencies. As has been noted, they are relevant in determining what counts as knowledge and performance, what is problematic and how the problematic shall be examined and responded to, what shall be the subject of policy proposals and how these shall be undertaken, and other issues. In such ways these agencies work at a social or cultural level, influencing definitions and conceptions, perceptions and interpretations, and ultimately modes of responding to situations. Thus they are key instruments in the management process.

Management activities and strategies in relation to these complementary agencies can be considered in two parts. One entails their internal management, as units in their own right. That is a little studied phenomenon, often dealt with incidentally in historical or other more general studies (e.g. Connell, 1980b) and so scarcely known about or understood in any systematic sense; nonetheless, it would seem to be reasonable to conclude that there would be many similarities with the management of other educational organizations. A second entails their external management by sponsors or controllers. That also is a little studied phenomenon; nonetheless it is dealt with incidentally in a number of studies (e.g. OECD, 1973) and so a topic that can be discussed more adequately and insightfully. As we shall see, this aspect relates much more to the more general political scene and to the major groups active in that scene.

One expression of that interest is in the establishment and operation of these specialist management agencies. In the main they are publicly sponsored and operated, often constituting units within a system of schooling, but sometimes as formally independent units. For example, many large systems of schooling have their specialist 'in-house' units to undertake curriculum development and implementation, research, teacher pre- and in-service education, policy development and implementation and so on. In addition are partially sponsored units such as centres for educational research and test development which obtain some support from governments and win considerable additional support from public and private sponsors of projects that they undertake. However, while formally autonomous and independent, they are clearly dependent on sponsors who are the public and private organizations with substantial resources. In such ways they are significantly dependent and susceptible to being steered in their operations. Different again are the privately established and operated organizations, often in the USA depending entirely on the resources they can attract from public and private sponsors. They are most dependent on 'market forces' and the people and organizations with substantial resources that largely determine the thrust of market operations. That means, in effect, that they are substantially interdependent on public systems of schooling and private organizations such as corporations and foundations. Inevitably, their independence is constrained while at the same time their formal independence is a useful token of impartiality.

These situations indicate strategies that top level managers employ in the operation of specialist management agencies. It is unfortunate that

The Social Dynamics of Schooling

they are little studied because such studies would yield valuable insights into the undertaking of those aspects of the management of educational systems. That significance has been illustrated in several earlier chapters when discussing the efforts of teachers and others to participate in particular specialist activities such as assessment and evaluation, and particularly in the management of the agencies involved. It is notable that in some societies their management has entailed considerable participation by diverse sets of specialists.

The present is of considerable interest because it has been characterized by substantial and sustained efforts to influence and even transform the operation of these agencies, together with the operation of the educational system as a whole. In the course of that being undertaken, more senior political and other managers have more openly exhibited their capacity to exercise influence. In that process, we are able to obtain a fuller understanding of the specific and relevant parts of political, professional, bureaucratic and other managers. It is useful to examine the activities and strategies of these senior managers in relation to mainstream and complementary agencies of management in the situation constituted by societies and their systems of schooling. It is useful to go further and consider extra-societal regional and international agencies such as OECD and the World Bank but these may be more appropriately identified as steering mechanisms and are therefore left for discussion in the next chapter. Of course, even the intra-societal activities and strategies that remain constitute a vast and complex topic that can be only indicated here. Fortunately, they have been tackled in recent years by a number of researchers (e.g. Sharp (ed.), 1986; Wirt and Harman (eds), 1986; Hunt, 1988), together with studies of some specialized agencies undertaking curriculum development and implementation, examination and evaluation, and the like (e.g. Broadfoot (ed.), 1984; Haywood, 1986; Goodson, 1987), and I shall draw upon those and other sources in making these comments. For illustrative purposes, I shall draw upon situations with which I am more familiar such as Singapore, England and the USA.

Distinctive features of Singapore include its very small land mass and lack of material resources, together with an industrious and competent population. Singapore's political managers have long recognized that prosperity requires the attraction of major international corporations to invest, establish industries and provide employment and incomes, exports and revenue for public and other services. Relevant to that is a range of financial and other policies but central is a competent and cooperative workforce. It is in that respect that schooling is of fundamental significance, although other concerns such as social, political and moral socialization also have considerable importance.

While the attention of Singapore's political managers has long been closely focused on its educational system, they have given it particular attention since the late 1970s. Responding to developments in technology, and anticipating implications for production, management and other activities, they generated a substantial reorganization and reprogramming. These included a substantial increase in the resources available for the operation of the educational system, particularly at the tertiary level. In addition, to remedy weaknesses in the learning of languages in particular, a drastic streaming policy was introduced from grade three primary schooling which meant that children would proceed at different rates with those continuing to progress slowly being eventually steered into the lower skilled sections of the workforce. A further initiative, largely to counter perceived possibilities of the development of anomie through the emphasis in schools on English language instruction and to ensure sound moral development which normally would be transmitted in large part through a mother language, literature and so on, was to promote programs of moral socialization. As Chew Oon Ai (1988) has shown, these substantially pervaded all aspects of school programs but also sustained incompatible elements which created sharp dilemmas for staff and students. Finally, for present purposes the political managers substantially expanded tertiary education, particularly in areas that developed competence with technology and thereby contributed increased competence to the workforce for modern modes of production.

Many other strategies of the Singapore government could be cited but these suffice to illustrate that it has given close attention to the management of the educational system and undertaken a comprehensive set of strategies that clearly structure the activities and experiences of staff and students. Of course, it remains difficult to establish the distinctive contributions of different types of managers; while political leaders announce the policies and monitor implementation and performance, conceivably interaction occurs between political, professional, bureaucratic and other managers in the development and undertaking of strategies for the operation of the school system. Certainly political managers are dominant formally although other managers may have considerable informal influence.

England constitutes quite a different situation of long established society with a long established system of education, a history of leadership in the world, a recent preoccupation with welfare state arrangements, and substantial transformation in priorities and strategies over the last twenty years. Through the 1950s and 1960s major political parties shared considerable agreement on the operation of the educational system, differing on the significance given to social integration and comprehensive schooling as against stratification and selective and residual schools. The consensus was far from complete and conservative views were asserted more vigorously from the late 1960s (e.g. Cox and Dyson (eds), 1969a, 1969b). Concerns became more widespread following the sharp increase in the oil price in 1973 with the associated onset of inflation, recession, unemployment and a need for public financial stringency. Government concerns, expressed for example in Prime Minister Callaghan's speech at Oxford in 1976, purportedly opening the 'Great Debate', reflected suspicions that the opposition would use educational issues at a forthcoming election. It also is arguable that the situation provided an opportunity for senior national government bureaucratic managers to assert their influence on the operation of schooling in England at a time when declining enrolments and financial stringency weakened the position of teachers and other professionals working in education.

Developments substantially changed with the election of the Thatcher government in 1979. Under her regime, financial stringency was greatly increased, constraining the operations of schools and impairing the quality of facilities in many cases. Complementary agencies such as the Schools Council were restructured to make them more directly responsible to the minister, while tertiary institutions were harshly restricted in resources and directed to work more closely with the private sector in order to obtain funding for research and other activities. Again, mechanisms such as the Council for the Accreditation of Teacher Education to more closely direct teacher education were established, and the Manpower Services Commission and other agencies were instituted or developed to ensure additional and different avenues for exercising influence on the operation of schooling. Most recently, the Thatcher government has taken its most distinctive and decisive action in transforming education with a major piece of legislation in the Reform Bill of 1988. Major provisions of the Bill include giving schools a right to opt out of local education authority control and receive funding direct from the national government, ending limits on parents' choice of schools, placing control of a school's budget in the hands of school governors, and establishing a national curriculum with three core and seven foundational subjects that would occupy from 70 to 80 per cent of each child's timetable, together with a national program of testing children at ages 7, 11, 14 and 16. In addition, some fundamental changes were made to tertiary institutions by abolishing academic tenure, and changing the methods of funding such institutions. In particular, polytechnical institutions were removed from local authority control and established as semi-independent corporations.

What remains unclear is the real thrust of these strategies. The claims of the government are in such terms as to improve the quality and relevance of schooling and to give parents more scope for exercising influence and enjoying choice. A plausible case can be argued, however, that the strategies serve to establish a particular entrepreneurial ideology and practice, and at the same time reduce bases of alternative views. Thus tertiary institutions have had their independence substantially reduced while local education authorities have also been severely constrained. And while parental influence may have been increased, it is likely to remain dispersed and weak as a total force. Meanwhile, there is no question of the greatly enhanced power of the centre, with the Secretary of State for Education having been granted some 190 new powers, and those to be exercised in conjunction with the professionals and bureaucrats of the Department of Education and Science.

Clearly, the basic framework within which school and system managers work, together with teachers and other specialists, has been dramatically transformed and, through modifications to rights and responsibilities, the basic roles of participants transformed. Again, the situation illustrates the overriding powers of the political manager and, in this case, most notably in a society which for decades prided itself on a relationship of partnership and the relative autonomy of schools.

At the same time, England provides evidence of the capacity of professionals to exploit situations, in a commendable manner, to achieve exemplary educational outcomes. For example, the introduction of the Technical and Vocational Education Initiative was widely seen as a mechanism for raising the emphasis of vocational education, and even for locating differentiation earlier in the school curriculum than was previously the case. As Barnes and others (1987) have shown, however, teachers were often effective in developing and undertaking programs that were highly regarded on educational grounds. Possibly that reflects a long experience of substantial autonomy and the development of considerable expertise in taking initiatives under difficult circumstances. It is to be hoped that in other situations now being created, teachers and school managers will be able again to use circumstances effectively to achieve educational rather than more limited technical outcomes.

The USA provides an interesting third example, essentially because it involves substantial local control with only a modest federal contribution to the management of its overall educational system. Nonetheless, that contribution is of substantial significance for particular groups in particular situations and circumstances. Moreover, its influence has been specifically directed to achieve particular ends and so illustrates the significance of central or national government in such a society.

The Social Dynamics of Schooling

The location of education as a local and state responsibility arises out of historical circumstances and experiences. The position was crystallized with the process of federation in the late eighteenth century and the production of a federal constitution that did not include responsibility for education. Even so, some federal influence was significant through such means as land grants for schooling and tertiary education, as with the Land Grant Colleges Act of 1862, and legally through the operation of the federal constitution and its Bill of Rights. In the twentieth century, federal contributions and influence have been steadily increased, establishing vocational education during World War I, providing youth employment and training during the depression of the 1930s, the amelioration of the impact of federal defence and other initiatives during and after World War II, the education of ex-servicemen after World War II, support for schooling in the cause of defence from the late 1950s following the Russian launching of Sputnik, and substantial contributions to primary and secondary schools from the mid-1960s, particularly for students from disadvantaged circumstances.

These trends reflect the operation of several factors but a principal one is the greater resources available to the federal government and their particular relevance for issues that transcend states or are of national significance. In particular, during the 1960s and early 1970s, a concern for children from disadvantaged circumstances was an important factor in justifying federal contributions to the undertaking of educational activity and can be credited with improving facilities and programs and the experiences and achievements of many children. In addition, of course, recourse to federal courts and other agencies constituted further means by which the influence of federal government on educational practices was magnified.

These thrusts were to change, however, during the 1980s under the influence of the Reagan administration. In general terms, its priorities involved reducing the supportive role of federal government for more vulnerable groups in society. The rhetoric emphasized that schooling was the responsibility of state and local authorities but that meant increasing the dependence of children and their schools on state and local resources with all their variability. Such a change in arrangements has little or no adverse impact on wealthier communities but bears disproportionately on poorer communities and states by reducing 'topping up' resources. Evidence (e.g. CDF, annual reports) indicates that as a result of the Reagan administration's policies poorer sections of US society suffered a substantial decline in resources and thereby in their access to opportunities to benefit from schooling.

The US experience thus testifies to the significance of national managers in determining the character of schooling and particularly the quality of its material resources. As Her Majesty's Inspectors' reports in England showed (e.g. HMI, 1984), such changes can bear upon the quality and style of teaching as well as of material facilities and resources. By exercising control over such a key element as resources, national managers can significantly influence the circumstances of undertaking schooling and thereby the quality and the modes of undertaking it.

While much can be said about the influence of senior political managers from the study of particular societies, more can be established on the basis of examining trends across a number of societies. Then one identifies, for example, widespread concern with economic priorities, including a disposition to see education as a commodity that can be produced and sold, and even 'exported' to improve the balance of a society's external transactions. From there it is but one step further to private sector forms of undertaking and managing schooling as with the 'cult of efficiency' that Callahan (1962) observed to emerge in the US in the early years of the twentieth century when the business ethos was especially dominant and school managers particularly vulnerable. Its concerns with establishing performance and quality in quantitative terms, and so giving primacy to quantitative indicators in the classroom, and in financial, personnel management and other areas of responsibility and activity have now been revived in such forms as corporate management which ignores differences between areas of activity such as education and commerce, limits the significance of human attributes and assigns exceptional competence and responsibilities to senior managers. Even they are seen as interchangeable, however, requiring little more than 'management training' or perhaps 're-programming'.

A second and possibly related thrust is expressed in the process of privatization and an associated strategy of making resources available to families in the form of vouchers (e.g. Coons and Sugarman, 1978). A salient feature of this strategy is, nominally at least, to place power in the form of resources in the hands of parents rather than the providing schools and systems. As such, it appears that a substantial shift in power is achieved with parents able to 'shop around' and select the school of their choice. However, the supermarket model that is often used in discussions of the operation of voucher systems also illustrates that suppliers can establish dominance and even a monopoly position in the market place so that parents and students, dispersed as consumers invariably are, can do little more than select from options made available to them.

In addition, governments can exercise considerable power separately from a voucher system. For one thing, while distributing resources and to that extent power to families, managers can also direct the operation of a schooling system through, as has been illustrated, examination, curriculum development and implementation, research and other complementary agencies. By such means they can structure the organization and operation of schools and thereby the experiences of students, and incidentally determine the options available to parents and their children.

Governments can also substantially structure opportunities in the course of dispersing resources. A common pattern has been to make comparable resources available for each student, either in the provision of schools or per capita grants; however, the deficiency in that approach is that the resources so allocated do little or nothing to redress disadvantages arising from poverty or other forms of handicapping circumstances. In contrast, a voucher system offers considerable scope for differentiated grants; for example, a government could decide to offer substantial amounts to poorer families and relatively little to wealthier families and thereby give reality to prospects of exercising choice in an educational market place.

The central point is that whatever strategy is pursued, it is nonetheless a crucial strategy in the management of schooling activity and one which ultimately can only be authorized by the political managers of schooling systems.

These ideas, conceptions and strategies do not usually arise among educational managers, however. The likelihood is that they are generated elsewhere in society, in government and in the private sector, in universities, 'think tanks' or other centres, and picked up and disseminated by agencies such as the OECD or the World Bank or through the work of foundations. That activity directs attention to the activity of people operating individually and collectively in organizations beyond schooling and so to the activities of steerers whom I shall consider in the next chapter.

Discussion

Management is undertaken from many types of positions, not all of which are formally identified as management. Thus teachers and associated specialists, together with political and bureaucratic managers, complement the activities of formal school and system managers. Correspondingly, their responsibilities and contributions are diverse, reflecting both hierarchical and vertical differentiation, at best complementary but often overlapping and even incompatible and conflictual and generative of tensions. Again, it is one thing for positions to be devised and responsibilities to be assigned but quite another as occupants of those and other related positions operate to exercise influence and possibly transform modes of operating. That is, there can be substantial discrepancies between the reality and the formally specified.

Management activities are structured by the forms of management employed, which reflect the distribution of power and the exercise of influence. The relevant power involves many elements and includes formal and social authority, and material, personal and social resources. Circumstances, ideologies and other factors are associated with the use of centralized or localized systems of management which then profoundly influence the operations by particular managers. While bureaucratization and rigidification are related to scale and complexity of operations, they are also related to circumstances and ideology. Systems vary on the basis of a multitude of factors in the extent that influence is exercised from the top but invariably that influence is significant even if, as with the reduction of US federal government support, its exercise is reduced. It is evident, too, that the central authorities exercise influence in a variety of ways, as by straightforward and closely monitored directives or by the extent to which resources are provided, and by establishing complementary agencies when they make particular operations such as examining and evaluating specialist technical operations.

Ultimately, power rests formally with the citizens of a society and particularly its parents but invariably it is preempted by political managers. Interestingly, their exercise of power has been significantly increased in the recent years of economically and politically turbulent times, reflecting the increased significance given to education. Ironically, that is also a period when those managers have often sought to reduce the scope of teacher preparatory programs, determining that such programs be focused more directly on technical issues and procedures.

The trend may be interpreted in terms of exigencies of prevailing circumstances but such direction has profound significance and implications. To the extent that teachers and other specialists are required to limit the issues which they consider and the factors that they take into account, managers reduce their responsibilities in decision-making and in determining how these activities will be undertaken. That limits their responsibility and increases the probability that they act in accordance with more or less explicit directives and even guidelines. But to do that, and accord authority to more senior political, professional and bureaucratic managers, is also to accept practices that were repudiated in the Nuremburg trials following World War II.

The position taken here upholds that managers and specialists have a responsibility for how they act, particularly in the case of professionals

The Social Dynamics of Schooling

for whom the case has persistently been made that responsibilities are to clients. In consequence, they continue to have responsibility for how they act in respect of their students and in obligations to parents, communities and society more generally. Nonetheless, political managers in particular are still able substantially to influence situations and circumstances, and how other managers and specialists operate as by controlling material resources available for undertaking schooling activities.

In this chapter I have sought to illustrate the many points and the diverse forms in which management is undertaken. In the light of the situation portrayed here, it is evident that the situation presented as constituting management, as in management training programs (e.g. Campbell and others, 1987), is often seriously limited. In such programs management is presented as involving a relatively limited range of tasks in the operation of schools and systems, and undertaken from a limited range of positions. Further, in highlighting issues with which such managers have scope to make decisions and by ignoring issues that have been considered and decided elsewhere, as by political and bureaucratic managers, such practices promote technical understanding and practice, but inhibit the development of fully professional practices among school and system managers.

Of course, these situations do not come about in any simple way. In part, for example, they reflect the practical orientations of school and system managers who see some urgency in 'getting on' with the practical tasks of management. But in part, too, they reflect the contributions of theorists, researchers, sponsors and others who contribute to the conceptions of what management involves and how it should be undertaken. These are, in those respects, the steerers of schooling activity and so it is appropriate that we now turn our attention to their activities.

Chapter 9

Steering

Although substantial responsibilities and authority are located within systems of schooling, it is also evident that schooling operates in relation to political, economic, religious and other systems of activity. Such relationships are readily apparent from historical and contemporary macro-studies of societies and the operation of their school systems, and have been dramatically demonstrated in the last decade or more during the period of turbulent economic and political circumstances. Thus schooling can be seen as part of a set of interdependent systems, and often dependent and substantially reactive to influences generated elsewhere.

A major task in this chapter is to identify and examine some of the sources and agencies of influence that act upon schooling from outside the system. So far we have considered the institutions of schooling, together with ministries or departments and some complementary agencies for their parts in the exercise of influence. But other ministries or departments, together with managerial units established at international levels, must also be taken into account. Attention must also be given to privately established and operated agencies such as the business sector, foundations and 'think tanks' that are centrally involved in determining modes of operating. Such public and private agencies often promote particular conceptions and modes of operating, and constitute less than obvious elements of the more extensive systems of which schools are part.

It has to be noted too, however, that, as with schooling, the identification of participants in steering is not a straightforward process. Some such as government and business, and some particular interest groups are readily identifiable from their activities. Others, however, such as consumers, investors or citizens have definite interests to which schooling is relevant but either, as with parents, teachers and others, operate in sectionalist groups reflecting particular kinds of interests, or remain simply immobilized and effectively passive in relation to schooling. That is, in identifying interest groups who constitute steerers, it is useful to recognize differences in competence, articulateness, power and other attributes and so in visibility, effectiveness and other respects.

In the examination of steerers, the usual task of differentiating between structures and people, acting individually or collectively as the major participants, has again to be tackled. As with schooling, it is convenient to take large-scale entities such as government or business, OECD, the World Bank, or the foundations as the major entities. However, again as with schooling and other systems of activity, these entities reveal, on closer examination, that they involve the dynamic interactions of people varying in competence, resources and other aspects of power, and correspondingly in the exercise of influence. Only sometimes, however, has the research on particular steerers been of a kind that identifies and reveals participants in those terms. Often, then, out of uninformedness we are limited to discussing activities in terms of crude structuralist entities.

As has been noted, the present is a particularly appropriate time to study the influence process and examine such participants and their activities. Due to recent turbulent economic circumstances, rapid developments in technology and possibly other factors, substantial efforts have been directed at transforming priorities and modes of operating schooling. For such reasons a second task undertaken in this chapter is to review briefly those developments and note their impact on schooling. In particular, attention is given to how those influences have been exercised, and agencies which have been significant in the influencing process.

Obviously, these two tasks are substantial undertakings and can only be undertaken here in an exploratory way. The point of the attempt to do so is to establish the significance of those agencies and their activities in relation to how schooling is undertaken. A serious limitation of school activity is that people commonly act on the basis of unconscious or at best semiconscious assumptions about other areas of activity, and so do not explicitly examine them and their implications. Were they to do so, they could be expected to operate in more informed and effective ways. The point of this section of the discussion, then, is to sketch a situation and indicate relationships between participants, and to illustrate that more conscious and systematic conceptions are necessary for sounder schooling activity. While such a discussion can only produce tentative findings and conclusions, it may be helpful in focusing attention on particular areas of activity, identifying elements of particular relevance and in leading to more useful questions that can then be taken up.

Steerers and Strategies

Beyond the school system are a number of structures operated in relation to schooling. They fall readily into distinct categories such as public and private, national and international, or political, economic and philanthropic. Thus public sector agencies include regional associations such as the European Economic Community, the Organization for Economic Cooperation and Development (OECD), the Association of South East Asian Nations (ASEAN), and the Council for Mutual Economic Assistance (Comecon) in Eastern Europe, and international agencies such as UNESCO and the financing agency, the World Bank. Private sector agencies include some specific large corporations, and associations or federations that constitute servicing umbrellas, philanthropic organizations in the major foundations, and policy centres or 'think tanks'. However, while such distinctions are plausible, closer examination shows them to be misleading due to close interaction between the organizations and connecting links through mediating people and institutions. Despite these interrelationships and complexities, we will proceed by taking them in their apparent separate categories initially, and explore their interrelationships later.

Formally the state is the mechanism of governance of a society, directed by the party or group that holds political dominance by electoral or other means. However, while formally the maker of laws and responsible for the management of a society, it is subject to considerable influence from its servicing bureaucracy, business, labour and other organized groups, including other governments. It is also constrained by a necessity to maintain legitimacy and credibility both internally and externally. While invariably involved in the management of schooling, although varying in extent and in degree from one society to another, the state also has responsibility for other areas of activity such as the economy and finance, law and order, social welfare and health, and which influence what is undertaken in respect of schooling. In recent years, the state of the economy and the availability or scarcity of resources, the extent of unemployment among youth and developments in technology have been areas with particular implications for schooling. In special circumstances, such as have prevailed in recent years, governments have employed exceptional and comprehensive strategies to reorganize many areas of society, including transforming the structuring and the operation of schooling, in the name of promoting economic growth and development. Thus the English government employed the Department of Employment's Manpower Services Commission to channel funds to schools and thereby modify curriculum offerings, while the Department of Education and Science has been greatly strengthened relative to local education authorities.

When Singapore appraised its school system in the late 1970s, it used a group of system engineers from the Department of Defence, brought in by the Deputy Prime Minister who was formerly Minister for Defence. Also, the Australian reorganization that places education in the Ministry of Employment, Education and Training has considerable ramifications for structural relationships and the influence of particular interest groups within the bureaucracy. Indeed, an important point of the efforts to control schooling and transform its priorities can be related to efforts by particular sectors within a bureaucracy to maximize their influence and prospects while incidentally limiting those of others.

In structural terms, however, probably the most influential steerers are in units such as the treasury whose responsibilities and authority in the allocation of resources often give it dominance in the determination of educational and other policies. On occasions, foreign relations, the environment and other interests can be asserted with particular force, but resources is a most persistent priority.

Governments are also involved in the establishment and operation of international arrangements which in turn can impinge on internal activities. Thus Western European societies have formed an economic and political community and reached a stage where community rules sometimes overrule local arrangements, bearing upon practices that involve discrimination and the availability of resources and programs for particular groups.

More to the point of this discussion, however, is their joining with other Western European, North American and Australasian societies and Japan to form the OECD and, within that, a section to service the organization and management of education in sponsoring societies. However, while the OECD has been very active in relation to education, and prodigious in producing studies and reports, and in proposing policy initiatives and kindred activities, its work has not been closely researched or appraised, other than in the course of internal management processes. This is unfortunate for it is clearly an important agency. In consequence, this brief examination is done on the basis of a long-term familiarity with OECD work in education, an examination of some recent reports, and discussions by outsiders such as Kogan (1979) of some aspects of its work.

Established in 1960, with the assistance of the Ford Foundation, and with employers and employees having observer status, reflecting their involvement in the production process, to promote economic development in member states, OECD gave attention to the economic relevance of education from the outset (e.g. OECD, 1962). Subsequently, that interest has been broadly defined and included work on unequal participation and discriminatory practices in respect of socio-economic, gender, ethnic and other characteristics of students and the expansion of opportunities to participate in schooling, and thereafter employment and other sectors of social activity. Some recent reports on compulsory and post-compulsory schooling (OECD, 1983, 1985a, 1985b) reflect an approach that is comprehensive in scope and sensitive to a wide range of social issues in respect of schooling. At the same time, they are preoccupied with managerial problems and issues and illustrate that OECD primarily serves political and educational managers as an informing, sensitizing, problem-identifying, researching and solutions-proposing agency. It can thus be argued that OECD's education section contributes to the development of a more perceptive management and hopefully to a more humane and sounder system of management. However, it does not identify basic faults in the wider system of social arrangements which may need transformation. Thus it can be seen as limited to contributing to more enlightened management practice within the more general status quo of societies.

Again, the national reviews are very much in-house affairs, drawing upon work from national or regional administrations and using former ministers, senior administrators and academic specialists as examiners. From the review of Kogan (1979) and other sources, there are no indications that, for example, members of marginal or minority groups participate in the more crucial stages of review processes, those being limited to senior officials and politicians. Again, for advice on management issues, it invariably draws upon senior administrators and established specialists rather than more critical or lower level participants in school activity.

Presumably these priorities and predispositions reflect the accountability of OECD to governments and a necessity to achieve credibility with and some degree of consensus among members of its governing body. However, it has not been a force for work in education for personal development, political education or in cultural aspects of schooling, except in that these can be related to economic priorities. To make that point, incidentally, is simply to recognize the basis on which OECD was established and has been operated. In relation to schooling, it illustrates the partiality of government interest which can be assessed by considering alternative contributions that might have been made by more broadly focused organizations, or by alternative types of organizations.

If OECD is a major agency of the more prosperous societies' 'club', then UNESCO, World Bank and some other agencies operate in relation to poorer societies. Fortunately, these have been examined by outsiders as well as insiders and so some debate has developed on their responsibilities and modes of operating. UNESCO's mandate is the broader, involving international cooperation in education; however, given its multi-governmental management, it is also more likely to be amorphous and ineffective in any particular respect. Thus one is not surprised by inconclusiveness in outcomes as noted by Coombs (1985) of the report of the Faure Committee (pp. 21–2) and of a literacy program for urban and rural workers (pp. 272–6). But observations such as that by Hoggart (1978: 164) that 'UNESCO's special function is to remind the rest of the UN system as well as its Member States that most major problems (of population, environment, development itself) have a more than economic dimension; that they involve more than one part of human experience, that value-implications, the social and individual costs of programs, are to be put in the balance', draw attention to some useful achievements as, for example, a forum where less powerful societies or sections of societies can address the more powerful on critical issues.

The World Bank is a much more directive agency in respect of schooling. Governments turn to it for financial support for projects in schooling and other areas of social activity, and it is required to establish the economic soundness of those projects. By the nature of its establishment, World Bank priorities are with economic achievement and private enterprise modes of operating, and only incidentally with social, cultural and other aspects of development. Beyond that point, is a fascinating but disturbing divergence in testimonies. Baum and Stokes (1985: Ch. 7), writing as insiders, presented an account of impressive achievement. However, most of their data are in aggregated forms which do not enable the experience of particular groups to be appraised. Such limitations give plausibility to concerned critiques such as by Payer (1982) and Hayter and Watson (1985), both of whom saw the World Bank as primarily an agency to ensure the accessibility of third world societies and their resources to managing and exploiting first world governments and corporations. Certainly its close links with the US government through financial support and the appointment of the Bank's presidents, and associations with other banks and corporations suggest primacy of concern with the exploitation of human and other resources. Again, Payer's account of the experience of social scientists concerned about the experiences and prospects of indigenous populations (1982: Ch. 12) sustains concerns that the Bank is a central agency in exploitative activity. Still again, in a restrained and moderate examination of the presidency of McNamara from 1968 to 1981, Ayres (1983: Ch. 10) made clear the dependency of the World Bank on the world's financial and political centres of power and the concern of such groups in the US that its activities are at least in harmony with US political and economic objectives and priorities. In consequence, its influence on education policies in recipient countries is to emphasize particular economic and political priorities.

Tertiary institutions constitute another constituency with certain general interests that bear upon schooling. To a degree, their interests approximate those of employers in valuing a graded school product, and so support such arrangements and processes as structured curriculum, and examinations that sift and sort students, particularly at the end of secondary schooling. An effective screening system, especially one that yields comparable measures of performance, saves tertiary administrators and employers considerable effort in appraising school leavers and deciding between them. Indeed, because of their great interest in selecting effective students, and their involvement in the production and control of knowledge, universities have traditionally been responsible for, or at least closely associated with, the conduct of final year school examinations. Growth in both the number of tertiary institutions and in the demand for more highly schooled students has generated separate examining bodies, with specialists to operate them, but they are still commonly subject to considerable tertiary influence.

A second less evident relevance of the tertiary sector for the operation of schooling arises from its being the agency which prepares many secondary teachers. Central here are the conceptions of knowledge either explicit to or implicit in the experience of prospective teachers. Often, it is the more positive conceptions involving knowledge as discovered, organized by subjects, and appropriate for transmission by specialists to students whose learning can be assessed by examinations. In such ways, tertiary institutions have exercised profound influence over the operation of schooling, and justify the usefulness of examining schooling in terms of cultural styles.

In relation to the private sector, of which business in one form or another is a major part, its operation and influence have already received considerable attention, but important areas of activity remain neglected, and here I will focus on a few points of particular relevance.

Business is a vast and complex sector of activity with many participants operating in remarkably varying circumstances and with extremely diverse concerns and priorities. Even so, certain of their concerns impinge more or less directly on the operation of schooling, and with sufficient force for schools to be obliged to give those concerns considerable significance.

The more direct relevance of business arises from its being an employer. With modern industrialized societies requiring differentiated and stratified workforces, equipped with different levels and kinds of skills and competencies, and different kinds of attitudes and commitments, the requirements of schools are for programs that involve levels of increasing difficulty, and which become differentiated into different types of programs and schools. By such arrangements, students can be sifted and sorted into categories and ranked relative to particular sectors of the workforce.

A second relevance of business has been as an example of practice. For example, business has been held up as a model, with one metaphor taking the factory as the exemplar case which schools employ in the organization of teaching and assessment, and thereby in conceptions of knowledge and modes of organizing schooling. Again, a study by Callahan (1962) showed the pervasiveness of the business model in the early twentieth century in the US in helping to form managerial conceptions and priorities, and giving rise to a 'cult of efficiency' in which relatively simplistic 'product' characteristics and logistical concerns were given priority. The business ethos is also the source for proposals to provide and operate schooling by a voucher system which has been presented in terms of a supermarket operation where customers can 'shop around' and exercise 'freedom of choice' (Friedman and Friedman, 1980: Pt 3).

Another aspect of the business sector, namely its operation as a supplier of goods and services, is also a major force in the production and supply of learning resource material for primary and secondary schools, and studies in the US (e.g. Anyon, 1979; Apple, 1986: Ch. 4) indicate consequences in terms of the treatment or even neglect of some controversial topics such as the experience of subordinate groups or of creation or evolutionary science. Again, Altbach and Rathgeber (1980) showed the dominance of first world publishers in third and fourth world societies, with profound consequences for the experiences of people in those societies, and prospects for their cultures and ways of living.

In a somewhat different relationship to schooling are sets of producers comprising textbook publishers, equipment and teaching material suppliers, media operators and others who are often parts of giant, multinational, multimedia corporations. In one respect, schools are part of their market in that they have an interest in servicing the schooling enterprise. In another sense, however, they are also potential supplanters of schooling, at least in its conventional forms, and so have considerable incentive to change the operation of schooling to enable them to move from being suppliers of materials to providers of educational programs. Conceivably, for such a transformation to be achieved, more basic changes would be necessary as in methods of allocating resources, and notably from treasury allocations to systems and schools to parents who could then 'shop around' and develop the market (or even supermarket) model where voucher and similar schemes would be particularly relevant. Such compatibilities also incidentally indicate the kinds of rationalizations, namely the 'free enterprise' capitalist *modus operandi,* that would be appropriate for establishing such methods of operation, and which were extensively documented for the Melbourne situation in the late nineteenth and early twentieth century by Clements (1979).

There has long been the commercial undertaking of schooling in such areas as occupational training. These continue to be important spheres of activity, and have been extended to include advanced level tertiary studies with commercially operated institutions awarding doctoral qualifications, usually in fields related to areas of business specialization as with communication technology (e.g. Eurich, 1985). In addition, a growing appreciation of the commercial value of knowledge is giving commercial significance to the tertiary sector in particular and is already well developed in terms of contracts with particular research departments. For example, recent developments illustrate new trends in the role of business that relate to its use of knowledge and a more assertive pursuit of developments in knowledge production. A long-standing academic practice has been to present research findings to colleagues in the 'market place of ideas' for appraisal and subsequently for use by relevant sectors of society. Possibly reflecting more aggressive approaches, some large corporations have negotiated agreements with particular kinds of research departments in tertiary institutions and provided substantial fundings in return for privileged access to findings. The magnitude of this activity in the US, indicated by Dickson (1984), is sufficient to be a major force in the determination of tertiary institutional priorities, and in influencing which areas of reality are researched or neglected. At the same time, entrepreneurial academics have also exploited opportunities by establishing their own companies as mechanisms for exploiting the commercial value of their discoveries. Concurrently, governments, recognizing the enormous resources available in the private sector, have been steering or even coercing tertiary institutions into seeking such funds and interlocking them integrally into the productive system. This trend is also developing in terms of operating such departments as parts of commercially operated tertiary institutions and profiting from students who seek training in those departments. Beyond that is a prospect for operating primary and secondary schooling which can be identified as a market with enormous potential and attractive to corporations with resources appropriate for exploiting such markets.

Another aspect of the corporation-schooling relationship is much more ominous, due to an inherent oppositional relationship between some elements of the media and schooling. These elements involve entertainment, marketing and other activities, and are dependent for support upon the audiences they can attract and hold. As a consequence, their basic thrusts can influence in ways that are dysfunctional to the achievement of such basic schooling responsibilities as the attainment of literacy and numeracy. As a further consequence, such organizations have considerable incentive to develop defensive strategies that denigrate schooling by undermining confidence in its efficacy, simply to direct attention away from their own influence on the learning or not-learning of basic competencies. In the light of that prospect, it is significant that throughout the critical appraisals of schooling during the 1970s and 1980s the media have been key avenues for the expression of often unfounded critical appraisals. At the same time, while television and other operations have been identified as sources of negative influence on levels of achievement, an interest in undermining the standing of schooling has not been established. Yet they have, at least potentially, the same counter-productive relationship to schooling as some other organizations and industries have to health, mothering and other socially valued conditions and processes.

We should not have any doubts about the readiness of corporations to act anti-socially to advance their interests or achieve disadvantages for rivals, or even for clients. For example, in an extensive survey of the health, oil, armaments, agricultural and financial industries, but unfortunately not of schooling or education more generally, Bayes (1982) documented serious and damaging malpractices and exploitation of situations and the formation of coalitions between public authorities and corporations to advance sectional interests at the expense of other social groups. An abundance of other studies (Sampson, 1977; Adams, 1980; Medawar and Freese, 1982; Braithewaite, 1983; *Newsweek*, 24 January 1983; White, 1988) document innumerable examples of exploitation, use of unsound practices, production of unsound goods, use of bribery, corruption and other socially unacceptable practices. Often these are used on politically uninformed and ineffective groups or sections of populations, often in third and fourth world societies. It is tempting to make further points concerning the inappropriateness of the profit motive in such sectors of activity as health and education; however, public officials in those areas often exhibit comparable behaviour testifying to the pervasiveness of ideologies and styles of acting across public and private structural arrangements.

For such reasons, the damaging role of the media in recent years in respect of schooling should not be treated as a chance affair. It has been a very potent force in launching damaging attacks on the public sector of schooling. Selective treatment of situations and events, the employment of poorly informed but ideologically bound critics, the preoccupation with negative comments on one sector of schooling or another all point to a partisan and negative role. Certainly they have a readily recognizable interest in discrediting schooling institutions as a strategy in moving both to deflect attention from their own activities and even to supplant them in their work.

Finally, it is useful to establish the magnitude of private sector organizations and appreciate the considerable power and influence they can exercise. Morgan (1986: 300), drawing on World Bank data from the early 1980s, showed Exxon and Royal Dutch/Shell followed nineteen nations in terms of Gross National Product or sales, and to be ahead of such nations as South Africa, Indonesia, Austria and Denmark. Indeed, of the 100 largest entities, nations comprised fifty-three and corporations forty-seven. That is, many corporations are more substantial and presumably more powerful and influential than many nations and so are able to dominate such societies and require them to be cooperative towards corporations.

However, while some multinational corporations are of considerable size and significance, and with extensive resources and influence, even the largest of them is not the ultimate in terms of coherently organized forces of action. Those are to be found among the coalitions of corporations comprising producers of goods and services, together with banks, insurance and other financial institutions, and organizations specializing in one or more of advertising, marketing, public relations, accounting, auditing, corporate counselling, research and policy development, including leading tertiary institutions (e.g. Ohmae, 1985: Ch. 9). Moreover, such coalitions often work cooperatively with governments, drawing upon political influence in their pursuit of corporate goals or assisting governments with information and other services. These vast and complex coalitions are particularly evident in the US but, as Ohmae showed, they are increasingly constituted of multiregional transnational corporations and other institutions. Such coalitions constitute units of enormous economic and political force and, at their most aggressive, tolerate few if any constraints upon their activities, and have been associated with the bringing down of governments. As such, they have to be seen as major generators of influence in contemporary societies and ultimately of considerable significance as influences on educational systems.

Such coalitions are particularly important beyond their sheer magnitude; they are the leading exponents of modes of production with a readiness to incorporate other producers, and exemplify a disposition towards dominance of situations to the extent of monopolization. But the greatest deterring attribute is their primacy of concern with their own benefit and to produce and market products that serve the growth and profit of the organization rather than the well-being of the client or of society as a whole. It is a radically different situation from a market place of small suppliers, confronted by customers in a real position to exercise choice, where Adam Smith's 'hidden hand' may operate for the common good. The present is a situation of giants in contestation where consumers are considered in the context of furthering a giant's advantage. Within that context, schooling is an arena with considerable significance on several grounds: as a market to which goods and services can be supplied, either through present institutions such as schools or directly through such corporations becoming suppliers in their own right, by profiting from the production of knowledge in its commercial applications, or perhaps most seriously by establishing learning systems that produce a compliant and even positively supportive population.

While business is a major private sector operator in respect of schooling, it is not the only such force. Closely associated are the foundations that employ resources derived from business and usually in ways compatible with the business mode of operating, if not directly servicing the business sector. The foundations arise from endowments from some more successful business people, and vary in the breadth and focus of their mandates, and in the resources available to them. The better known and more fully studied ones are based in the US, but substantial foundations operate from Europe, Japan and elsewhere. Because of the lack of research on foundations in most societies, what can be said derives mostly from research on a few US foundations. The major foundations are attracting growing research interest (e.g. Arnove (ed.), 1980), but are still far from adequately researched or understood. Even so, it is sufficient to establish them as primary influences on the operation of schooling.

Their significance can be appreciated in part from their resources: Arnove (1980: 6) reported that in 1978 the Ford Foundation was the largest with assets of $2.3 billion, while the Rockefeller Foundation was fifth with assets of $740 million, and the Carnegie Foundation was eleventh with $274 million in late 1977. They constituted the three largest foundations contributing to education. Some important points can be made by examining some areas where they have contributed, such as in the measurement of personal attributes, and in promoting particular kinds of social research.

Research and development work in the measurement of individual attributes and its use or abuse in discrimination by class and ethnicity and in the classification and treatment of students have been discussed on a number of occasions (e.g. Kamin, 1977). Less well known, and often neglected in those discussions, is the role of the foundations that supported such work. Karier (1972) suggested links arising from the interests of business managers in classifying the workforce and selecting more efficient employees. Lagemann (1983) related Carnegie support to the personal interest of Pritchett, first president of the Carnegie Foundation for the Advancement of Teaching, who thought sound measurement and classification might provide a more efficient basis for selecting students for admission to higher education. Nonetheless, as a concept relevant to efficiency it reflected employers' concerns in making effective use of a labour force. Of interest, too, is the work of the Carnegie Foundation in establishing similar work together with appropriate research and test development centres in New Zealand, Australia and South Africa in the early 1930s, and later associating with the establishment of the National Foundation for Educational Research in England. All of these, incidentally, showed a preference for a particular style of research, the more behaviouristic, empiricist and quantitative approach that I will discuss next.

A second area of critical significance in education where foundations have made substantial and crucial contributions is in the development of research. The full story has not been told, and the role of foundation support and influence has often been omitted from discussions of particular studies; however, several studies enable some understanding to be achieved. For example, Collier and Horowitz (1976: 143), in their account of the Rockefeller dynasty, noted the efforts of Rockefeller Foundation officers, working with academics at Chicago University, to establish behaviouristic social science in the late 1920s. Fisher (1980) indicated that that interest was part of a substantial international project; in the period between the two world wars, the Rockefeller Foundation undertook a substantial role in the direction of the development of social science in England. It selected several leading institutions in England and some other societies for special support, encouraged research that might help achieve more stable social and economic conditions, and the use of perspectives such as functionalism that were more compatible with managerial perspectives and priorities. In addition, the Rockefeller Foundation provided fellowships for promising scholars, grants to undertake appropriate research and assistance with the publishing process. Thus scholars attracted to the Foundation network were greatly assisted in their career advancement and able to exercise considerable influence in their subsequent spheres of activity. Given the paucity of other support for social science in Britain in that period, these efforts meant that the Rockefeller Foundation played a major part in shaping the development of social science in England. Seybold (1980) extends the story in his examination of the development of behavioural political studies in the US in the 1950s and 1960s. In that case, the Ford Foundation contributed scholarships and grants for both researchers and institutions to enable programs of research, teaching and training to be undertaken, thereby building up a body of specialists with relevant expertise to promote the development of the approaches and the area of research activity.

In retrospect, and with the benefit of an understanding of the range of issues and approaches that could have been supported, it is evident that the foundations supported projects that related more to management priorities and concerns, were essentially conservative and did not get to basic issues that might have generated those problems and justified efforts to restructure social arrangements. There was, too, a neglect of the problems of Blacks, women and other groups whose concerns existed but generally were not established until the 1960s. Again, new developments in the social sciences that drew upon interpretivist approaches were neglected. The priority was for behaviouristic, empirical, quantitative studies that were of particular relevance for bureaucratic social managers. By preempting scholars and focusing their efforts on particular kinds of problems and along particular lines, the foundations delayed developments that nonetheless emerged in the 1960s and 1970s. Their efforts also had considerable implications for other systems of activity such as schooling as we shall see presently.

Foundation contributions to other areas of schooling and higher education, discussed in several contributions to the volume edited by Arnove (1980), indicate that individually and collectively they contributed substantially to exercise influence in most areas of US education, as well as in many developing societies. In addition, the work they promoted had further implications in exemplifying particular conceptions of knowledge to which students and teachers are exposed and which are taken into schooling. That is, both lines of development sustain conceptions of knowledge as objective, discoverable, transmissible and learnable, and testable, which contrasts with conceptions of knowledge as interpretation and personal, and less amenable to testing, at least in simple ways. Thus foundation support for particular kinds of research helped to sustain particular ways of undertaking teaching and operating schooling.

A further significant point arises from the nature and modes of operating of the foundations. While formally constituted as independent or autonomous organizations, they invariably draw upon leaders in business and academic administration for trustees, and work very much in an 'establishment' milieu. While that does not necessarily imply conservatism, it does suggest cautiousness and a fundamental preference to modify rather than radically change basic social structural arrangements. Moreover, with their considerable financial and human resources, they are well placed to exercise influence at critical points in processes, and in ways that encourage one kind of development, as in research, rather than others. As Marks (1980: 116) argued on the basis of his review of foundation-supported work on establishing and measuring individual traits, that work produced a framework that 'emphasised not only innate rather than acquired differences, but also individual (i.e. psychological) rather than social traits, individual differences rather than individual similarities, and particular differences (e.g. intellectual differences rooted in the needs of the social order) rather than other differences.' That conception of traits and differentiation was then used to justify differentiated and discriminating programs and types of schools. As private and sometimes self-perpetuating organizations, foundations are not accountable to society generally but rather to particular sector managers and so located outside the public system while operating effectively and influentially upon it. Ultimately, they have to be seen as constituting, directly in the US and either directly or indirectly in other societies, major vehicles for the exercise of influence by the business sector on schooling and other areas of activity (e.g. Fisher, 1983).

Another unit in the network of steering agencies to be considered here is the policy centre or 'think tank'. These range from some that are long established and highly regarded to others that are little more than cells within special interest groups or organizations or within government or corporation departments. Many attract considerable resources and competent scholars and are associated with a substantial output of publications, seminars, conferences and other contributions. They vary in being associated with liberal or conservative positions but, reflecting the source of resources, are preponderantly conservative; more radical centres tend to eke out an existence and sustain more modest programs. At the same time, the significance of their output and contributions does not directly reflect resources and expertise available to them as some draw more heavily on normative commitment. While many of them can have a significant impact on a particular issue at a particular time, some are much more formidable and continuing in their contributions and influence. Again, the better known centres are in the US, possibly because they are more substantially funded but probably because they have been more extensively researched.

These centres have proliferated in the recent years of economic turbulence and been exceptionally active in promoting interpretations of trends and strategies for responding in accord with those interpretations. For example, the Heritage Foundation in Washington, substantially funded by a former business man, produced policy statements congenial to the Reagan administration and disseminated them through substantial publications such as *Mandate for Leadership* (Heatherly (ed.), 1981), together with many pamphlets and lesser publications. Similarly, the Adam Smith Institute in London has been credited with a considerable influence on the development of policy initiatives, operating through task forces that shadowed particular government departments and generated reports indicating radical ways of introducing competition, deregulation, high growth and lower taxes (Rusbridger, 1987). While initially their proposals often seemed as coming from a lunatic fringe on the extreme right, subsequently many have been adopted and implemented by particular ministers.

Such centres, largely reflecting the preponderance of conservative institutions and the turbulent and uncertain conditions of the 1970s and 1980s, have been credited with substantially establishing agendas for discussing schooling. They have been associated with effective efforts in identifying and focusing attention on such issues as standards, excellence, basics, discipline and the relevance of schooling to economic productivity and prosperity, and to undermining confidence in public systems of schooling. Certainly, trade unions and other organizations of the 'left' of politics have identified themselves as being in need of such centres to identify issues and provide concepts, data and theories with which to contend with opponents on such issues, and to determine the agenda for schooling debate.

One further point of significance is the close links between participants in these various steering mechanisms. Colwell (1980) contributed interesting data on such connections, identifying trustees who served on several foundations, or linked foundations with recipient organizations or with high status business, social and professional organizations. Thus, for example, of 205 directors of the Committee for Economic Development, responsible for producing *Investing in Our Children* (CED, 1985), ninety-seven were also on foundations while almost all were chief executives or their immediate subordinates in major US corporations. This considerable and extensive system of connections indicates an 'establishment' sector in US society, as Silk and Silk (1980) and others have identified them, involving high status families, particular schools and tertiary institutions, and associations with major organizations, including clubs, policy centres and other meeting points. Of course, that does not ensure any considerable degree of consensus on any or even most issues, but nonetheless such participants do relate more to each other than they do with minority, working-class and some other groups of people. At the same time, the Silks portrayed this sector of US society as a relatively liberal establishment, distinguishing it from more conservative groups in business, politics, academia, professional life and elsewhere.

To students of power and the governance of societies, this is a familiar phenomenon. In an extensive review of US research available to the mid-1960s, Domhoff (1967) identified elite members, associations and modes of exercising influence, and generally substantiated the operation of a governing class. He also made the point that the distinctive feature of elites in a democracy is the divisions between them so that they have some necessity to compete for political support from the general populace. In that way a modicum of choice becomes available to the general citizenry.

Relevant to this discussion, too, are the theorists, researchers and other intellectuals who contribute to the development of understanding, the construction of theories and strategies, and the production of social and mechanical technology that can have profound influence on the undertaking of social activities and ultimately on a way of life. Clearly, people such as Darwin, Marx, Freud, Einstein, Keynes and others have profoundly influenced human activity by providing either insights, theories, strategies and technologies or the bases for developing them, and so steered human activity. Numerous others, less significant in their contributions and influence, have exercised more direct influence or sustained the exercise of influence in particular areas of activity such as education. Often, particularly in contemporary societies, they are located in particular institutions such as universities, policy centres or think tanks. Often, too, a distinctive feature of their activities is undirected in character as with fundamental research and theorizing that may have no purpose beyond understanding at a particular time, and only become consciously useful at some later time. This is in distinct contrast with practical and action research and theorizing which can be directed at identifying and resolving particular problems.

At the same time, of course, such participants are the objects of considerable efforts, sometimes entailing substantial resources, to influence their activities and the outcomes of their research and theorizing. Thus, as we have seen, foundations, corporations, governments and other major sponsors establish institutions, centres or other organizational arrangements to work on specific problems, possibly in specific ways. They can exercise influence too by selectively recruiting theorists and researchers congenial with their priorities and so likely to produce insights, understandings, strategies and technologies of value to the sponsors.

Currently, these efforts are most apparent in the reorganization of universities. For example, the Thatcher government in England is notable for its efforts to reduce funding so that researchers are obliged to obtain resources from more directive private sponsors. Simultaneously, the security of staff has been removed so that unwanted staff can be removed or disposed of, or employed on contract when they perform to some sponsor's more direct requirements. Similar trends are evident in other, hitherto more progressive societies so that differences between these and more authoritarian societies are now more in the subtlety of relationships involved in directed strategies.

In addition to these are groups who would seem to have legitimate interests in schooling but who do not articulate concerns or organize themselves to exercise influence. They are relevant to a discussion of steerers because of their potentiality rather than the actuality of their influence. One such group is the workforce, as distinct from managers, and who would seem to have several legitimate interests in schooling. One is for their own development in terms of knowledge, skills and competencies that enable them to be more effective and to obtain higher returns on their labour, take up more interesting and satisfying positions, or extend their understanding of the situations in which they work. A second is to ensure that children of employees receive quality schooling through the public provision of a high quality system of schools to which they can have satisfactory access. In particular, this means assistance to enable children from poorer families to have good quality facilities and opportunities. While there is interest along those lines, it appears to be more in terms of conditions of employment. This is even more the case when teachers' associations affiliate with the larger trade union movements, and follows from representatives of those associations undertaking to draft trade union policies on education, using the opportunities to ensure priority is given to concerns about conditions of employment. Quality education for all may be a common concern but it has to take a place alongside concerns about conditions of employment so that in situations of conflicting priorities, labour organizations are, not surprisingly, concerned about members' circumstances and prospects, and children's interests, even those of working-class children, can take second place.

It is also the case that trade union movements are particularly caught up in the substantial changes occurring in the world economy, and in social arrangements and culture more generally. Their situations have been affected by increased unemployment on the one hand, and the opening up of new industries with different occupational requirements and orientations on the other. For a variety of reasons, labour movements are finding major shifts and changes in priorities necessary. Also, as with the establishment of superannuation or pension funds, and the accumulation of resources for investment into vast amounts, they are becoming conscious of another strategy for exercising influence on the economy, namely through control over the use of those funds. Either industrially through work participation or economically through influence over the use of resources, they are facing the prospect of being able to exercise substantial influence over the operation of the economy, and possibly over other systems of activity such as schooling.

A further factor operating on the workforce is a change in the central character of employee organizations. In some cases, as in Australia and England, umbrella-type trade union organizations have been joined by relatively high status professional and technological specializations, so that the blue collar worker becomes something of a minority within the trade union movement. For several reasons, then, this diverse collection of employees has an interest in employment and the regulation of conditions and services, and an incentive to capture and use political parties and governments to promote a regulatory rather than a market-type society. This trend has most important implications for the operation of societies and for the prospects of other groups within societies.

One can go on to identify other groups within a society that have interests and potentiality to act to steer the operation of schooling. For example, consumers of goods and services can argue concerns with the quality of goods and services produced and so with the calibre of the workforce and the management of production and service agencies. However, they appear commonly to focus on cheapness and convenience, and rarely to act in any organized sense with exceptions involving decisions to buy 'home' society products or not to buy some types of product. That is, customers generally do not interrelate to constitute a coherent force and in any case are substantially influenced by personal convenience factors.

Another category comprises savers who, incidentally, are investors through banks, insurance policies, investment and other means. As such, they supply the financial resources that fund economic activity and so have the potentiality to determine the character of economic activity. Typically, however, their priorities are with security of investment and financial return, and they are readily martialled and influenced in the use of their resources by investment managers of one kind or another.

Members of a society are also citizens and as such have interests in the operation and development of a society, and particularly with its provision of housing, employment and health, education and other social services. To a substantial extent, however, they act individually or sectionally, rather than as a community. Moreover, their collective activities are likely to be orchestrated by the operation of political parties and coalitions which in turn are largely polarized around particular sets of positions relating to class, ethnicity, rural or urban location and similar characteristics, circumstances and interests.

In so many cases, then, collective interests can be identified but invariably participants are fragmented. Class, gender, ethnicity, religion, and rurul-urban location are some major bases of division and grouping but the influence of these can be tenuous with fractionization extending to sustain divisions within communities and even to families and ultimately to individuals. Even individuals can express different priorities and positions with their different strategies over time, and even at a particular time. In such ways, a population is a diverse fragile entity unlikely to pursue collectively common interests. At the same time, obviously specific political, economic, investment and other interests can be mobilized and managed, giving significance to the managers who emerge in these areas of activity.

Discussion

A primary purpose of this chapter has been to consider participants who operate from beyond or outside systems of schooling, and the agencies used to exercise influence on schooling. In the first instance, they are identifiable in terms of being public or private, commercial or political and so on, but examination reveals them to be interrelated with adept participants acting individually or collectively through any or several of them, according to circumstances and in relation to purposes and opportunities.

I have surveyed a few examples of a substantial range of units used to influence social functioning but it would be unwise to assume that all or even the major ones have been identified. The most important social units may well be social clubs or gathering places, or even informal networks. Silk and Silk (1980), writing on the American establishment, noted the significance of the Council of Foreign Relations in New York as an agency for exercising influence on international political issues. Again, Collier and Horowitz (1976) in their account of the Rockefeller dynasty gave significance to the Trilateral Commission as an agency for interrelating influential groups from North America, Western Europe and Japan. Still again, Ohmae (1985: Ch. 9), considering strategies for multinational corporations in the same three major market regions, illustrated the role of particular business consultancy firms in analyzing situations and devising strategies for corporations to pursue. His contribution is also a reminder of the remarkable growth of Asian and more particularly Japanese corporations which have now emerged as among the more substantial both as corporations and in coalitions, and have to be recognized as major steering agencies in the world economy and ultimately on social activities such as education. A major point to be noted from this discussion is the difficulty and perhaps the impossibility of tracing out all the centres and linkages of significance used in exercising influence. In addition, such work is complicated by their changing character as particular individuals and organizations gain or lose influence in those networks. At the same time, many other groups, lacking wealth, organization, competencies or other resources, remain ineffective in the influence process.

On the surface, then, political leaders and governments have taken the initiatives and introduced and implemented the policies being pursued. At the same time, they have done so in contexts shaped by the activities of many people operating in business, through the media and policy centres, and through academic and other workplaces and forums. Certainly, it is not difficult to find advocates of proposals and generally they have had a conservative thrust and been assisted by the operation of an abundance of agencies such as policy study centres and supportive media that have been notable for sensational claims and efforts to undermine confidence in public systems, whether of schooling or other forms of activity. It is also evident that those agencies are more active at this time, presumably because the environment is more receptive or supportive of their efforts.

It is here that material circumstances appear to be critical. The recent turbulent economic and political circumstances have encouraged feelings of uncertainty about personal and organizational prospects and achievements. That appears to have fostered caution and conservatism in attitudes, and recourse to more structured and controlled forms of schooling, and to steering students into particular sectors of the workforce and of society more generally.

For such reasons, we operate on a sound basis by focusing attention on participants in situations and in relation to issues, and seeking to establish the personal and social factors that influence their activity. On that basis, we can expect to achieve some understanding of their dynamics and strategies which can be meaningful, even without a full understanding of the situations in which they operate.

Chapter 10

Interpretation

The discussion so far has involved a particular kind of analysis of schooling, reflecting the particular assumptions that have formed the basis of the study. These entail assumptions about the nature of the person and of social reality that rest in turn on ontological, epistemological and moral assumptions regarding the nature of reality, how that reality may be known, the status of the interpreter, and his or her relationships with other participants and other aspects of reality. In turn, important elements of testing the soundness of an understanding are coherence and consistency between aspects of the interpretation, and its usefulness as a guide to effective action. However, given subjectivity in relation to selecting criteria for determining effectiveness, and the salience of power and compliance in achieving purposes, this latter is not a straightforward task. Indeed, correspondence and coherence and consistency need to be taken together, as in a process of triangulation, to increase confidence in an interpretation.

As has been indicated, people are seen here as inherently active, curious, exploratory and interpreting, and acting in the pursuit of interests. These interests include such concerns as to develop as a person and achieve competence and fulfilment, together with forms of aggrandisement such as to increase status, wealth and power in the terms used by Weber (Gerth and Mills (eds), 1964: Ch. 7). Some such as the development of competence may, as White (1959) argued, derive essentially from characteristics of the person and be expressed in efforts to improve performance in activities which humans are inherently capable of such as crawling, walking, communicating, reasoning and so on. Others such as differentiating one's self or group from others, and accumulating resources that are of social significance as in achieving aggrandisement, reflect social influences. So while inherent and learned elements are involved in the constitution of interests, they are largely inseparable. The important point is that interests constitute important forces that influence the activities of people, serving as goals which they pursue through their various social activities.

At the same time, social arrangements such as the symbolic cultural beliefs and interpretations and the manifest social structural and procedural arrangements or modes of operating by which people act are seen to be constructed arrangements. Indeed, they are not simply constructed but sustained, modified, neglected or transformed according to the actions of people in relation to particular needs, circumstances and so on. That is, they are not perceived as immutable social reality but as social agencies or forms of social technology, complementary to the mechanical technology that is another part of the constructed equipment that people use.

Central to this conception of social activity are the concepts of competence and power. People vary in their competencies as a consequence of differences in inherent and acquired attributes and other forms of personal, social, cultural and material resources. As a consequence, they differ in their interactions with social reality with less effective participants obliged to accommodate and comply with existing arrangements, more effective people able to master and use them, while some rise beyond existing forms of social and mechanical technology and invent or innovate and thereby generate changes and new developments. It is difficult to establish what gives rise to differential capacity and effectiveness but it is a crucial element in understanding people-situation interactions and relationships, and establishing the ultimate significance of human activity.

At the same time, to perceive situations and activities in terms of structures and processes can be useful as a step in the process of examining and interpreting what is happening in social activity. They constitute useful 'short-hand' terms for identifying main areas of activity. But they are essentially terms of convenience for when those situations are examined more closely they turn out to involve a population of participants acting dynamically and coherently, in relation to their contexts but also in the pursuit of their interests, as they understand those, and to the extent they are able to pursue them.

Yet even that interpretation is still inadequate as a representation of what is going on. It is inadequate in that participants do not act simply or solely in terms of their interests and their competencies and resources; one commendable feature of human activity is a propensity to take account of the circumstances and concerns of others, and show compassion and concern, or exercise a sense of social justice. The reality of that is often difficult to perceive with so much activity seeming to indicate the unadulterated pursuit of self-interest and the uncompromising use of power.

Interpretation

Nonetheless, it is always possible to see individuals and groups acting with concern for the interests of others such as poorer and weaker sectors of one's own or other, often third world societies, or victims of political and other forms of violence, and even of other species as with animal liberation movements and environmentalists. Such participants constitute significant and enduring reminders of the reality of such concerns. In consequence, any examination of social reality must be guided in its perceptions and interpretations by the knowledge of such kinds of activity.

In the present situation that has meant in particular that a special effort has been made to identify participants so that not only the more active or visible have been included. That is, attempts have been made to identify groups or even collections of people who might have common interests and so be relevant in an area of activity even though they are not visible as participants. For one thing, to include them helps to clarify how power, for example, is employed in promoting efforts to serve the interests of some rather than others.

The development of an understanding of the operation of schooling, involving the identification of participants who pursue personal and shared interests, operate individually and collectively, and use social structural and processual arrangements or forms of social and mechanical technology in the pursuit of those interests, has much in common with the development of an understanding of other systems of activity. More particularly, however, education is integral to the activities of many people such as to families for the development of their children, to employers for the production of a labour force, to political managers for the production of citizens, to teachers, specialists and school managers as a situation of rewarding activity and careers, to social theorists for its role in reproducing or transforming aspects of the social status quo, and similarly for other groups of people. In consequence, it is a crucial social situation and the activities associated with it are inevitably the focus of many and usually divergent interests, and so ultimately it is of considerable social and political significance.

In setting out now to offer an interpretation of educational activity, the discussion will be undertaken at two levels. The first will be in more limited and concrete terms, and involve a discussion of the situations and participants who constitute schooling, focusing on teachers and students, parents, specialists, managers and the steerers who exercise substantial influence on what happens in schooling. The second will be in more general terms that interrelate activity in schooling with activity in other sectors of society. While not obviously theoretical in character, it nonetheless reflects the theoretical position taken here which emphasizes

191

participants and their priorities and strategies. In taking that form, it also serves as a basis for the development of proposals and strategies and courses of action in the final chapter.

The Operation of Schooling

Schooling can be perceived as constituting a system or set of systems of activity, involving people acting individually and collectively in the pursuit of interests, usually in relation to the power they can mobilize but sometimes exhibiting a degree of concern for others, or a sense of justice. Being formally organized, people can be seen as acting in groups on normative, calculative or coercive bases in contract and other types of relationships, in the terms used by Etzioni (1975). Such groups are invariably established and operated by more effective participants in relation to the pursuit of individual and collective interests, and so serve as parts of processes of control and domination, and even of exploitation. I will explore this interpretation situation by situation, starting with the more visible and readily experienced classroom involving teacher-student interaction, and moving through to the school, the system and thence to society and the world as a system. Analytically, each constitutes a dynamic system of activity in itself, involving people pursuing interests in their personal development, advancement and aggrandisement, and seeking to influence the undertaking of schooling in part or in whole. But the participants in any one are also involved in other parts, or interactive with those other participants so that the concept of a system as a whole has validity.

In portraying each situation, the usual difficulties arise in identifying participants. Some are more specific to particular situations as with students in the classroom, while others such as major steerers can be influential although unidentified forces in all situations. To avoid repetition in discussing these latter and so to simplify presentation, situations will be discussed in terms of their more specific participants, and more general participants will be considered at a later stage as parts of society or world entity. It will then be straightforward to go on to review the rationales and strategies, including structures and processes, employed in the undertaking of schooling.

The classroom, involving the interaction of a teacher and students, is a most visible and familiar aspect of schooling and also most extensively studied. On the basis of such studies, common assumptions of competently managed teaching and learning activity readily give way to perceptions of intense interactions that reflect control and management concerns of teachers and social and other concerns of students. While teachers have legal authority to act as such, they have to gain acceptance or social authority from students who ultimately are required to participate. Invariably, relationships reflect the background circumstances and experiences of students and their related aspirations and perceptions of prospects, giving rise to types of classroom situations. Partly reflecting the backgrounds and social circumstances of students, but partly also reflecting characteristics of resources provided, together with cultural, economic and other more general influences, classrooms are invariably situations of differentiation among students and differential treatment on such bases as class, gender and ethnicity, varying in the expectations of students held by teachers and the character of experience provided for them. In consequence, classrooms provide microcosms of schooling, collectively portraying the range and diversity of school experience.

The school community constitutes a second entity that is useful for identifying participants and examining their activities. Here students and teachers are again highly visible participants but the structuring of their activities and relationships is more evident as within any individual school they are grouped by age into grades and forms, and then further into streams or programs, and further into different types of schools on performance and other bases. School managers are significant in generating policies and procedures, particularly in larger schools where activities are more routinized and regulated. These principals and their deputies, departmental heads and other managers exercise substantial influence on the basis of their legal authority, and while students and teachers contest and negotiate with their managers, invariably size, age level of students, and other often constructed entity characteristics influence how schooling is undertaken in a particular situation.

The concept of school community is also useful in drawing attention to parents, prospective employers and others who participate in one way or another in the operation of a particular school. Of these, parents are the more specifically related, being directly involved in the upbringing and forming of their children who are the students of the school, and concerned with what the school is doing with their children. A major feature of recent developments is that their scope for exercising influence has been greatly increased so that they are more likely than heretofore to be involved in the appointment of principals and in other aspects of the work of undertaking schooling. Even so, their major influence is undoubtedly in how they form their children, from promoting development and positive orientations to impairing development and generating negative and even destructive orientations, and as an influence on the performance of their children in the programs and activities of schooling. In consequence, they are a major set of participants in the operation and achievements of any school.

The system constitutes a further unit that is useful in enabling further structuring and patterning and additional participants to be identified and examined. One obvious aspect is the differences among systems in their size and scale of operations with larger systems invariably publicly operated with limited resources and substantially regulated, partly reflecting negotiations between staff and managers, and partly as a consequence of managers securing the system and themselves against legal initiatives. Smaller systems are common in the public sector of the US, although much less so than heretofore as pressures to economize operate, but are particularly evident among private schools. There they often reflect affluence and the capacity of patrons to support expensive modes of operating and allow characteristics of specialness, exclusiveness and even elitism to be achieved. Small systems are also associated with particular religious, political and other groups who share a commitment to a way of life and see separateness as essential to its perpetuation.

But even though schools are differentiated by the administrative sectors of which they are parts, they still form an overall collectivity of an educational system, and as such exhibit diversity and structured characteristics and relationships. Thus schools vary by the communities they serve in ways reflected in their clientele, staffing, programming, resources and management ethos and modes of operating and so are rural or urban, working- or middle-class or elite, substantially of one or many ethnic groups or of one or another religious affiliation and so on. Such groupings are significant influences on the organization, operation and day-by-day activities of a school.

But such characteristics of schools reflect the decisions of managers and the sponsors of schools. Thus more affluent groups can readily establish and operate special schools to meet their requirements. Again, particular religious or other communities can also usually manage to sponsor a particular school or system to serve their needs. Public sector systems emerge through the political process with central political, bureaucratic and professional administrators, together with interest groups such as staff and parent associations, employers and other groups, negotiating and perhaps agreeing on ways of organizing and operating them. Thus decisions concerning the organization of schools, programs, resources, staff or other aspects of a system are made by these managers, while in more participatory political systems, parents, teachers, employers and others may exercise influence. Ultimately, however, the responsibility and authority of operating and managing systems of schools, and determining the arrangements that structure the activities of teachers, students and others, rest with the political, bureaucratic and professional managers, and formally with the first of these.

It is the managers, too, who establish and operate the complementary examination, curriculum development and implementation, teacher education and other agencies that are so useful in steering teaching and learning processes, thereby influencing the operation of schooling. In establishing such agencies, however, they also create entities with staff and managers, clientele and other interested parties that then become additional forces influencing the operation of the overall educational system. The specialists, for example, give significance to responsibilities and authority, to status and career structures, and opportunities to influence school practices. Teachers, administrators and others often find it convenient to participate in the work of these agencies to gain experience, exercise additional influence, and sometimes enter into different and possibly more interesting careers.

Collectively, these agencies greatly complicate the organization of an educational system and influence its operations, partly as a consequence of the work they do but partly also by the structured ways in which they undertake their work. Thus efforts to achieve status, careers and opportunities bear upon and can restrict the situations and prospects of teachers, school managers and others. At the very least, they represent ways of using resources and, in simply existing and operating, constitute a drain on the resources available to schools.

In discussion of the classroom, schools, the system and other entities, it has been useful at times to note the activities of some such as employers who operate primarily in political, economic and other systems of activity. To catch the full range and ascertain the full force of their influence, it is useful to go beyond the system and examine schooling in relation to society. Thus we find a further plethora of groups comprising not only employers but also suppliers of school materials, potential competitors in the provision of school programs, and a multitude of others with political, economic and other social involvements, and who, on the basis of those involvements, have an interest in the operation of schools. Their interests can be basic and fundamental, as with the moral character of material used in schools or with the attitudes and loyalties being established with students, to more general concerns such as the political or economic value or usefulness of schooling. Collectively, they span an extensive range in types of interests and in the extent to which they pursue them, the resources available to them, and the mechanisms they employ in pursuing their interests.

Business managers, for example, operate as individuals on the basis of positions in particular corporations, on behalf of a corporation, through umbrella associations for particular industries, or through entities that their corporations sponsor. These last are often the more influential, having an aura of autonomy and independence in the formation and promotion of a point of view, expression of priorities or set of policies. Probably the most significant among these are the policy centres or 'think tanks' to which specialists are attracted and provided with resources and facilities to undertake particular projects. In that mode of operating, resources are of particular significance, evidenced in the preponderance of conservative and the paucity of more liberal centres.

But the policy centres are again a more visible agency. More substantial in terms of resources and influence over extended periods of time are the foundations established by particular philanthropists and then progressively taken over and operated by managers from business, the professions and academia, in conjunction with the managers they appoint to operate the foundations. Primarily historical evidence testifies to the extensiveness and pervasiveness of the influence of these agencies. For example, studies of the efforts of foundations to influence social research methodologies indicate that their efforts bear upon the staffing, programming and operation of university departments and subsequently on their research and publications and other forms of productive activity. It is important to recognize, too, that many of the students from those departments become teachers and thereafter help to form conceptions of what constitutes history, geography, economics and other aspects of social science in schools. Similarly, foundation supported work on the conceptualizing and measuring of human attributes and the establishment and operation of centres to promote such work has found its way through to examination and monitoring agencies, and so helped to structure requirements of schools and incidentally teachers' conceptions of their tasks. Thus they exercise influence indirectly and even covertly with teachers often unaware of the priorities or concerns that steer such efforts. That is, by such programs of research and development, foundations and other agencies shape the perceptions, expectations and criteria of performance or, more generally, the culture of schooling.

It is also useful to identify the world as a sector relevant to what goes on in schools. While foundations and policy centres are usually located in particular societies, their activities extend into other societies and constitute key mechanisms for exercising influence and even direction. It is at the international level, too, that such organizations as OECD, the World Bank and UNESCO have been established and operated as regional and international organizations to influence activities within and across societies. In examining them, it is useful to note their different modes of operating, largely reflecting variations in the status, resources and other attributes and circumstances of societies. Thus more industrialized societies are joined in a more or less cooperative relationship of which OECD is an example. In contrast, the World Bank is more an instrument of direction and coercion that first world societies employ in dealing with third and fourth world societies.

These developments and practices reflect more extensive developments that in turn reflect pressures or incentives to move towards larger, more inclusive regional and international entities. These are many and diverse, and an adequate consideration of them is beyond the scope of this discussion. However, it is important to note that they constitute regional responses to expansion in economic units and the operation of multinational corporations. Other factors such as environmental issues are also constituting imperatives for international policy responses and drawing attention to limitations of nation-states, as was discussed in Chapter 8. Indeed, nations may be losing some of their significance so that regional organizations such as the European Commission and OECD, and world organizations such as UNESCO and the World Bank may be given greater significance in the management of social activities, including, of course, education. Concurrently, ethnic groups, often as minorities within a society or across several societies, may find greater scope for the assertion of their identity and priorities and emerge as a greater force in the undertaking of schooling and other social activities.

In the light of the operation of these organizations, one has to recognize that steering agencies become silent and invisible participants in schooling, substantially determining how it is undertaken. In consequence, any consideration of school or classroom activity that focuses on the obvious and visible participants and ignores the strategies, materials and processes they employ and the priorities and concerns implicit to them, falls substantially short of developing a comprehensive or even adequate understanding of what is going on in schooling. One has to recognize that many other participants exercise influence in the classroom and in effect constitute silent participants in classroom activities. Indeed, their relationships are complex with sets of participants effectively constituting coalitions on the basis of shared priorities and concerns, and so having a concerted effect on what occurs in schooling. Thus some employers, together with particular media specialists, academics and others, constitute a 'new right', while others, comprising again some media specialists, academics, teachers and others, form a 'left' grouping.

The existence of coalitions and shared perspectives and interests raises the issue of the bases on which participants operate, and is useful in understanding the priorities and positions of participants, including the divisions between some groups, such as parents, who might be thought to share certain interests and priorities, and the coalitions found across sets of participants in other cases. I will return to this point later but for the present wish to consider the dynamics of participants' activities, particularly in relation to the structures and processes involved in social situations.

Before leaving this topic it is relevant to note that although the interpretation is ultimately made in terms of participants, invariably one moves readily and frequently to employ structural arrangements in discussing the operation of schooling. Primarily, as has been noted, that is for reasons of convenience in that the structures are the agencies through which or by means of which actions are taken and power is exercised. Commonly, that in turn reflects the paucity of research on key structures, particularly those at higher levels of decision-making and the use of power. Some progress has been made with the foundations and the World Bank, although much of that is historical and so one is generally working speculatively from it. In other cases, such as the European Commission, UNESCO, the influential Bank of International Settlements and OECD, insider knowledge on the operation of individuals and groups is slight or unavailable. The significant and reassuring circumstance is that, as has been illustrated repeatedly in the closer and more detailed historical and sociological studies, individuals and groups invariably are found to be the movers and operators of these organizations as they pursue individual and collective interests and take account of the situations and circumstances in which they operate. For such reasons we can be confident in giving primacy to their significance.

The Social Dynamics of Schooling

A central issue in examining the social dynamics of schooling involves establishing the relative significance of people and social entities as determinative entities. While analytically separable, they are closely and complexly interrelated, with each reflective of the other. At the same time, as has been noted, developing an understanding of them draws upon psychological, biological, social and other research and theories regarding the person and sociological, political, economic and other research and theories regarding social entities. Those in turn rest on ontological, epistemological and moral assumptions and theories regarding the nature of reality, how it may be known, and relations between interpreter and other participants and their situations. In consequence, developing an interpretation is a substantial and complex task that cannot be fully undertaken here; rather, a few major points will be made to indicate essential elements of an interpretation of the undertaking of schooling. Discussion will be organized first in terms of the person and then in terms of social entities. Subsequently, points will be made regarding the undertaking of social activities.

Of several main points to be made about the person, some have already been indicated. For example, the person is accepted as being active and dynamic, curious, exploring and enquiring, experiencing and interpreting that experience, developing and adapting, and sustaining, modifying and transforming ways of acting. With development, inherent and acquired attributes interrelate and interact and the attainment or achievement of competence in social, physical and other activities, of a sense of self and of others, a degree of individuality and a concern for others, of economic, political and social aggrandisement, and other personal and social goals become important concerns or interests. Moreover, these are pursued individually and collectively, in cooperative actions with some and in competition and even conflict with others. Again, because people are differentially competent and effective, reflecting differences in personal attributes and competence, including a sense of self and self-worth, stage of development and other elements of personal, social, cultural and material resources, they vary greatly in asserting and pursuing their interests, and in the competence and effectiveness of their impact on the situations of which they are part.

At the same time, their development, performances and achievements are not simply matters of chance. In particular, parents vary greatly in their effectiveness in promoting the development and achievements of their children with some employing considerable competence and other resources in their efforts within the home, in working with schools and other agencies, and generally in managing their children's lives. Indeed, the efforts of some parents to advance their children's development and give them a comparative advantage generate much of the differentiation among schools, and in particular sustain elite schools that constitute centres of advantage and privilege and which operate to assist their students to gain advantages during and subsequent to schooling. In contrast, other parents may be inept and ineffective in promoting the development of their children, with still others who, through abuse in one form or another, actively pervert the development of their children and contribute to the production of 'problem' children. Where patterns of access to resources, competence and effectiveness in social activities, use of particular types of elite schools, and continuities between family of origin and subsequent status and achievements in society are coherent, then conceptions of a ruling class with concomitant lower and middle classes become viable. These may be linked with further groupings on the basis of ethnicity, gender, religion or other circumstances.

As a consequence of these different kinds of situations, circumstances and experiences, children are substantially destined from the outset for different types of prospects, careers, forms and degrees of achievement. In particular, they are varyingly able to exercise influence with some readily able to progress to positions of significance and exercise influence on both their own situations and those of others, and others destined to be essentially ineffective and obliged to comply or to operate antagonistically or even disruptively, and eventually be restricted by confinement in prisons or other institutions.

Thus competence and effectiveness reflect the operation of inherent or acquired characteristics, together with situations and circumstances which, collectively, substantially account for the different prospects and achievements of people. At the same time, the experience of disadvantaging and handicapping experiences illustrates that there is scope for efforts to improve the effectiveness of families and their children. But such efforts are dependent on a sense of concern for others or social justice by those who are more able and effective and with greater resources, and who are prepared to act in the interests of less effective people. That much occurs along those lines testifies to the reality of such concerns and establishes social justice as an important factor, along with power, in the working out of social situations and relationships. That is, participation in social situations is not solely a reflection of 'survival of the fittest' types of ethos or situations.

At the same time, many of the activities of parents and their children, and the more general process of the production of people, relate directly to the societal and other situations in which they are active and which some identify as the primary social reality and use to offer interpretations in cultural, structural, functional and other terms. Certainly, that social reality, comprising symbolic cultural elements such as values, beliefs and worldviews, perspectives, perceptions and interpretations, rationalizations and ideologies, and strategies that provide formulae for acting, together with manifest social structural arrangements such as family and community, political, economic, religious and other organizations, and caste, class, ethnic, gender and other groupings, along with processes such as socialization, the maintenance of values and traditions and social cohesion, and modes of producing goods and services, undertaking governance and other tasks, is persistent and obdurate. It pre-exists and succeeds individuals and is clearly established, ongoing and determinative as an influence on social activities.

However, it is readily apparent that cultures, social structures and processes are not stable entities but continually change. Indeed, more careful examination, as with holistic historical and contemporary studies, reveals these phenomena to be elusive realities and located ultimately in the conceptions, interpretations, actions, constructions and artefacts of people. In consequence, they vary greatly in detail and their similarities and continuities are often of most general kinds. The reality is of almost infinite diversity, derived from individual variations at a time or over time, as people adopt, employ, modify or neglect concepts, processes and arrangements. Indeed, as attention is focused more closely on people's activities, it becomes apparent that concepts such as culture, social structure and processes are again substantially terms of convenience, useful for short-hand references to situations, arrangements and actions, likely to divert attention from the more dynamic and significant actions of participants who construct, modify, sustain or transform these cultural and social forms of reality.

Nonetheless, there is no question that societies, communities, organizations and other major social entities with their cultural and social elements have considerable force and significance. And that force and significance derive substantially from expectations, practices, sanctions and other elements of interaction that have their bases in tradition, law and other sources of authority. They also vary not only in their stability or changeableness but also in the elements given priority such as religion, political or economic activity, or in other ways. It is also apparent that there are links or patterns between these and so in the character of particular types of societies. Two types in particular, 'traditional' and 'modern', are useful for making some essential comments.

Societies commonly identified as traditional are noted for their social stability and the persistence of cultural and social features. But they are also usually closed, particularly from external influences, and exhibit considerable unity in the dominant doctrine or ideology and associated practices. Less evident is a firmly established system of control and domination by particular elites who are able to restrict thought and expression in action. That is, traditional societies are invariably characterized by a concentration of power, the promotion of a particular doctrine, the repression or exclusion of challenging outside influences, and restriction of the participation of most members of a society. Inevitably, they are authoritarian and repressive, with conformity facilitated by some central doctrine that gives meaning and force to established and sustained arrangements.

In contrast, modern societies are characterized by a dispersal of power and relative openness and diversity. Usually, their situations reflect

The Social Dynamics of Schooling

the efforts of hitherto repressed or restricted groups in asserting their priorities and distinctive interests. As a consequence, larger proportions of a population experience development, aggrandisement and achievement. Their diversity also undermines any single doctrine, and favours a shift to secularity. People may also be seen as more enterprising, reflecting limitations to efforts to restrict and control.

It should not be assumed, however, that development follows a particular pattern as from traditional to modern or from restricted to open or from scope for only a few to develop to scope for many. Regressions are always possible, depending on developments in understandings and in knowledge and its applications in social and mechanical technology, and in situations and circumstances. For example, periods of economic recession are seen to favour increased exclusionary practices and the emergence of other-worldly views, and the acceptability of simplistic political solutions from demagogic types of leaders.

However, it is evident that efforts to individualize in one's development and to exercise greater influence over one's life, achieve greater autonomy and participate more effectively in social situations are persistent and powerful forces. Moreover, in the modern world these focus around political and economic activities and associated sets of resources, and are expressed in the venues of the forum and the market place respectively. In the contemporary world, these two distinct forms of operating can be identified as socialism and capitalism in one form or another. But the tensions between individualization and participation, with a concern for the other on the one hand, and dominance and exclusion with associated discrimination and exploitation on the other, also persist so that both political and economic developments have their inclusionary democratic and exclusionary and oppressive and exploitative forms.

In any understanding of these two major modes of operating, it is useful to distinguish between rhetoric and reality. The rhetorical version of capitalism as presented by Friedman (1962), Novak (1982), Berger (1986) and others emphasizes freedom for the individual to produce and trade goods and services, and so engage in transactional negotiations in a market place. As presented, it is an attractive mode of operating and can be plausibly linked with democracy. The reality, however, is that because people vary in their competencies and other resources, some manipulate and even control the market place so that interactions entail domination and exploitation of weaker, more vulnerable groups, or operate in harmful and damaging ways through the use of particular methods or in the production of particular kinds of goods and services. That is, a common and perhaps inevitable tendency for the capitalist mode of operating is to become monopolistic, predatory and exploitative. When markets become dominated by particular suppliers or are avoided by people without resources, then their operations are distorted and they do not constitute authentic markets.

In the contemporary world this tendency is often expressed through large corporations that operate trans-societally or as multinationals. Such is their magnitude that some are more substantial than many societies (e.g. Morgan, 1986: 300). They are further magnified when, as Ohmae (1985: Ch. 9) illustrated, they associate together in very much larger coalitions, combining substantial multinational corporations in industry, commerce, the media, banking and other financial services, insurance, research, transportation, armaments and other activities. With their capacity to mobilize massive resources and other elements of power, their pursuit of collective interests can be all-embracing, all-pervasive and overwhelming of all but the most powerful states, and particularly damaging to smaller, weaker and sometimes desperate states and their populations. Indeed, such is their improbity and ruthlessness in the pursuit of not simply profit but the endless goal of growth that they have achieved a considerable reputation for disastrous impact, as a multitude of studies, noted in the previous chapter, illustrate.

It is also evident that many corporations are operated with clear concerns regarding their impact on people, the environment and other aspects of reality. However, pressures from a competitive mode of operating and the operations of less scrupulous rivals are a constant challenge to probity and responsibility. At the same time, the emergence of environmental and other problems of fundamental significance for the continuation of life on this planet is generating individual and collective state sponsored regulatory arrangements to control at least some of their more damaging practices.

The socialist rhetoric emphasizes the social unit as a situation where all can experience opportunity and achieve development (e.g. Bowles and Gintis, 1976: Ch. 11). It is epitomized in the supportive society, characterized by altruism and justice. The reality, however, entails individuals and groups struggling to achieve political dominance and establish stratified statist systems that reflect inequalities in competencies and other resources, and the dominance and exploitation of some by others, essentially through regulatory processes. Commonly, socialist societies become coercive and exploitative and are distinguishable from capitalist societies mainly by their emphasis on political as against economic activity and strategies, and involving the use of massive, ruthlessly operated departments, including the military, secret police and other agencies. Nazism, fascism, communism and other developments in the twentieth century illustrate the awesome character of excessive or perverted statism in the abuse of political power and in the concomitant use of oppression and exploitation.

Encouraging, however, are the relatively exemplary practices of some states with their emphasis on human rights and the development of monitoring mechanisms and checking agencies. It is of considerable significance and cause for optimism that some such societies have been able to combine moderation of behaviour in both political and economic activity and constitute examples of prosperous and humane societies (e.g. Gastil, 1982; Wright, 1982).

These forms of social arrangements and processes can be further understood by examining them more closely and identifying the individuals, groups and coalitions who constitute and drive them. That is, societies, like organizations and other social entities, break down to reveal participants in action, but who vary greatly in their resources and in the competence and effectiveness with which they use those resources in the pursuit of individual and collective concerns or interests. We then see that general concepts constitute the conceptualizations and modes of operating which are sustained primarily by the more powerful who seek to retain particular modes of operating, but partly also by less powerful members of social units who value stability and continuity and predictable prospects. Thus commercial arrangements and activities are endorsed by investors, employees, customers and others because benefits are satisfactory or convenient, and alternatives are difficult to conceive and establish. Again, political arrangements are sustained by subjects or electors, together with professional and bureaucratic managers and their subordinate operatives, because the benefits they provide or because the task or cost of establishing and operating alternatives puts them out of consideration. Similarly with religious, educational and other systems of activity. That is, beyond the simple polarities of leaders and subordinates, or classes, are more complex situations within organizations and systems of activity, involving people who seek to maximize their returns as best they can. Among these are the 'willing workers' who seek advancement to a wider range of intermediate positions in political, commercial or other organizations, and who come to constitute the crucial force of specialists, operatives or technocrats who ensure that organizations and other social arrangements operate effectively. In education, I have identified these as the teachers, specialists and professional and bureaucratic managers and they have their equivalents in other systems of activity. In return for their contributions to operating the system, they obtain personal and social benefits in terms of careers, with increases in status, income and influence, largely reflecting access to the considerable resources available in organizations. Thus organizations and systems of activity constitute, to a degree, coalitions of participants, working on a variety of bases, and with great variations in the distribution of benefits from some that are collegiate groups of more or less equals to others that are hierarchical and extreme in the extent of domination, exploitation and even abuse of lower level participants. Indeed, as caste systems, Nazism and other extreme cases of oppression, abuse and exploitation illustrate, operators of these systems can invariably attract accomplices who are willing to cooperate, regardless of the consequences and cost of their activities for others. In pursuing their interests, many readily take advantage of gender, ethnicity and other bases for achieving advantages for themselves and disadvantages for others. That is, differentiation and discrimination and the structuring of relationships are not simply top-down or system-driven phenomena but derive considerable force and effectiveness from widespread recourse being made to them by many types of participants.

Nonetheless, those who occupy the upper echelons of such systems of social arrangements are of critical significance in determining how activities are undertaken. They have access to greater resources, and are in a position to exercise greater influence directly on the operation of their organization and indirectly on other organizations and systems of activity. As has been illustrated with education, these constitute a diverse array that can be seen as varying from slight to considerable importance. At their most formidable, they occupy senior positions in government or in a department or a corporation. Often they occupy several organizational positions and operate through both the public and private sectors, and through commercial, financial, philanthropic and other organizations, as with the Rockefellers, the Fords, the Carnegie managers and others who have been seen as major influencers through much of the late nineteenth and twentieth centuries. Concurrently, major participants are likely to include people who operate from Western Europe, Japan or other East Asian locations. But while, for example, Silk and Silk (1980) provided a helpful discussion of the American establishment during the mid-twentieth century, Sampson (e.g. 1977, 1981) provided similarly helpful discussions of some major international corporations and their managers, and other comparable contributions have been made, we are a long way from an adequate guide to a 'world establishment'.

However, although such managers as we have identified are extremely significant as determiners of social arrangements and parties, they are not the only major influencers. Of considerable importance, too, are inventors, discoverers, conceptualizers, synthesizers and others who initiate or innovate and extend understanding, technologies and capabilities in fundamental ways. Exceptional contributors such as major researchers or inventors are readily recognized but a multitude of lesser participants significantly influence developments and trends by their cumulative efforts and activities. Thus the technological revolution of the late twentieth century which is having such a profound impact on production, management, communication and other areas of activity reflects the contributions of numerous researchers and technologists in many societies. But integral to those developments, too, are sponsors who, by allocating resources and other benefits, steer the development and use of ideas and conceptions, and their application in social and mechanical forms of technology.

As the world becomes a more integrated economy, and environmental and other issues generate measures for coordinated political action, it is difficult to anticipate future trends. On the one hand, more constraints from a wider spectrum of competitors are probable, together with greater uncertainty and unpredictability. At the same time, developments in technology facilitate the control and direction of ever larger organizations and corporate empires, and ultimately increase the influence that their managers can exercise. Of these, some such as media operators with their television and radio networks, publishing houses and other communication facilities can bear more directly on how schooling is undertaken by influencing perceptions, understandings, interpretations and the like. But then again, major operators in other sectors of the political, commercial and industrial worlds exercise influence indirectly by influencing conceptions of public responsibility, financial policies and the like.

At the same time, some major differentiations and coalitions are discernible. Reference was made earlier to 'left' and 'right' positions and orientations and much is said and done on the basis of such conceptions. While membership of each group can be quite diverse, patterns have been discerned and bases of coherence argued. Thus Berger (1986: 68) argued that the entrepreneurial and exploitative production sector of capitalism is being challenged by a more radical and liberal knowledge class, associated with knowledge production and its application and exploitation in technology.

The division upheld here employs the more general capitalist-statist dichotomy, emphasizing those who resort to material resources, production and the market place, and those who employ regulatory modes of operating and who work through the forum. The latter is attractive to those such as employees whose members lack material resources and so find strength and exercise influence through organization and collective action. Both sets of coalitions can readily employ social justice, democracy and other inclusionary principles in achieving their priorities. But each is also constituted of participants who can be sectionalist and pursue advantages and domination, and even seek to oppress and exploit. In the process of contestation between the two major groups, the tendency is for a third major group of less effective, disadvantaged people to emerge and become a vulnerable under-class experiencing poverty, hardship, exploitation and oppression in a generally affluent and prosperous society.

Even so, in many situations, and increasingly in the present with remarkable developments in technology and its use in modes of production, communication, management and so on, education is a particularly important process. As the process of fostering learning and the development of understanding and competence, involving knowledge, skills and other attributes, it is crucial to effective performance in contemporary societies. But that very significance gives education particular kinds of significance to particular groups, with education for the acquisition of knowledge, skills, and the development of competence a simple and basic view. More sophisticated perceptions see education as a crucial means in securing advantages in relation to others. For example, those who have achieved high status positions in a society regard education as critical in ensuring the achievements and successful activity of their children and act to support schools of advantage and privilege which function to perpetuate differential performance and achievement and which incidentally are often given unwarranted credit for the achievements of students who, very clearly, are the beneficiaries of well resourced, competent and effective parents. Employers, being a diverse group, have a multitude of views with some valuing schooling for its provision of basic training and socialization, and others valuing a 'ladder-like' system of schools and tertiary institutions that sift and sort according to performance, conformity and other criteria. Still others look to particular institutions and programs to provide specialists, managers and other special-type 'products' for higher level sectors of the workforce. Again, political, bureaucratic and other societal managers appear increasingly to look to educational systems to provide comparative advantages relative to competitors through enhancing the work skills and competencies of their 'human resources'. Still other groups look to schools to provide religious or other kinds of indoctrination of the young.

It has been argued that such concerns with differential provision and opportunities follow from capitalist forms of undertaking economic activity with their reliance on a differentiated and stratified workforce (e.g. Bowles and Gintis, 1976; Sharp (ed.), 1986). However, the reverse, namely that capitalism follows from the tendency of people to develop individually and operate in the pursuit of individual and sectional interests, is also arguable (e.g. Berger, 1986). Certainly, a formidable argument can be developed that people are disposed to seek autonomy and flexible conditions which are compatible with some capitalist forms of operating. However, that tendency can also be related to the development of democracy which can be seen as a form of operating that gives scope for the expression of individuality and degrees of autonomy and self-determination. When these tendencies are reinforced by sentiments of concern for others which attribute rights to all people and so sustain a concern with social justice, they are important factors in the generation of conceptions of socialism as a system of arrangements for handling social situations and opportunities.

But such practices exist precariously in that varied sentiments are held. Many people hold and express such sentiments in their actions. At the same time, some particularly vigorous participants give little significance to the well-being of others and preoccupy themselves with the pursuit of sectional interests. Such dispositions are associated with experiences in political and economic activity with economic exploitation and oppression in the one case, and political manipulation and exploitation in the other.

If a primary force is the priorities and dispositions of people, pursued with different degrees of effectiveness, then a differentiated and discriminatory school system can reflect those attributes and tendencies rather than derive from the economic mode of production or a counterpart form of political activity. Such attributes and dispositions can sustain the human basis of differentiation and discrimination that is a universal characteristic of schooling, despite differences in political, economic, religious and other systems of values and beliefs and the modes of operating they are held to sustain.

One further notable trend of the present is to see education as a commodity, useful in utilitarian terms and amenable to commercial exploitation. These perceptions are expressed through strategies to emphasize basic skills and competencies and vocationalism in schooling, and to use educational institutions to serve the productive sector by giving priority to the production of commercially useful knowledge, and by undertaking research that yields saleable knowledge and skills. The priorities and strategies are sustained by the prospects for exceptional prosperity for entrepreneurs and the significance given to marketable competencies by students and their parents. Concurrently, those priorities incidentally sustain a corresponding neglect of political, cultural, social, personal and other aspects of schooling. It is a time when many people see considerable prosperity and affluence as a prospect and connive in the use of all systems of activity in the pursuit of such ends.

The understanding that emerges then is that schooling is characterized by complex activities reflecting the pursuit of diverse interests by a variety of participants. In part, it entails educational activity and reflects efforts in the pursuit of personal and social development, the attainment of competencies and qualifications and the opportunities they give access to, together with the failure and alienation of less effective students. But it is also a situation strongly influenced by operators from economic, political and other systems of activity. That is, schooling is subject to contending forces promoting not only alternative forms of educational ideology and practice but also utilitarian priorities in the development of vocational and other competencies and commitments. Invariably, the groups supporting the latter are well resourced and powerful, and strongly committed to using schooling in relation to their primary priorities. In contrast, proponents of more educational approaches are dependent on public and private sources for the resources required to undertake schooling. Accordingly, educators are very much dependent on others and in particular on the general circumstances and the climate of opinion and concerns that are substantially influenced by those circumstances. Thus while schooling evolved towards being a more supportive and developmental process in the relatively prosperous 1950s and 1960s, it has been steered to be a more production-oriented process in the economically turbulent 1970s and 1980s.

Moreover, future prospects for educational as distinct from training or socializing activity are not promising. Producers have constructed exceptionally large-scale organizations in multinational corporations and joined these together in working relationships as commercial mega-coalitions so that their managers now direct organizations that are larger and more powerful than many societies. At the same time, states express the priorities and serve the concerns of more effective political groups which, incidentally, may be producers or their political allies or, alternatively, political as distinct from economic entrepreneurs and operators. In either case, substantial proportions of populations are effectively disenfranchised so that their interests are inadequately or inappropriately served. Ironically, however, these disenfranchised majorities have considerable potential to exercise influence and in a multiplicity of ways — as citizens or as workers, as savers and investors, as customers, parents and educators or in other capacities. Of course, the tasks involved in acting more effectively are considerable and include establishing clearer understanding of what individual and collective developmental interests entail, recognizing the scope for action in different sectors of one's life, and acting coherently both individually and collectively to develop and promote policies and practices that will establish the conditions necessary for development to be achieved. But central to these efforts must be a concern for others or a sense of justice; given that, then the objectives can

The Social Dynamics of Schooling

be achieved either through the market place or in the forum or both. Increasingly, this has to be achieved not simply within a particular society but regionally and internationally in more substantial economic and political entities such as Eastern and Western Europe, North America, Australasia or Southeast Asia.

At this point it is appropriate to note the relevance of a fourth period of social change, referred to in Chapter 1, that appears to be emerging and which, to that extent, can be expected to have a profound impact on social activity, including schooling. The problems derive from some modes of producing goods and services and some aspects of consumption patterns, and the use or production of particular elements such as dioxins and chlorofluorocarbons that have extremely damaging effects on the environment, together with consequences of the depletion of rain forest and other resources. Brown and others (1989) indicate that persistence with such practices could justify extensive regulatory activity by governments in order to constrain human activity and limit the damage caused by modes of producing and consuming. That is, the situation emerging favours regulatory activity and the constraint of individualistic and sectionalist activity that has particular kinds of harmful consequences. Of course, it is only realistic to recognize that the regulatory activity will reflect not simply nor solely safety imperatives but include initiatives taken by political, bureaucratic and other managers in the pursuit of sectionalist interests to achieve or remain in government, or extend one department or undermine another.

It is also only realistic to recognize that a similar surge of activity will occur in respect of the undertaking of schooling. Teachers, specialists, managers, steerers and others can be expected to act, from a variety of motives, to pursue courses of action in respect of programs in particular, but also other aspects of schooling, in the pursuit of personal and sectionalist interests as well as the imperatives arising from efforts to achieve sustainable ways of life. The central point is that efforts to achieve developmental education and other opportunites to promote development may be facing the prospect of limitation and abortion from another thrust that seeks to advance particular sectionalist interests at the expense of the interests of others. For such reasons, developmentalists have to be alert, perceptive and flexibly responsive in their efforts to achieve their goals.

Discussion

The interpretation of the undertaking and operation of schooling developed here emphasizes the part of people as participants in social processes. In doing so, however, it recognizes differences between participants in their resources and in their effectiveness and so sees some as more significant determiners of social activity than others. Indeed, those with fewer resources and generally ineffective as participants may have few options other than to comply with or passively resist the requirements confronting them. At the same time, access to resources, competence and effective performance are not the sole determinants of outcomes; in addition, a concern for others or sense of social justice is an important factor in many situations resulting in weaker, vulnerable sectors of a population faring better than would otherwise be the case.

To emphasize people and participants is not to dismiss culture and social structures and processes. However, it is important to recognize that they are constructed, modified, transformed or sustained by human actions. As such, they have reality and significance in their own right, and can entail legislation and regulations, contracts, expectations, practices and customs and other elements. Nonetheless, they are sustained or otherwise by the actions of people, reflecting power and competence, and expressing intentions, ideologies and other elements. It is most important to recognize that they are ultimately mechanisms of more effective operators. At the same time, they are often also supported by less powerful or effective participants due to complacency, the convenience of the arrangements, the advantages they make available, or the opportunities they provide for advancement or aggrandisement, or to obtain other benefits. That is, the durability, significance and effectiveness of a culture, an organization or other form of structure, and the processes employed can be understood in terms of the activities of participants acting individually or in groups, sectionally or in coalitions in relation to such entities.

A further step in the process of determining the soundness of interpretation is by looking to the effectiveness of solutions or responses they sustain to problematic situations. Thus, for example, to interpret in terms of structures is to imply that structural changes constitute the critical step in achieving reform. However, revolutions and other attempts to change structures testify to the limited effectiveness of such strategies as those with resources and effective as participants readily adapt to operate effectively through the newly established structural arrangements so that little change occurs from one situation to another.

More effective strategies involve changing sentiments and redistributing the resources available to participants and improving the competence and effectiveness of less effective participants. Such strategies reduce the possibility of some dominating others and increase the necessity for the formerly dominant to negotiate and achieve accommodation with others. In addition, the promotion of a concern with social justice can be helpful in weakening a reliance on resources, competence and other aspects of power and in promoting a readiness to consider others. But greater reliance must be placed on increasing the effectiveness of hitherto less effective people.

That is not a simple or straightforward process. It entails redistributing resources, but the development of competence and effectiveness can be a most complex and extensive undertaking. It can entail such diverse elements in improving performance as the articulation of issues and positions, developing negotiating skills, analyzing and synthesizing abilities and so on. In many ways, it entails much of what good education entails, namely the development of competent and effective people in themselves and as participants in political, economic, social or other processes and arrangements.

The task is complicated further by its two-step nature. One involves devising educational programs that are developmental and promoting of competence and effectiveness. A second, more difficult task involves constructing and operating systems of educational institutions and programs that achieve those ends. That is difficult at least substantially because it is a priority that can be contrary to the priorities of groups who favour advantage for some rather than others, a stratified and so differentially qualified school 'product', or socially, politically and in other ways compliant school leavers, or for other similar reasons. That is, a major obstacle to achieving good educational programs is that it is incompatible with the priorities of some major interest groups. It is to issues associated with that matter that I turn in the last chapter.

Chapter 11

Strategies for Developmentalism

The concerns addressed in this study arise from a developmentalist position that recognizes that people from the outset have attributes and the potentiality to develop, and accords them the right to develop and achieve their potentialities. Obviously, important issues concern which attributes, competencies and other qualities are to be developed and which are to be restrained or discouraged because of their harmful or other undesirable characteristics. Despite such restrictions, there remains considerable scope for development. For example, the full development of children and youth includes emotionally, cognitively, socially, culturally and in other ways. It means both the development of inherent attributes, together with education with the learnings and achievements of their communities and societies so that they develop as competent and cultivated people. It includes the development of a clear and positive sense of identity and a capacity to relate to and empathize with others, and of abilities to interact and communicate, to observe, reflect and reason, and develop interpretations of experience and systems of beliefs and ideas within which to devise and undertake courses of action. It means the development of capacities to act effectively, individually and collectively, informedly, sensitively and in other ways. And the development of these should be in ways that respect the rights of others to develop comparably.

Of critical importance too, of course, is insulation or even protection from negative or even damaging practices and experiences. They can occur through physical, psychological, social and other forms of abuse, through restriction from developmental experiences, through limiting experiences and opportunities such as being restricted to narrow and bigoted views and ideologies that promote unsound and even distorted perceptions and understandings, and expectations and aspirations. But we must be mindful, too, of less direct and less obvious practices, operated through social, cultural, economic, political and other systems of arrangements and processes, and which can be seriously damaging, and have a 'silent' impact through the impersonal operation of regulations or other forms of social technology. In such ways, individuals and societies can be extensively and pervasively damaged, and development impeded or obstructed.

Now while development can be promoted by the family, local community agencies, a multitude of social, cultural, recreational and other associations, the media and other agencies, schooling is especially important because it has been specifically established by communities and societies to promote the development of young people. Unfortunately, however, the reality is that schools operate poorly in this respect, differentiating among students and providing excellent facilities and programs for some but poor quality facilities and programs for others, and so constituting a mechanism that channels children, largely by circumstances, into differentiated situations and opportunities, and so contributes to the stratification process. Accordingly, this study was undertaken specifically to examine the dynamics of schooling in order to ascertain why it operates as it does, with such developmentally negative consequences for many, and hopefully to establish a basis for developing sounder strategies and courses of action.

Reflecting a developmentalist perspective, schooling has been examined in terms of participants and the interests they pursue, the strategies they employ, and the courses of action they undertake. In general, it has found that participants pursue a diverse range of often sectionalist and even conflicting interests, with different degrees of resources, competence and effectiveness. In consequence, some participants are much more effective than others and the less effective are excluded from attractive situations and opportunities. As a consequence, many young people and society as a whole are deprived, the former of opportunities and achievements, and both of the personal and social benefits that follow from the fuller development of young people. Indeed, society also carries costs from their frustration, alienation and impairment, and the damaging social activities some become involved in.

At the same time, these outcomes arise not simply from differences in access to resources and in competence and effectiveness in action, and the self-serving and exclusionary action of some to the detriment of others; to a degree, consequences are also a product of indifference, insensitivity, uninformedness, unawareness or lack of concern with the implications of actions for others as people act on the basis of convenience or the minimization of costs and the maximization of benefits. That is, some probably considerable amount of activity is not necessarily deliberately sectionalist and self-serving but mindless or thoughtless, and could well be otherwise, once damaging consequences for others are identified. In addition, the cause of social justice has some appeal and is a conscious concern of many and could be so for many more. Perhaps the best indicators of that possibility are given by the efforts and achievements of those who have taken up the issues of differentiation and discrimination on the basis of gender and ethnicity. Certainly, social justice and other grounds for concern have been elements in the debates and courses of action pursued in attaining increased opportunities and improved prospects. At the same time, however, it has to be recognized that the participation of more effective, often middle-class participants in the cause of gender and ethnic concerns has been a particularly significant factor, and goes a long way to establishing why such concerns, although starting on the basis of class, have been more effective in terms of gender and ethnicity. That is, one can realistically hold only modest expectations for what can be achieved on the basis of a concern for social justice and on more effective participants acting in support of less effective participants.

It is also apparent that to be a more satisfactory institution schooling requires much more than changes to its organization, operation and undertaking. The influence of steerers, the situations from which they operate, the structural and other mechanisms they use, and the general preoccupation with personal and sectionalist interests and priorities indicate that changes in priorities and concerns are necessary so that those people in particular, but all to some degree, reflect greater concern for others in their actions. Such changes can be expressed in terms of aspects of general culture, structural arrangements and the like, but ultimately they have to be in the assumptions, beliefs, orientations and actions of participants.

As Scheffler (1985) pointed out, social arrangements that start from a basic concern for others ultimately require a type of society, with distinct modes of operating in governing, producing goods and services, determining acceptable and unacceptable forms of behaving and how transgressions will be dealt with, and other matters. While some have argued that these outcomes can be best achieved through capitalism, socialism or other system of arrangements, the position taken here emphasizes the importance of a concern for social justice and anticipates that elements of capitalism, socialism and other systems of arrangements can contribute to the operation of a humane, just and developmentally-oriented society.

In the remainder of this chapter, consideration will be given to strategies for generating such developmental arrangements. In the first instance, that entails considering how schooling can be organized and operated as a more developmental agency. But beyond that it is necessary to direct strategies towards establishing a more developmentally-oriented society, which, incidentally, must also be a sustainable society with priorities compatible with those pursued here. In particular, these involve strategies that bear more directly on participants and in particular on steerers in other systems of activity. Here attention is directed at social, economic, political and personal action, partly because they are common to all people and partly because they illustrate strategies that can be employed elsewhere. One could easily go further; for example, there is considerable scope for more effective action in respect of religious activity where doctrines vary in the extent to which they endorse developmentalism with some being little concerned with prospects and opportunities in this world or with the situations and circumstances of other people and emphasizing spiritual salvation, while others are more concerned with worldly issues and the improvement of present human situations and circumstances. The areas of activity selected for consideration here are adequate to illustrate possibilities as well as deal with some major common areas of activity.

Fortunately, as we develop the discussion, it becomes apparent that many people have already achieved considerably in efforts along those lines (e.g. Bastian and others, 1986). Hence, the thrust of present efforts is primarily to indicate desired directions, identify what has been and is being achieved, and encourage further efforts and their more effective undertaking.

Educational

The critical issue in achieving developmental education through schooling is not so much in determining what it involves but in achieving its universal availability. High quality staff, facilities and programs have often been provided in particular schools and many children and youth have benefitted from such provision. However, it has invariably been provided through privileged publicly or privately operated institutions for students from more favourably circumstanced families. Occasionally, public systems of education have achieved a reasonable quality of educational provision but, as has been illustrated throughout this discussion, powerful interests and pressures work against achieving and maintaining such standards. Generally, the outcomes involve provision in relation to the situations and circumstances of particular categories of students so that schooling works to differentiate and stratify students, and thereby substantially to perpetuate established social arrangements.

In achieving developmental outcomes, the most critical element is clearly the staff who work with students. At the same time, competent and effective teachers and administrators need good quality facilities and resources, together with forms of organization and an operating culture that promote students' development and do not, for example, channel students to more and less favourable situations and opportunities in accordance with preconceived assumptions, or restrict their development in other ways. For example, a common practice has been to stream children into different types of programs, classes or even schools so that their prospects and opportunities are largely determined by decisions made on behalf of them, often quite early in their lives.

There are several strategies that can be employed to avoid such outcomes. One involves ensuring that students and their parents achieve a sound understanding of educational arrangements and processes, and are well prepared to deal with situations they encounter. A second entails maintaining an open structuring of schooling so that crucial decisions bearing upon opportunities and prospects are not made prematurely or ill-informedly and unwittingly at such early stages as senior primary or even junior secondary levels. During the more prosperous 1950s and 1960s, efforts in many societies succeeded in delaying those critical points for decision-making to later in secondary schooling. Currently, at least in more prosperous and often, incidentally, more technologically sophisticated societies, a point at around senior secondary school level would seem to be an appropriate time for clarifying interests, competencies and other attributes in relation to kinds of situations and opportunities in work and other sectors of activity.

The quality and appropriateness of teaching, resources, organization and other aspects of developmental education also reflect less obvious but fundamentally significant factors such as the allocation of resources across education and ultimately across a society. Insofar as education is concerned, patterns of allocation tend to reflect the growth of educational systems, and the influence of particular interest groups on that growth. Public provision of schooling began, generally, with the provision of primary education for all, followed by secondary education for some and tertiary education for a few. The latter levels have been successively extended to include larger proportions of relevant student groups, and with larger proportions of resources going to those who stay longer at schooling, and who, incidentally, are invariably from more affluent families. Such arrangements are particularly damaging when it is evident that important needs of children from poorer families cannot be met because of inadequate public resources. And when it is recognized that wealthier families would ensure that their children are educated, even if they have to meet the full costs themselves, then it is apparent that, under conventional arrangements, public resources are used both unfairly and ineffectively in that a considerable proportion of them does not achieve additional education.

Of course, systems of arrangements are in place and the patterns of current beneficiaries make it difficult to change situations substantially. Nonetheless, it is useful to review the soundness of priorities so that strategies may be devised to transform progressively practices to enable resources to be used more equitably and effectively. To that end the following observations have some pertinence.

In determining priorities within education for support from public resources, research and other evidence (e.g. Colclough, 1982) suggest that the basic education provided in compulsory schooling, entailing literacy, numeracy and communicacy, together with scientific, social and cultural, moral and other aspects of education, is a sound investment both for the development of youth and the better operation of society and its organizations and institutions. That is, a sound policy is to ensure that every child has a good basic and general education from around 5 or 6 years of age through to early or mid-adolescence when interests, talents and other attributes and competencies should be established, and appropriate avenues for further educational and training experiences can be identified.

The extension of full provision beyond primary and junior secondary schooling is more problematic. As has been noted, a common pattern of extending the availability of schooling 'up' the age range by providing upper secondary and various forms of tertiary education from public resources substantially reflects the expression of 'demand' by more articulate and competent participants in educational and political activities. However, as again has been noted, when resources are limited, such policies can be at the expense of children from less effective families, operating from disadvantaged circumstances, and who can be substantially disadvantaged even before they commence schooling.

It is now evident that a more effective step beyond primary schooling is to work with children at pre-school ages in order to increase their capacity to make effective use of schooling. Parents, for example, vary greatly in their abilities and opportunities to assist their children to develop, and range from some who have a good understanding of child development and considerable expertise in undertaking developmental activities to others, possibly represented in such studies as *Children in Adversity* (Wedge and Essen, 1982), who have limited understanding, expertise or resources. In addition, some, possibly substantial proportions of parents, actively damage or impair their children's development by the practice of abuse in one form or another, and cause incalculable damage to their children and costs to society both through the loss of potential and through the damaging and even destructive activities such children subsequently enter into. Indeed, whole lives can be perverted to damaging and destructive courses of action.

Evidence that is emerging suggests that that does not have to be the case. Programs reported by the Consortium for Longitudinal Studies (1983), Berrueta-Clement and others (1984), Hechinger (ed.) (1986) and others indicate that efforts with pre-school children from disadvantaged situations, and likely to include impaired children, can achieve substantial improvements in their subsequent performances in schooling. Hence a valuable investment for a society is staff, facilities and programs that enable the early development of all children to be fostered.

Taking account of effective and equitable use of resources, then, a set of priorities can be devised as follows. First, to ensure that all children experience a high quality basic and general education program through to early or mid-adolescence. Before that is made freely available to all, however, resources should be allocated to ensure the fuller early development of all children. And before either is made freely available to all, supplementation of resources could enable children from less affluent families to participate in upper secondary and tertiary levels of education.

A further point to recognize is that the provision of a good system of educational institutions and facilities does not necessarily imply a publicly operated system. The interests of society can be expressed in principles or specifications and children required to meet those requirements. To a degree, how those requirements are achieved is not a crucial issue for the state that manages societal affairs. Indeed, there are good reasons for schooling being undertaken by religious, communal, employee and other groups and organizations within a society when they have strong commitments to promote the education and development of their children. At the same time, there are limits to the extent that schooling can be privatized as when particular groups with restricted or even harmful views and practices damage their children. There are also good grounds, as we shall see presently, for avoiding the commercialization of schooling with its dangers of perversion or vitiation of integrity out of concern for profit, growth or simply to serve other sectors of a substantial corporation or perhaps component of a major coalition of corporations. As we shall see in more detail presently, there are also good grounds for a society operating a system of schools as an integrative and cohering mechanism to promote its own development, coherence and achievements.

To nominate such a set of strategies for the more effective and equitable use of resources is one thing; to achieve their introduction is much more difficult. Present policies persist largely because major beneficiaries in staff, parents and students are articulate, competent and effective operators in the political process, and effectively oppose substantial changes in existing arrangements which would mean major changes in the flow of the benefits and costs. Yet they would also benefit from more economically effective arrangements; while wealthier parents would have to meet costs directly, there could be a reduction in taxation because public funding requirements for direct support and administration would be less. Again, staff would be freed from some of the requirements associated with working in large bureaucratic systems and able to operate more in the way of autonomous specialists in other areas of practice. Finally, more equitable and effective use of resources would be achieved by directing limited funds to the early development of children from less well-off parents, thereby enabling them to make better use of later educational facilities and opportunities.

Unfortunately, however, the provision of high quality staff, facilities, programs and arrangements is not enough of itself to ensure maximization of developmental education. Ultimately, schooling has to take account of the world beyond schooling and in particular the working of the economy, the political system and other sectors of activity. At this time, with economic priorities being emphasized and particular importance given to entrepreneurialism and competitiveness, it has to be recognized that the comparable improvement of education and increases in the effectiveness of its work with students by itself can only mean increased competition for opportunities and prospects in the workforce and elsewhere. That is, increasingly competitive styles of operating in society inevitably impinge on the school both directly through being relevant to the results that graduating students achieve, and indirectly by affecting the expectations and orientations of parents and students, and even of teachers and administrators.

That is unfortunate because there are substantial grounds for operating schooling as a socially unifying or integrating mechanism that fosters a sense of coherence among people and compassion towards fellow members of a society as well as humankind as a whole. Such considerations indicate the importance, as many societies have acknowledged historically, of creating a 'common school' as a socially integrating institution. It is particularly important that prospective leaders of a society experience that kind of education, preferably in association with students of whom they are likely to be leaders, so that all have first-hand experience of each other and are not dependent on misconceptions and unsound stereotypes. In recent times, the concept of the common school has been neglected and even fallen into disrepute, very much as a consequence of efforts to transform societies, and their educational systems in particular, into more competitive and productive units. If personal and social developmental priorities are to be emphasized, then the integrative possibilities of schooling need to be given greater priority, and provision made for it to do so. At the same time, it would seem to be necessary that the pattern for providing full public support on social grounds follows the sequence of steps, to the extent that funds allow, that was indicated for partial support.

Acknowledgement of the interdependence of schooling and society indicates that efforts to improve and incidentally transform schooling so that it operates as an agency of developmentalism must be directed at sectors of society beyond schooling. In the first instance, it is useful to identify these as the economy, the political system, the state and other sectors of activity, but ultimately concern must be with how influence can be exercised within or through those systems. In consequence, it is now time to extend this discussion of strategies to ones that can be directed to the steerers of schooling and the agencies they employ in that activity.

Social

If the schooling process is to have a prospect of operating developmentally for all, it must be situated in a social world that requires or at least supports such modes of operating. That means a world in which developmentalism is part of the ethos, reflecting basic values and priorities and expressed in the everyday practices of people acting individually or in groups, be they in communities, organizations or a society. It entails the development of a way of life and the expression of that way of life in values and priorities, practices, customs and laws of the society.

However, it is not a task that has to be undertaken from the beginning. A sense of justice or fairness to others has a long history in many societies, and in major religious and secular systems of thought. Indeed, there is an abundance of contributions that constitute elements for such programs of action. Relevant points are expressed in religious precepts as with the Golden Rule of Christianity to 'do unto others as you would have them do unto you', in the statements of philosophers such as Kant with his moral imperative to treat others as ends, not as means, and in everyday maxims such as 'fair go'. It is expressed, too, in the work of critical theorists that presupposes scope for others to participate and contribute. It is evident in Kohlberg's conception of moral development, including the possible seventh stage of acting on the basis of *agape* (Carter, 1987), and in the perceptions of the nature of the person in the work of Rogers and Maslow. It is evident in a wealth of studies of the participation of the active child from the embryo stage on, and in studies of discrimination in schools, employment, politics, religion and other social situations.

Now while such sentiments have not been part of a dominant credo, they have been and continue to be important in the lives of many people. Thus there are widespread movements as in acting on behalf of women's rights, of the rights of ethnic minorities, of politically oppressed individuals and groups, for particular sectors of a society such as children or the poor, as well as for other species, and of the environment more generally. While it is not difficult to find exponents of some of these causes who, as their opponents are readily disposed to point out, are less than worthy, there is in each case a substantial proportion of people whose sincere and responsible commitment to these expressions of a sense of justice testify to the integrity and authenticity of such concerns.

It has to be recognized, too, that human dispositions and impulses are integral to the types of social systems that have been developed. While common patterns reflect inequalities and differences in competence and effectiveness, a significant contrary force has been to achieve a wider sharing of rights and responsibilities. Thus it is arguable that political democracy, capitalism and socialism, as model or ideal types, each reflects a concern for the other and involves a recognition and respect for their rights and obligations. Unfortunately, it is also evident that the practical working out of these modes of operating invariably reflects the efforts of some who pursue sectionalist goals and economic, political or other advantages and benefits, including personal and group aggrandisement, to extreme degrees, and thereby generate considerable degrees of inequality and promote the solidification of these over time into structural arrangements such as castes, classes, minority and other groups. In such ways, social relations become distorted and function differentially with some benefitting greatly and others being seriously disadvantaged.

In respect of developmentalism, then, it needs to be recognized that the issue is not so much one of developmentalism versus some opposite such as non-developmentalism but rather of whether only a minority or all shall have prospects to develop. There have been select minorities within most if not all societies who have ensured extensive developmental opportunities for some children; the reluctance has been to ensure such opportunities for all. One can take encouragement from the emergence of groups and movements that pursue programs of action to advance the well-being of others although, at the same time, one has to be conscious that the overall situation may still be worsening. Thus many societies have established legislation over at least a century or more to improve conditions for children yet currently an incredible amount of harsh and even brutal treatment is dealt out to children, and often by people from supposedly more enlightened societies, either directly in various forms of child abuse, or by neglect and abandonment in pitiful circumstances, or by the treatment of the communities or societies of which they are members.

At the same time, the extent of inequality in the quality of life and opportunities for better lives may well be a major deterrent to responsive action. People can be well-intentioned to the extent of being concerned about the well-being of people within their own group or community but overwhelmed by the incidence of poverty and ill-treatment of people in other societies and the world more generally. For such reason, the concept of a program to achieve equality of treatment and prospects on a world basis has little prospect of being readily accepted. A more likely prospect is a compromise, accepting one set of goals and levels of effort for one's own community or society, and other goals and sets of levels for other societies. But given that the circumstances of one society are commonly, in part, the consequences of the practices of people in other societies, even that can be a major step. So while it may be unrealistic to consider equalizing opportunities and prospects on a world scale, there is much that can be done within a particular society to reduce the harmful effects of individual and group actions on the lives of people in other societies.

Economic

Some would argue that the economy is the most powerful force operating on social activities, and clearly it is of considerable significance. That significance arises from its being the system of producing goods and services, and incidentally a major source of employment and the provision of livelihoods, as well as for accumulating wealth and achieving aggrandisement. It is in these latter respects that economic activity is distorted as exceptionally competent and effective but unscrupulous participants exploit economic activity for the returns, advantages and benefits that they can extract from it. At worst, such participants establish economic considerations as the primary or even the only considerations, overriding or even excluding social, cultural and other priorities and considerations.

Such participants are particularly convenienced by or able to exploit the movement towards the establishment of a single world economy. For one thing, it gives them much more scope in the accumulation of corporations and other resources, and in the exercise of influence. Some, specializing in an area such as the media, are able to assemble global networks from which they have the prospect of exercising considerable influence on culture generally and particularly on political, educational and other forms of activity. In those developments, they are particularly well served by developments in technology which aid the undertaking of production, communication and management, and indeed are largely a product of their interests and support in sponsoring research and development. Others indulge not so much in the operation of productive corporations but in the buying and selling of them, or what Reich (1983: Ch. 8) identified as 'paper entrepreneurialism', thereby generating the symbols rather than the reality of wealth, to their particular and often considerable advantage.

At the same time, these forms of economic activity are incompatible with universal developmentalism and so subvert the efforts of developmental educators. However, the strength and appeal of these forms of entrepreneurialism is in providing considerable scope for more competent and effective participants who are able to use situations and circumstances effectively to enhance their own opportunities and prospects, often to the considerable disadvantage of others. These are, of course, the worst cases and it needs to be remembered that a considerable proportion of managers and corporations are socially responsible and moderate in their expectations and actions.

It is also important to appreciate that the achievements of more predatory participants depend only in part on their competence and effectiveness as managers. To a considerable extent they benefit from the witting or unwitting cooperation of investors, customers, employees and others who are involved in the economic sector in one way or another. At the same time, such cooperating participants have considerable scope for exercising influence if they commit themselves to doing so. For example, the employees of a corporation who readily differentiate into a range of types and levels, including the managers but also professional specialists, administrators and supervisors, and various categories of skilled workforce through to relatively unskilled employees, are crucial to the operation of a corporation. However, while they appear to have limited scope for independent action, largely because they depend on a corporation for employment and a livelihood, their dependence also varies over time, as with changing economic circumstances and the availability of alternative employment, or with the degree of organization of the labour force in a union movement. Again, while employees are differentially able to exercise influence on an organization, there is little doubt that they could be more effective as a social force, discouraging management from operating in damaging ways, or in producing dangerous products, or in using practices that are anti-developmental in their impact. Clearly, they are not so attentive or conscientious on these matters as they are on conditions of employment and so less a force on social issues than they might be.

Consumers constitute a second major force whose significance rests on the fact that they accept the output of the productive system and so are an essential element of its operation. However, while producers pay considerable attention to consumers, aggregating their demands in terms of a 'market' and competing for shares in it, consumers tend to behave individually and even be manipulated by producers. Correspondingly, practices that are quite reprehensible to some people such as the utilitarian exploitation of labour, the brutal farming of livestock, unsound production methods and the production of dangerous goods are sustained because people find those products cheaper or convenient, or because they ignore harming or disadvantaging consequences for others. However, occasional efforts such as campaigns against particular industries or modes of producing or even against types of social arrangements, such as apartheid in South Africa, illustrate that consumers have enormous potential to influence the production process. A potential consumer strategy, then, entails differentiating among products on grounds such as those associated with their production or effects of their use, and not simply in terms of price or availability.

Another activity undertaken by many people is to save and invest and accumulate assets or resources for the future against personal mishap, retirement or other constraining or disadvantaging circumstances. In acting as an investor, however, it is all too easy to follow established practices and rely upon the advice of bankers or other investment advisers and managers. However, they are guided by modes of thinking that give priority to growth, profit and other sectionally benefitting considerations, and neglect social or moral considerations in investing. As a consequence, such networks gather together substantial resources and channel them into investments, with some of the major investment organizations holding substantial shareholdings in most of the major corporations in a society. In that process, savings of socially responsible people can be channelled into types of productive activities that they find unacceptable and would not want to be associated with. That is, there is considerable scope for people to be more socially discerning and selective in their role as investors, and seek to use their influence to promote demands that provide more scope for developmentalism in the operation of the economy.

On this issue, some recent developments are encouraging. Selective investment in ethical or socially responsible investments has grown substantially in several societies in recent years, and entails a large proportion of investment in the US. Some obvious targets that have been avoided include tobacco, nuclear energy, armaments and South Africa, although such a selection scarcely touches the surface of what can be defined as ethically dubious economic activity. It is also the case that ethical investments can be used unscrupulously by investment managers to attract investors but not necessarily assiduously to pursue investments in any systematic and socially discriminating way. However, the emergence of investment analysts such as those who work at the Ethical Investment Research and Information Service in London (e.g. Ward, 1986) is a step in the process of making information available in a more systematic way. Again, the recourse to other than financial and economic criteria opens the ways for both scrupulous and unscrupulous practices, and is no assurance in itself that investments are being directed scrupulously and responsibly.

A second development that has considerable significance is the extension of superannuation schemes to many employees. Such schemes mean the accumulation of substantial amounts of capital for investment and when the contributors are also associated in large industrial organizations, they then have a mechanism for monitoring and directing the use of those resources in such ways as to support local industry and employment or for use elsewhere, or to exclude particular types of industries and employers. Potentially, this development is a major challenge to existing forms of investment, although it does not necessarily open up an era of ethically or socially responsible investment.

However, while much can be attempted by significant interest groups to influence the operation of economic organizations, such actions always confront a critical dilemma. One feature of a thoroughgoing competitive situation is that it constitutes a force for efficiency in productive activity. Its value is indicated when attention is given to overly regulated activities where it is evident that particular groups act to protect their interests at the expense of others, generating incompetent and inefficient entities. The widespread endorsement of deregulation in recent years has gained much of its momentum from the widespread recognition that regulation enabled some groups to exploit situations of protection to provide for their own well-being and advantage, often at considerable cost to the wider social community. The market place then becomes a convenient mechanism for establishing the more or less efficient. At the same time, it has to be monitored to ensure that particular individuals, groups and organizations do not establish dominance and so come to distort its operations, employ unacceptable production practices, produce harmful products or in other ways subvert or undermine opportunities for all to develop.

Political

The political sector constitutes a major alternative mechanism for the assertion of priorities and the attainment of ends. Of course, it is not altogether separate from economic activity as those with considerable material resources have an advantage in political activity. Even so, people without such resources can be effective through organizing their efforts, building coalitions and so mobilizing political power. That is, political and economic activity are only loosely connected so that the political forum constitutes a significant alternative venue for the attainment of goals. Hence for the promoters of developmentalism it is an important sector through which to operate and the concern here is to identify some of the strategies that may be useful.

A first and minimal step is in one's role as an individual citizen. In that capacity one can support and even encourage political participants and their organizations to promote a more developmental society and types of schooling, or take initiatives oneself and attempt to lead development. But in what has aptly been termed the organizational society, usually only a limited amount can be achieved through actions by an individual. Of more significance are efforts through the organizations of which one is a member or which are available as mechanisms for exercising influence. In that respect, almost any group or organization offers scope for the exercise of influence.

More directly relevant and important either for action from within or drawing together in coalitions are teacher and other school-related organizations. The possibilities here are considerable, particularly as such organizations operate at national and international levels, and have to be effective at each if they are to exercise significant influence. In some societies, too, teacher organizations have joined with other employee organizations to marshall greater influence which of course involves compromises and trade-offs. At the same time, members of employee organizations benefit from good quality developmentally-oriented school systems, provided as part of a social wage, as Tawney (1964) argued in his classic statement on equality.

Parents are another major group associated with schooling with considerable potential as a force in the political arena. A major critical issue is whether they segment, as by type of school, and contest with each other for available resources, or whether they are able to find common causes on which they work together and strengthen the education lobby. That strategy applies also to teachers and other interest groups associated with schooling. The potentiality for such groups to divide is well understood by opponents of developmental schooling for all and so a strategy of divisiveness is an attractive option for them. The major challenge for teachers, parents and other educational interest groups is to find bases for unity and concerted action.

A second set of strategies involves developing links with kindred or complementary organizations. People involved in health and child welfare, in recreational, cultural and other creative and expressive activities, in human rights and in some religions share elements of the developmentalist concern and have grounds for forming coalitions to promote the formulation and implementation of developmental policies. While corporations and their managers have been credited with substantial responsibility for the present thrust towards utilitarian and exploitative schooling, it is also evident that they constitute a diverse population, and that some favour the more developmentally educated school leaver or tertiary diplomate or graduate. That is, developmentalism has the potential to draw support from many sections of a population and traditional or conventional divisions should not be allowed to sustain stereotypes that separate or estrange possible members of a coalition.

The formation of coalitions and the mobilization of support constitute one form of strategy. Of crucial importance, too, is the development of an understanding of problems and issues, of programs to be worked for, and of obstacles to the implementation of such programs. More predatory groups have been particularly effective in establishing policy centres or 'think tanks' and developing comprehensive rationales and sets of strategies, and are well on the way in transforming social arrangements and processes, including systems of educational institutions, to provide services for their activities. In addition, particular entrepreneurs have accumulated very large media empires wherein they employ a substantial collection of specialist economic, financial, political and other writers and commentators to purvey their sectionalist and predatory views and thereby establish a political climate. Developmentalists have some achievements to their credit but are at a considerable disadvantage and there is a need to marshall resources to support research into the development process, including conditions that facilitate or obstruct development, together with the production of strategies to establish developmental priorities on political agendas, and mobilize support for the implementation of developmental strategies. Ultimately, there is a need for an articulated theory and rationale or ideology that presents the developmentalist position cogently and coherently, and in forms that can be taken up and espoused by specialists in the media, by political spokespeople and others involved in developing political climates and agendas.

The construction of these phenomena incidentally establishes a political culture that can then have a salient influence on the actions of participants. At best, it provides priorities, interpretations, programs, strategies and rationalizations that can be readily drawn upon, saving the need to return to first principles for any additional initiative. It also provides a comprehensive account which can attract supporters and so strengthen movements for particular causes.

It is at that point that interactions with political parties become crucial. While they have priorities, positions and agendas as parties, they are dependent on support and so impelled to seek such support. In those circumstances, educational interest groups are more effective to the extent that they can gain a party's acceptance of their concerns, priorities and policy proposals. That is the essence of the political process with the forum or meeting place central in establishing strengths and prospects. It is also imperative that the education lobby attends not just to the rationality or plausibility of its case but also gives close attention to its justness. To do otherwise is to approximate their opponents in promoting sectionalist interests and thereby compromise and even subvert their own efforts.

But given influence in the political process, it is then possible to exercise influence at the societal and sometimes even at the international level in the determination of priorities and strategies, the formulation and implementation of policies, the allocation of resources, the construction of laws and the adjudication of issues, and the overall determination of a society's agendas and courses of action. For example, the state is a most useful mechanism through which to direct or steer the economy and all societies use it to do so to some extent. A major opportunity for developmentalists is to steer entrepreneurs into the production of useful and helpful goods and services, using safe and developmental modes of production, and away from activities that are more relevant to personal and group aggrandisement. Most important too, of course, is the use of resources to promote developmental priorities and policies, such as were identified for education, in health and other social services. Probably the most important task that the state can be used to undertake is to steer economic, educational, social, political and other activities to create optimal conditions for the development of all people.

Personal

The discussion so far has been constituted substantially in terms of groups, organizations and sectors of activity. However, central has been the concept of the person as a participant in the many social situations associated with education, with emphasis on competence and effectiveness in performance. Left at that point, however, the discussion would be seriously deficient in that working with the concept of participant can encourage a perception of the person as a segmented entity, participating in different sectors of activity and not having a unity or integrity or other important attributes. For such reasons it is important, as this discussion is drawn to a conclusion, to return to the person who is a participant in many situations and identify ways in which they may increase their overall personal competence and effectiveness.

A first point to be made is that the person has many avenues to contribute towards the achievement of priorities and interests. People typically are members of families and communities, employees in organizations, citizens, savers and investors, consumers, and members of recreational, cultural, religious, special interest and other groups and organizations. However, what is striking about these memberships is that they are often undertaken in segmented ways or in isolation from each other. One consequence of that practice is that people sometimes, possibly often, act in different and possibly even incompatible ways in different situations and circumstances. Thus, for example, a person may be very much concerned with environmental issues in one aspect of life but as a saver, investor or contributor to a superannuation fund support organizations that act irresponsibly and damagingly in respect of the environment. Again, a person may be concerned as a parent, a teacher or in other ways with the development of children and people generally but as a customer and consumer support unhealthy products and production processes.

In acting in these different, sometimes incompatible ways, people can be seen to have multiple personal styles. These constitute interesting phenomena in themselves, and presumably reflect concern for convenience, economy and perhaps simply thoughtlessness or unawareness of the interrelations and counter-productiveness of pursuing such incompatible modes of acting. In some cases, of course, they are pursued as parts of a set of strategies intended to serve one's own interests and exploit the situations available to one. However, where they are unintentional, then the person has much to gain by reviewing their styles of acting in the different aspects of their lives, establishing their primary priorities, and developing a coherent set of courses of action and strategies in all sections of one's life in order more effectively to pursue those priorities.

Such a step may well be the most important single step a person can take in the pursuit of priorities and interests. At one time, resources and other sources of support are removed from courses of action one does not endorse or support and made available for those to which priority is given. However, the social ramifications are also considerable in that the decisions of a few people to act in a particular way such as to buy environmentally friendly, safely produced or other particular kinds of goods or to invest in companies that have socially responsible employment and production policies can constitute a significant signal in the market place and draw the attention of producers, marketers and others associated with the production process to those priorities and concerns, and encourage their responsive action.

That is, economic, political and other systems of activity are usually responsive to concerns and priorities. Typically, however, the producers and managers take the initiative and persuade or manipulate their investors, customers, constituents or other publics for their own convenience and advantage. The important point is that that does not have to be the case; indeed, it is often in the person's own interest to assert their priorities and seek the kind of services that they require. That may essentially entail a mobilization of one's efforts and resources and direction of their usage in a coherent way so that personal priorities are favoured and they are not exploited or used in the service of other priorities, and possibly ones which the person does not endorse and may actually reject.

Discussion

An attempt has been made in this final chapter to indicate what can be achieved to make schooling a more developmental process for all children. Consistent with the perspective employed and the analysis and interpretation made of schooling, the proposals are directed towards what participants can achieve, working directly in educational situations or to change economic, political and other priorities, by acting individually and collectively as citizens, investors, consumers and in other ways. Of considerable importance in these efforts is the achievement of coherence in one's own activities and endeavours and thereby the concentration of one's influence in support of the programs endorsed and the withdrawal of support and resources from, and even mobilizing opposition to organizations and courses of action that are contrary and even counterproductive to one's priorities and efforts.

Such a charting of possible courses of action is, of course, to produce a most ambitious program. Its usefulness is to draw attention to ways in which the effectiveness of the efforts of many people could be increased. The main strategies of achieving greater personal integration and coherence of effort, of developing more explicit and targeted organizational policies and strategies, and building coalitions of kindred organizations are essentially strategies of maximizing effectiveness, and incidentally of providing more rewarding experiences that serve to stimulate further participants' efforts and activities.

At the same time, it is only realistic to be sceptical as to how much can be achieved by such strategies. Apathy, indifference and other attitudes mean that many people do not make an effort to improve prospects and opportunities for others. For while a sense of justice has been a significant force for many people in many situations, it is often not so powerful as self or sectional interests. When these latter are taken up by competent and effective participants, they can be remarkably successful and also used to express not only their own and others' interests but to mobilize the efforts and energies of others into organized entities. In the present, this has been developed to an exceptional level as when corporations set goals in terms not simply of profits but in an open-ended concept of growth which can mean expansion at an exponential rate and be virtually insatiable.

Perhaps the most useful point to the discussion is the identifying of what needs to be tackled if something significant is to be achieved. In that respect proposals such as these constitute a profile or template that is useful in considering reform proposals and evaluating their usefulness and likely effectiveness. From such a template or profile, it may be easier to recognize that many efforts at reform can hardly be taken as seriously intended initiatives. That is, if we have a thoroughgoing analysis of situations and a setting out of a comprehensive set of strategies for changing those situations, we have a basis for judging whether particular proposals are realistically constructed or are largely rhetorical in character, or possibly designed essentially to exploit opportunities in particular situations.

Bibliography

Adams, Stanley (1980) *Roche versus Adams,* London, Cape.
Aikin, M., Bennett, S.N. and Hesketh, Jane (1981) 'Teaching Styles and Pupil Progress: A Re-analysis', *British Journal of Educational Psychology,* 51, June, 170–86.
Alexander, Robin J. (1984) 'Innovation and Continuity in the Initial Teacher Education Curriculum', in Robin J. Alexander, Maurice Craft and James Lynch (eds), *Changes in Teacher Education: Context and Provision Since Robbins,* London, Holt, Rinehart and Winston.
Altbach, Philip G. and Rathgeber, Eva-Marie (1980) *Publishing in the Third World: Trend Report and Bibliography,* New York, Praeger Publishers.
Althusser, L. (1972) 'Ideology and Ideological State Apparatuses', in B.R. Cosin (ed.), *Education, Structure and Society,* Harmondsworth, Penguin Books.
Anderson, D.S. and Vervoorn, A.E. (1983) *Access to Privilege: Patterns of Participation in Australian Post-Secondary Education,* Canberra, Australian National University Press.
Anyon, Jean (1979) 'Ideology and United States Textbooks', *Harvard Educational Review,* 44, 3, 361–86.
Anyon, Jean (1981) 'Social Class and School Knowledge', *Curriculum Inquiry,* 11, 1, 3–39.
Anyon, Jean (1983) 'Interactions of Gender and Class: Accommodation and Resistance by Working Class and Affluent Females to Contradictory Sex Role Ideologies', in Len Walker and Len Barton (eds), *Gender, Class and Education,* Lewes, Falmer Press.
Apple, Michael W. (1979) *Ideology and the Curriculum,* London, Routledge and Kegan Paul.
Apple, Michael W. (1980–81) 'The Other Side of the Hidden Curriculum: Correspondence Theories and the Labor Process', *Interchange,* 11, 3, 5–32.
Apple, Michael W. (1986) *Teachers and Tasks: A Political Economy of Class and Gender Relations in Education,* New York, Routledge and Kegan Paul.
Archer, John and Lloyd, Barbara (1982) *Sex and Gender,* Harmondsworth, Penguin Books.
Armstrong, Michael (1980) *Closely Observed Children,* London, Writers and Readers.
Arnott, Madeleine (1983) 'A Cloud over Co-education: An Analysis of the Forms

of Transmission of Class and Gender Relations', in Len Walker and Len Barton (eds), *Gender, Class and Education*, Lewes, Falmer Press.
Arnove, Robert F. (1980) 'Foundations and the Transfer of Knowledge', in Robert F. Arnove (ed.), *op. cit.*
Arnove, Robert F. (ed.) (1980) *Philanthropy and Cultural Imperialism: The Foundations at Home and Abroad*, Boston, Mass., G.K. Hall and Co.
Ayres, Robert L. (1983) *Banking on the Poor: The World Bank and World Poverty*, Cambridge, Mass., MIT Press.
Ball, Stephen J. (1980) 'Initial Encounters in the Classroom and the Process of Establishment', in Peter Woods (ed.), *Pupil Strategies*, London, Croom Helm.
Ball, Stephen J. (1981) *Beachside Comprehensive: A Case Study of Secondary Schooling*, Cambridge, Cambridge University Press.
Ball, Stephen J. (1985) 'English for the English Since 1906', in Ivor F. Goodson (ed.), *Social Histories of the Secondary Curriculum: Subjects for Study*, London, Falmer Press.
Ball, Stephen J. (1987) *The Micro-Politics of the School: Towards a Theory of School Organisation*, London, Methuen.
Ball, Stephen J. and Lacey, Colin (1980) 'Subject Disciplines as the Opportunity for Group Action: A Measured Critique for Subject Sub-cultures', in Peter Woods (ed.), *Teacher Strategies*, London, Croom Helm.
Barker Lunn, Joan C. (1970) *Streaming in the Primary School*, Slough, Bucks, National Foundation for Educational Research.
Barnes, Douglas and others (1987) *A Second Report on the TVEI Curriculum: Courses for 14–16 Year Olds in Twenty-six Schools*, Leeds, University of Leeds School of Education, October.
Bastian, Ann and others (1986) *Choosing Equality: The Case for Democratic Schooling*, Philadelphia, Pa., Temple University Press.
Baum, Warren C. and Stokes, Tolbert M. (1985) *Investing in Development: Lessons of World Bank Experience*, New York, Oxford University Press.
Bayes, Jane H. (1982) *Ideologies in Interest-Group Politics: The United States as a Special Interest State in the Global Economy*, Novato, Calif., Chandler and Sharp.
Bellaby, Paul (1977) *The Sociology of Comprehensive Schooling*, London, Methuen.
Bennett, Neville (1976) *Teaching Styles and Pupil Progress*, London, Open Books.
Bennett, Neville (1987) 'Changing Perspectives on Teacher-Learning Processes in the Post-Plowden Era', *Oxford Review of Education*, 13, 1, 67–79.
Berger, Peter L. (1986) *The Capitalist Revolution: Fifty Propositions about Prosperity, Equality and Liberty*, New York, Basic Books.
Berger, Peter L. and Luckmann, Thomas (1966) *The Social Construction of Reality*, New York, Doubleday.
Berlak, Ann and Berlak, Harold (1981) *Dilemmas of Schooling: Teaching and Social Change*, London, Methuen.
Bernstein, Basil (1971) 'On the Classification and Framing of Educational Knowledge' in Michael F.D. Young (ed.), *op. cit.*
Berrueta-Clement, J.R.B. and others (1984) *Changed Lives: The Effects of the Perry Pre-school Program on Youths through Age 19*, Monograph 8, Ypsilanti, Mich., High/Scope Press.
Blau, Peter M. and Scott, W. Richard (1962) *Formal Organizations*, San Francisco, Calif., Chandler Publishing Co.

Bourdieu, Pierre and Passeron, Jean-Claude (1977) *Reproduction in Education, Society and Culture*, London, Sage Publications.
Bowles, Samuel and Gintis, Herbert (1976) *Schooling in Capitalist America*, London, Routledge and Kegan Paul.
Braithwaite, John (1983) *Corporate Crime in the Pharmaceutical Industry*, London, Routledge and Kegan Paul.
Brantlinger, Ella (1985) 'What Low-Income Parents Want from Schools: A Different View of Aspirations', *Interchange*, 16, 4, 14–28.
Broadfoot, Patricia (1979) *Assessment, Schools and Society*, London, Methuen.
Broadfoot, Patricia (ed.) (1984) *Selection, Certification and Control*, Lewes, Falmer Press.
Bronfenbrenner, Urie (1958) 'Socialization and Social Class through Time and Space', in Eleanor E. Maccoby and others (eds), *Readings in Social Psychology*, 3rd ed., New York, Holt, Rinehart and Winston.
Brown, Lester R. and others (1989) *State of the World, 1989*, A World Watch Institute Report on Progress toward a Sustainable Society, Melbourne, S. and W. Information Guides.
Burrell, G. and Morgan, G. (1979) *Sociological Paradigms and Organisational Analysis*, London, Heinemann.
Bush, Tony and Kogan, Maurice (1982) *Directors of Education*, London, George Allen and Unwin.
Buss, Dennis C. (1980) 'The Ford Foundation in Public Education: Emergent Patterns', in Robert F. Arnove (ed.), *op. cit.*
Callahan, Raymond E. (1962) *Education and the Cult of Efficiency*, Chicago, Ill., University of Chicago Press.
Calvert, Barbara (1975) *The Role of the Pupil*, London, Routledge and Kegan Paul.
Campbell, Roald F. and others (1987) *A History of Thought and Practice in Educational Administration*, New York, Teachers College Press.
Carnegie Council on Policy in Higher Education (1979) *Giving Youth a Better Chance: Options for Education, Work and Service*, San Francisco, Calif., Jossey Bass.
Carnegie Forum on Education and the Economy (1986) *A Nation Prepared: Teachers for the Twenty First Century*, The Report of the Carnegie Forum on Education and the Economy's Task Force on Teaching as a Profession, Washington, D.C., The Forum.
Carter, Robert E. (1987) 'Beyond Justice', *Journal of Moral Education*, 16, 2, 83–98.
Chew Oon Ai, Joy (1988) Moral Education in a Singapore Secondary School, Unpublished PhD thesis, Melbourne, Monash University.
Children's Defense Fund (CDF) (annually) *A Children's Defense Budget*, Washington, D.C., CDF.
Cicourel, A. and Kitsuse, J. (1963) *The Educational Decision-Makers*, Indianapolis, Ind., Bobbs-Merrill.
Clements, McKenzie A. (1979) Relationships between the University of Melbourne and the Secondary Schools of Victoria 1890–1912, Unpublished PhD thesis, Melbourne, University of Melbourne.
Colclough, Christopher (1982) 'The Impact of Primary Schooling on Economic Development: A Review of the Evidence', *World Development*, 10, 3, 167–85.
Coleman, James and others (1966) *Equality of Educational Opportunity*, Washing-

ton, D.C., Department of Health, Education and Welfare.
Coleman, James S., Hoffer, Thomas and Kilgore, Sally (1982) *High School Achievement: Public, Catholic and Other Private Schools Compared*, New York, Basic Books.
Collier, Peter and Horowitz, David (1976) *The Rockefellers: An American Dynasty*, New York, Holt, Rinehart and Winston.
Collins, Randall (1975) *Conflict Sociology*, New York, Academic Press.
Collins, Randall (1979) *The Credential Society: An Historical Sociology of Education and Stratification*, New York, Academic Press.
Collins, Cherry W. and Hughes, Phillip W. (1982) 'Where Junior Secondary Schools Are Heading: Research and Reflections', *Australian Education Review*, No.16, Hawthorn, Australian Council for Educational Research.
Colwell, Mary Ann Culleton (1980) 'The Foundation Connections: Links among Foundations and Recipient Organisations', in Robert F. Arnove (ed.), *op. cit.*
Committee for Economic Development (CED) (1985) *Investing in Our Children, Business and the Public Schools: A Statement by the Research and Policy Committee of the Committee for Economic Development*, New York, Committee for Economic Development.
Connell, R.W. (1985) *Teachers' Work*, Sydney, George Allen and Unwin.
Connell, R.W. and others (1982) *Making the Difference: Schools, Families and Social Divisions*, Sydney, George Allen and Unwin.
Connell, W.F. (1980a) *A History of Education in the Twentieth Century World*, Canberra, Curriculum Development Centre.
Connell, W.F. (1980b) *The Australian Council for Educational Research, 1930–1980*, Hawthorn, Australian Council for Educational Research.
Consortium for Longitudinal Studies (1983) *As the Twig Is Bent ... Lasting Effects of Pre-School Programs*, Hillsdale, N.J., Lawrence Erlbaum Associates.
Cookson, Peter W. and Persell, Carolyn H. (1985) *Preparing for Power: America's Elite Boarding Schools*, New York, Basic Books.
Coombs, Philip H. (1985) *The World Crisis in Education: The View from the Eighties*, New York, Oxford University Press.
Coons, John and Sugarman, Stephen (1978) *Education by Choice: The Case for Family Control*, Berkeley, Calif., University of California Press.
Cornia, G.A., Jolly, Richard and Stewart, Frances (eds) (1987) *Adjustment with a Human Face: Protecting the Vulnerable and Promoting Growth*, Oxford, Clarendon Press.
Cox, C.B. and Dyson, A.E. (eds) (1969a) *Fight for Education: A Black Paper*, London, Critical Quarterly Society.
Cox, C.B. and Dyson, A.E. (eds) (1969b) *Black Paper Two: The Crisis in Education*, London, Critical Quarterly Society.
Cremin, Lawrence A. (1961) *The Transformation of the School*, New York, Alfred Knopf.
Curriculum Development Centre (CDC) (1980) *Core Curriculum for Australian Schools*, Canberra, CDC.
Davies, Bronwyn (1982) *Life in the Classroom and Playground*, London, Routledge and Kegan Paul.
Davies, Lyn (1984) *Pupil Power: Deviance and Gender in Schools*, Lewes, Falmer Press.
Delamont, Sara (1976) *Interaction in the Classroom*, London, Methuen.

Delamont, Sara (1983) *Sex Roles in the School,* 2nd ed., London, Methuen.
Delamont, Sara and Galton, Maurice (1986) *Inside the Secondary Classroom,* London, Routledge and Kegan Paul.
de Mause, Lloyd (1974) 'The Evolution of Childhood', in Lloyd de Mause (ed.), *The History of Childhood,* New York, The Psychohistory Press.
Denscombe, Martin (1985) *Classroom Control: A Sociological Perspective,* London, George Allen and Unwin.
Dershimer, Richard A. (1976) *The Federal Government and Educational Research and Development,* Lexington, Mass., Lexington Books.
Dickson, David (1984) *The New Politics of Science,* New York, Pantheon Books.
Domhoff, G. William (1967) *Who Rules America?* Englewood Cliffs, N.J., Prentice-Hall.
Dore, Ronald (1976) *The Diploma Disease: Education, Qualifications and Development,* London, George Allen and Unwin.
Eastman, Moira (1989) *Family: The Vital Factor,* Melbourne, Collins-Dove.
Eisner, Elliot W. (1985) *The Educational Imagination: On the Design and Evaluation of School Programs,* 2nd ed., New York, Macmillan.
Essen, Juliet and Wedge, Peter (1982) *Continuities in Childhood Disadvantage,* London, Heinemann.
Etzioni, Amitai (1975) *A Comparative Analysis of Complex Organizations,* rev. ed., New York, Free Press.
Eurich, Nell P. (1985) *Corporate Classrooms: The Learning Business,* Princeton, N.J., Carnegie Foundation for the Advancement of Teaching.
Evetts, Julie (1973) *The Sociology of Educational Ideas,* London, Routledge and Kegan Paul.
Finn, Dan (1984) 'Leaving School and Growing up: Work Experience in the Juvenile Labour Market', in Inge Bates and others, *Schooling for the Dole? The New Vocationalism,* London, Macmillan.
Fisher, Donald (1980) 'American Philanthropy and the Social Sciences in Britain, 1919–1939; The Reproduction of a Conservative Ideology', *Sociological Review,* 28, May, 277–315.
Fisher, Donald (1983) 'The Role of Philanthropic Foundations in the Reproduction and Production of Hegemony: Rockefeller Foundations and the Social Sciences', *Sociology,* 17, 2, 206–33.
Foucault, Michel (1972) *The Archaeology of Knowledge,* London, Tavistock Publications.
Fox, Irene (1985) *Private Schools and Public Issues,* London, Macmillan.
Fraser, George MacDonald (ed.) (1977) *The Way of the Public School,* London, Weidenfeld and Nicolson.
Friedman, Milton (1962) *Capitalism and Freedom,* Chicago, Ill., University of Chicago Press.
Friedman, Milton and Friedman, Rose (1980) *Free to Choose,* Melbourne, Macmillan.
Galton, Maurice, Simon, Brian and Croll, Paul (1980) *Inside the Primary Classroom,* London, Routledge and Kegan Paul.
Gannaway, Howard (1976) 'Making Sense of School', in Michael Stubbs and Sara Delamont (eds), *Explorations in Classroom Observation,* Chichester, John Wiley and Sons.
Garnier, Maurice A. and Raffolovich, Lawrence E. (1984) 'The Evolution of

Equality of Educational Opportunities in France', *Sociology of Education*, 57, 1, 1–11.
Gastil, Raymond, D. (1982) 'The Comparative Survey of Freedom', in *Freedom at Issue* (Special Issue), No. 64, January-February, 3–14.
Gerth, H.H. and Mills, C. Wright (eds) (1964) *From Max Weber*, London, Routledge and Kegan Paul.
Giddens, Anthony (1984) *The Constitution of Society*, Cambridge, Polity Press.
Gilbert, Rob (1984) *The Impotent Image: Reflections of Ideology in the Secondary School Curriculum*, Lewes, Falmer Press.
Ginsburg, Mark B., Meyenn, Robert J. and Miller, Henry D.R. (1980) 'Teachers' Conceptions of Professionalism and Trade Unionism: An Ideological Analysis', in Peter Woods (ed.), *Teacher Strategies*, London, Croom Helm.
Goodlad, John I. (1983) *A Place Called School*, New York, McGraw-Hill.
Goodson, Ivor (1987) *School Subjects and Curriculum Change*, rev. ed., Lewes, Falmer Press.
Grace, Gerald (1978) *Teachers, Ideology and Control: A Study in Urban Education*, London, Routledge and Kegan Paul.
Grace, Gerald (1985) 'Judging Teachers: The Social and Political Contexts of Teacher Evaluation', *British Journal of Sociology of Education*, 6, 1, 3–16.
Gray, John (1981) 'From Policy to Practice — Some Problems and Paradoxes of Egalitarian Reform', in Brian Simon and William Taylor (eds), *Education in the Eighties: The Central Issues*, London, Batsford.
Greeley, Andrew M. and Rossi, Peter H. (1965) *The Education of Catholic Americans*, Chicago, Ill., The Aldine Press.
Gregory, R.P. (1984) 'Streaming, Setting and Mixed Ability Grouping in Primary and Secondary Schools: Some Research Findings', *Educational Studies*, 10, 3, 209–36.
Griffiths, Morwenna (1986) 'Hirst's Forms of Knowledge and Körner's Categorical Frameworks', *Oxford Review of Education*, 12, 1, 17–30.
Gronn, Peter (1983) 'Talk and Work: The Accomplishment of School Administration', *Administrative Science Quarterly*, 28, 1, 1–21.
Gross, N., Mason, W.S. and McEachern, A.W. (1957) *Explorations in Role Analysis: Studies of the School Superintendency Role*, New York, John Wiley.
Habermas, Jürgen (1978) *Knowledge and Human Interests*, 2nd ed., London, Heinemann.
Halsey, A.H., Heath, A.F. and Ridge, J.M. (1980) *Origins and Destinations*, Oxford, Clarendon Press.
Halsey, A.H., Heath, A.F. and Ridge, J.M. (1984) 'The Political Arithmetic of Public Schools', in Geoffrey Walford (ed.), *British Public Schools: Policy and Practice*, Lewes, Falmer Press.
Hammer, Joshua (1989) 'The Myth of Global Synergy', *Bulletin-Newsweek*, 27 June.
Hansen, Ian (1971) *Nor Free Nor Secular*, Melbourne, Oxford University Press.
Hargreaves, A. (1984) 'The Significance of Classroom Coping Strategies', in Andy Hargreaves and Peter Woods (eds), *Classrooms and Staffrooms: The Sociology of Teachers and Teaching*, Milton Keynes, Open University Press.
Hargreaves, David H. (1967) *Social Relations in a Secondary School*, London, Routledge and Kegan Paul.

Hargreaves, David J. and McColly, Ann (eds) (1986) *The Psychology of Sex Differences*, London, Harper and Row.
Hatton, Elizabeth J. (1985) 'Equality, Class and Power: A Case Study', *British Journal of Sociology of Education*, 6, 3, 255–72.
Hayter, Teresa and Watson, Catherine (1985) *Aid: Rhetoric and Reality*, London, Pluto Press.
Haywood, Roy (1986) 'The Life and Death of Two National Agencies: Implications for Curriculum Reform Strategies', *Journal of Curriculum Studies*, 18, 2, 185–96.
Heath, Anthony and Ridge, John (1983) 'Schools, Examinations and Occupational Attainment', in June Purvis and Margaret Hales (eds), *Achievement and Inequality in Education*, London, Routledge and Kegan Paul.
Heatherley, Charles L. (ed.) (1981) *Mandate for Leadership: Policy Management in a Conservative Administration*, Washington, D.C., The Heritage Foundation.
Hechinger, Fred M. (ed.) (1986) *A Better Start: New Choices for Early Learning*, New York, Walker and Co.
Henriques, Julian and others (1984) *Changing the Subject: Psychology, Social Regulation and Subjectivity*, London, Methuen.
Her Majesty's Inspectors (HMI) (1984) *Education Observed 2*, A Review of Published Reports of HM Inspectors on Primary Schools and 11–16 and 12–16 Comprehensive Schools, London, HMSO.
Hess, Robert D. (1970) 'Social Class and Ethnic Influence upon Socialization', in Paul H. Mussen (ed.), *Carmichael's Manual of Child Psychology*, Vol. 2, 3rd ed., New York, John Wiley and Sons.
Hirst, Paul H. (1965) 'Liberal Education and the Nature of Knowledge', in R.D. Archambault (ed.), *Philosophical Analysis and Education*, London, Routledge and Kegan Paul.
Hirst, Paul H. (1974) 'The Forms of Knowledge Re-visited', in Paul H. Hirst, *Knowledge and the Curriculum*, London, Routledge and Kegan Paul.
Hoggart, Richard (1978) *An Idea and Its Servants: UNESCO from Within*, London, Chatto and Windus.
Hollingshead, August B. (1949) *Elmtown's Youth*, New York, John Wiley and Sons.
Holmes, Brian (1973) 'Leicester, United Kingdom', in OECD (1973), *op. cit.*
Holt, John (1965) *How Children Fail*, New York, Pitman.
Hunt, F.J. (1979–80) 'The Reality of Childhood — and Some Policy Implications', *Interchange*, 10, 4, 53–71.
Hunt, F.J. (1986) 'Bases of Educational Action', *Education Research and Perspectives*, 13, 2, 67–74.
Hunt, F.J. (1988) *The Incorporation of Education*, London, Routledge.
Hurn, Christopher J. (1985) *The Limits and Possibilities of Schooling*, 2nd ed., Boston, Mass., Allyn Bacon.
Husén, Torsten (ed.) (1967) *International Study of Achievement in Mathematics: A Comparison of Twelve Countries*, Stockholm, Almqvist and Wiksell.
Husén, Torsten (1974) *The Learning Society*, London, Methuen.
Jackson, Philip W. (1968) *Life in Classrooms*, New York, Holt, Rinehart and Winston.
Jencks, Christopher and others (1972) *Inequality: A Reassessment of the Effect of Family and Schooling in America*, New York, Basic Books.

Johnson, Susan M. (1984) *Teacher Unions in Schools*, Philadelphia, Pa., Temple University Press.
Jones, Adele M. (1989) Dependence, Domination and Legitimacy: Educational Planning in a Frontier Zone, Unpublished PhD thesis, Melbourne, Monash University.
Kamin, Leon J. (1977) *The Science and Politics of I.Q.*, Harmondsworth, Penguin Books.
Kapferer, Judith L. (1981) 'Socialization and the Symbolic Order of the School', *Anthropology and Education Quarterly*, 12, 4, 258–74.
Karabel, J. and Halsey, A.H. (1977) 'Educational Research: A Review and an Interpretation', in Jerome Karabel and A.H. Halsey (eds), *Power and Ideology in Education*, New York, Oxford University Press.
Karier, Clarence J. (1972) 'Testing for Order and Control in the Corporate Liberal State', *Educational Theory*, 22, 2, 154–80.
Keddie, Nell (1971) 'Classroom Knowledge', in Michael F.D. Young (ed.), *op. cit.*
Kelly, Alison (ed.) (1981) *The Missing Half: Girls and Science Education*, Manchester, Manchester University Press.
Kerckhoff, Alan C. (1986) 'Effects of Ability Grouping in British Secondary Schools', *American Sociological Review*, 51, 6, 842–58.
Kerr, Norman D. (1964) 'The School Board as an Agency of Legitimation', *Sociology of Education*, 38, 1, 34–59.
Kogan, Maurice (1975) *Educational Policy Making: A Study of Interest Groups and Parliament*, London, George Allen and Unwin.
Kogan, Maurice (1979) *Educational Policies in Perspective: An Appraisal*, Paris, OECD.
Kohn, Melvin, L. (1963) 'Social Class and Parent-Child Relationships', *American Journal of Sociology*, 68, January, 471–80.
Kohn, Melvin L. (1977) *Class and Conformity*, 2nd ed., Chicago, Ill., University of Chicago Press.
Kulick, C.C. and Kulick, J.A. (1982) 'Effects of Ability Grouping on Secondary School Students: A Meta-Analysis of Evaluation Findings', *American Educational Research Journal*, 19, 3, 415–28.
Lacey, Colin (1970) *Hightown Grammar*, Manchester, Manchester University Press.
Lacey, Colin (1977) *The Socialisation of Teachers*, London, Methuen.
Lagemann, Ellen Condliffe (1983) *Private Power for the Public Good: A History of the Carnegie Foundation for the Advancement of Teaching*, Middleton, Conn., Wesleyan University Press.
Lareau, Annette (1987) 'Social Class Differences in Family-School Relationships: The Importance of Cultural Capital', *Sociology of Education*, 60, 2, 73–85.
Lawn, Martin and Ozga, Jenny (1986) 'Unequal Partners: Teachers under Indirect Rule', *British Journal of Sociology of Education*, 7, 2, 225–38.
Levin, Henry M. (1978) 'The Dilemma of Comprehensive Schooling Reform in Western Europe', *Comparative Education Review*, 22, October, 434–51.
Liffman, Michael (1978) *Power for the Poor*, Sydney, George Allen and Unwin.
Lortie, Dan C, (1975) *School Teacher*, Chicago, Ill., University of Chicago Press.
Lynd, Robert S. and Lynd, Helen M. (1929) *Middletown*, New York, Harcourt, Brace and Co.

Bibliography

Lynd, Robert S. and Lynd, Helen M. (1937) *Middletown in Transition*, New York, Harcourt, Brace and Co.

Maccoby, Eleanor E. and Jacklin, Carol Nagy (1974) *The Psychology of Sex Differences*, Stanford, Calif., Stanford University Press.

McNeil, Linda M. (1986) *Contradictions of Control: School Structure and School Knowledge*, New York, Routledge and Kegan Paul.

McPherson, Gertrude H. (1972) *Small Town Teacher*, Cambridge, Mass., Harvard University Press.

MacPherson, Stewart (1987) *Five Hundred Million Children: Poverty and Welfare in the Third World*, Brighton, Wheatsheaf Books.

Marks, Russell (1980) 'Legitimating Industrial Capitalism: Philanthropy and Individual Differences', in Robert F. Arnove (ed.), *op. cit.*

Masters, G. N. (1988) 'Educational Measurement: Prospects for Research and Innovation', *Australian Educational Researcher*, 15, 4, 23–34.

Mattelart, Armand (1979) *Multinational Corporations and the Control of Culture: The Ideological Apparatuses of Imperialism*, Brighton, Harvester Press.

Measor, Lynda and Woods, Peter (1984) *Changing Schools: Pupil Perspectives on Transfer to a Comprehensive*, Milton Keynes, Open University Press.

Medawar, Charles and Freese, Barbara (1982) *Drug Diplomacy*, London, Social Audit.

Montgomery, Robert (1978) *A New Examination of Examinations*, London, Routledge and Kegan Paul.

Morgan, Gareth (1986) *Images of Organisation*, Beverley Hills, Calif., Sage Publications.

Mortimore, J. and Blackstone, Tessa (1982) *Disadvantage and Education*, London, Heinemann.

Mortimore, Peter and others (1988) *School Matters: The Junior Years*, Wells, Open Books.

Musgrave, Peter W. (1987) *Socialising Contexts: The Subject and Society*, Sydney, Allen and Unwin.

Nachmias, Chara (1980) 'Curriculum Tracking: Some of Its Causes and Consequences under a Meritocracy', *Comparative Education Review*, 24, February, 1–20.

Nash, Roy (1973) *Classrooms Observed*, London, Routledge and Kegan Paul.

Nash, Roy (1976) 'Pupils' Expectations of their Teachers', in Michael Stubbs and Sara Delamont (eds), *Explorations in Classroom Behaviour*, Chichester, John Wiley and Sons.

Newson, John and Newson, Elizabeth (1963) *Infant Care in an Urban Community*, London, Allen and Unwin.

Newson, John and Newson, Elizabeth (1970) 'Changes in Concepts of Parenthood', in Katherine Elliott (ed.), *The Family and Its Future*, London, Longman.

Newson, John and Newson, Elizabeth (1976) *Seven Years Old in the Home Environment*, London, Allen and Unwin.

Newson, John and Newson, Elizabeth (1977) *Perspectives on School at Seven Years Old*, London, Allen and Unwin.

Newsweek (1983) 'All Work and No Play', 24 January.

Nisbet, John (1985) 'Introduction', in John Nisbet (ed.), *World Yearbook of Education: Research, Policy and Practice*, London, Kogan Page; New York, Nichols Publishing Co.

Novak, Michael (1982) *The Spirit of Democratic Capitalism*, New York, American Enterprise Institute/Simon and Schuster.
Oakes, Jeannie (1985) *Keeping Track: How Schools Structure Inequality*, New Haven, Conn., Yale University Press.
Ogbu, John U. (1982) 'Socialization: A Cultural-Sociological Approach', in Kathryn M. Borman (ed.), *The Social Life of Children in a Changing Society*, Hillsdale, N.J., Lawrence Erlbaum Associates.
Ohmae, Kenichi (1985) *Triad Power: The Coming Shape of Global Competition*, New York, Free Press.
Organization for Economic Cooperation and Development (OECD) (1962) *Policy Conference on Economic Growth and Investment* (Washington, 16–20 October 1961), Paris, OECD.
Organization for Economic Cooperation and Development (1973) *Case Studies of Educational Innovation: 11. At the Regional Level*, Paris, OECD.
Organization for Economic Cooperation and Development (1983) *Compulsory Schooling in a Changing World*, Paris, OECD.
Organization for Economic Cooperation and Development (1984) *Educational Trends in the 1970s: A Quantitative Analysis*, Paris, OECD.
Organization for Economic Cooperation and Development (1985a) *Education in Modern Society*, Paris, OECD.
Organization for Economic Cooperation and Development (1985b) *Education and Training after Basic Schooling*, Paris, OECD,
Patrick, Helen (1986) 'From Cross to CATE: The Universities and Teacher Education over the Past Century', *Oxford Review of Education*, 12, 3, 243–61.
Payer, Cheryl (1982) *The World Bank: A Critical Analysis*, New York, Monthly Review Press.
Phenix, Philip H. (1964) *Realms of Meaning: A Philosophy of the Curriculum for General Education*, New York, McGraw-Hill.
Plowden Report (1967) *Children and Their Primary Schools*, A Report of the Central Advisory Council for Education (England), London, HMSO.
Pollard, Andrew (1980) 'Teacher Interests and Changing Situations of Survival Threat in Primary School Classrooms', in Peter Woods (ed.), *Teacher Strategies*, London, Croom Helm.
Popkewitz, Thomas S. (1987) 'Ideology and Social Formation in Teacher Education', in Thomas S. Popkewitz (ed.), *Critical Studies in Teacher Education: Its Folklore, Theory and Practice*, Lewes, Falmer Press.
Pring, Richard (1976) *Knowledge and Schooling*, London, Open Books.
Radford, W.C. (1962) *School Leavers in Australia, 1959–60*, Melbourne, Australian Council for Educational Research.
Radford, W.C. and Wilkes, R.E. (1975) *School Leavers in Australia, 1971–1972*, Melbourne, Australian Council for Education Research.
Ramirez, Francisco O. and Boli, John (1987) 'The Political Construction of Mass Schooling: European Origins and World Wide Institutionalization', *Sociology of Education*, 60, 1, 2–17.
Ramsey, Peter and others (1983) 'Successful and Unsuccessful Schools: A Study in Southern Auckland', *Australian and New Zealand Journal of Sociology*, 19, 2, 272–304.
Reich, Robert B. (1983) *The Next American Frontier*, New York, Times Books.
Reynolds, David (ed.) (1985) *Studying School Effectiveness*, Lewes, Falmer Press.

Reynolds, David and Sullivan, Michael (1979) 'Bringing Schools Back In', in Len Barton (ed.), *Schools, Pupils and Deviance*, Nafferton, Driffield, Nafferton Books.

Reynolds, David, Sullivan, Michael and Murgatroyd, Stephen (1987) *The Comprehensive Experiment*, Lewes, Falmer Press.

Richardson, Elizabeth (1973) *The Teacher, the School and the Task of Management*, London, Heinemann.

Rist, Ray C. (1973) *The Urban School: A Factory for Failure*, Cambridge, Mass., MIT Press.

Roach, John (1971) *Public Examinations in England 1850–1900*, Cambridge, Cambridge University Press.

Rusbridger, Alan (1987) 'A Thought for Tomorrow', *Guardian*, 22 December.

Rutter, Michael and others (1979) *Fifteen Thousand Hours*, London, Open Books.

St John-Brooks, Caroline (1983) 'English: A Curriculum for Personal Development', in Martin Hammersley and Andy Hargreaves (eds), *Curriculum Practice: Some Sociological Case Studies*, Lewes, Falmer Press.

Sampson, Anthony (1977) *The Arms Bazaar: The Companies, the Dealers, the Bribes; From Vickers to Lockheed*, London, Hodder and Stoughton.

Sampson, Anthony (1981) *The Money Lenders*, London, Hodder and Stoughton.

Scarth, John (1983) 'Teachers' School-Based Experience of Examining', in Martyn Hammersley and Andy Hargreaves (eds), *Curriculum Practice: Some Sociological Case Studies*, Lewes, Falmer Press.

Scheffler, Israel (1985) *Of Human Potential*, Boston, Mass., Routledge and Kegan Paul.

Schilling, Marie (1986) 'Knowledge and Liberal Educational: A Critique of Paul Hirst', *Journal of Curriculum Studies*, 18, 1, 1–16.

Schneider, Barbara L. (1987) 'Tracing the Provenance of Teacher Education', in Thomas S. Popkewitz (ed.), *Critical Studies in Teacher Education: Its Folklore, Theory and Practice*, Lewes, Falmer Press.

Sedlak, Michael W. and others (1986) *Selling Students Short: Classroom Bargains and Academic Reform in the American High School*, New York, Teachers College Press.

Seeley, John R., Sim, R. Alexander and Loosely, Elizabeth W. (1956) *Crestwood Heights*, New York, Basic Books.

Seybold, Peter J. (1980) 'The Ford Foundation and the Triumph of Behavioralism in American Political Science', in Robert F. Arnove (ed.), *op. cit.*

Sharp, Rachel (ed.) (1986) *Capitalist Crisis and Schooling*, South Melbourne, Macmillan.

Sharp, Rachel and Green, Anthony (1975) *Education and Social Control*, London, Routledge and Kegan Paul.

Shipman, M.D. (1974) *Inside a Curriculum Project*, London, Methuen.

Sikes, Patricia J., Measor, Lynda and Woods, Peter (1985) *Teacher Careers: Crises and Continuities*, Lewes, Falmer Press.

Silk, L. and Silk, M. (1980) *The American Establishment*, New York, Basic Books.

Skilbeck, Malcolm (1984) *School-based Curriculum Development*, London, Harper and Row.

Skilbeck, Malcolm (ed.) (1984) *Readings in School-based Curriculum Development*, London, Harper and Row.

Smith R.A. and Knight, J. (1978) 'MACOS in Queensland: The Politics of

Educational Knowledge', *The Australian Journal of Education*, 22, October 225–48.
Spaull, Andrew and others (1986) 'Teacher Unionism in the 1980s: Four Perspectives', *Australian Education Review*, No. 24, Hawthorn, Australian Council for Educational Research.
Spender, Dale and Sarah, Elizabeth (eds) (1980) *Learning to Lose: Sexism and Education*, London, Women's Press.
Stedman, Lawrence C. (1985) 'A New Look at Effective Schools Literature', *Urban Education*, 20, 3, 295–326.
Steedman, Jane (1983) *Examination Results in Selective and Non-selective Schools*, London, National Children's Bureau.
Stenhouse, Lawrence (1975) *An Introduction to Curriculum Research and Development*, London, Heinemann.
Stone, Lawrence (1977) *The Family, Sex and Marriage in England, 1500–1800*, London, Weidenfeld and Nicolson.
Stubbs, Michael (1976) 'Teaching and Talking: A Sociolinguistic Approach to Classroom Interaction', in Gabriel Chanan and Sarah Delamont (eds), *Frontiers of Classroom Research*, Slough, Bucks, National Foundation for Educational Research.
Sutherland, Margaret R. (1981) *Sex Bias in Education*, Oxford, Basil Blackwell.
Tawney, R.H. (1964) *Equality*, London, Unwin Books.
Tomlinson, Sally (1982) *A Sociology of Special Education*, London, Routledge and Kegan Paul.
Turner, Glen (1983) *The Social World of the Comprehensive School: How Pupils Adapt*, London, Croom Helm.
Walford, Geoffrey (1984) 'The Changing Professionalism of Public School Teachers', in Geoffrey Walford (ed.), *British Public Schools: Policy and Practice*, Lewes, Falmer Press.
Walford, Geoffrey (1986) *Life in Public Schools*, London, Methuen.
Waller, Willard (1932) *The Sociology of Teaching*, New York, John Wiley and Sons.
Ward, Sue (1986) *Socially Responsible Investment*, London, Directory of Social Change.
Wedge, Peter and Essen, Juliet (1982) *Children in Adversity*, London, Heinemann.
Wehlage, Gary C. and others (1989) *Reducing the Risk: Schools as Communities of Support*, Lewes, Falmer Press.
Wentworth, William M. (1980) *Context and Understanding: An Inquiry into Socialization Theory*, New York, Elsevier.
Werthman, C. (1963) 'Delinquents in Schools: A Test for the Legitimacy of Authority', *Berkeley Journal of Sociology*, 8, 1, 39–60.
White, Larry C. (1988) *Merchants of Death: The American Tobacco Industry*, Guildford, Beech Tree Publishing.
White, R.W. (1959) 'Motivation Reconsidered: The Concept of Competence', *Psychological Review*, 66, September, 297–333.
Whiting, Beatrice (ed.) (1963) *Six Cultures: Studies in Child Rearing*, New York, John Wiley and Sons.
Williams, G.G. (1981) Teachers' Evaluations and the Reproduction of Schooling, Unpublished PhD thesis, Melbourne, Monash University.
Willis, Paul (1977) *Learning to Labour*, Westmead, Saxon House.

Willms, J. Douglas (1987) 'Patterns of Academic Achievement in Public and Private Schools: Implications for Public Policy and Future Research', in Edward H. Haertel, Thomas James and Henry M. Levin (eds), *Comparing Public and Private Schools*, Vol. 11, *School Achievement*, Lewes, Falmer Press.

Wilson, Bryan R. (1965) 'Essay Review: Religion and Career', *School Review*, 73, 2, 156–72.

Wirt, Frederick M. and Harman, Grant (eds) (1986) *Education, Recession and the World Village*, Lewes, Falmer Press.

Wolcott, Harry F. (1977) *Teachers vs. Technocrats*, Eugene, Ore., University of Oregon, Center for Educational Policy and Management.

Woods, Peter (1979) *The Divided School*, London, Routledge and Kegan Paul.

Woods, Peter (1983) *Sociology and the School: An Interactionist Perspective*, London, Routledge and Kegan Paul.

Woods, Peter and Pollard, Andrew (eds) (1988) *Sociology and Teaching: A New Challenge for the Sociology of Teaching*, London, Croom Helm.

Wragg, E.C. (1982) *A Review of Research on Teacher Education*, Windsor, Berks, National Foundation for Educational Research/Nelson.

Wright, Lindsay M. (1982) 'A Survey of Economic Freedoms', *Freedom at Issue* (Special Issue), No. 64, January-February, 15–20.

Young, Michael F.D. (ed.) (1971) *Knowledge and Control*, London, Collier-Macmillan.

Zeigler, L.H., Jennings, M.K. and Peak, G.W. (1974) *Governing American Schools*, North Scituate, Mass., Duxberry Press.

Index

advantaged parents
  and schooling, 78–9
assessment and evaluation, 127–31
  management and, 129
  purposes and, 129
  social and political character of, 127–8
  steerers and, 130
attainment levels, 60–1
attendance patterns, 59–60

business
  and the commercialization of schooling, 178
  and foundations, 178
  and steering, 173–8

capitalism
  as a mode of operating, 202–3
children's rights, 68
circumstances
  and school achievement, 214–15
citizenry
  collective, 227
  individual, 227
classroom, 192–3
  differentiation and discrimination, 96–7
coalitions
  and economic exploitation, 224
    shared perspectives and interests, 197–8
  of participants, 204–5
  political, and developmental society, 228
  social, and strategies, 206–7
commercialization
  and teaching, 102
complementary agencies of management, 195–6
conflict theories, 11–12
consultancy
  and dependency, 143
  and entrepreneurialism, 144
consultants, 143–4
consumers
  and developmental society, 225
control
  of teachers, 100–1

development, 213
  conditions for, 213–14
developmental schooling, 216
  educational strategies for, 216–21
  priorities in provision of, 217–20
  social conditions for, 215
  sponsorship and, 219
developmental society, 221–2
  consumers and, 225
  economic strategies for, 223–7
  employees and, 224–5
  investors and, 225–6
  personal strategies for, 230–1
  political
    coalitions and, 228

education and, 228
  organization and, 228
  strategies and, 227–9
 prospects for, 222–3
 social strategies for, 221–3
developmentalism, 12–15
 and the right to develop, 13
 and implications of approach, 14
 positions compatible with, 14
disadvantaged parents
 and schooling, 77–8

economic activity
 as exploitative, 223–4
educational strategies
 for developmental schooling, 216–21
effective schools, 39–40
employee organizations
 and steering, 184
employees
 and developmental society, 224–5
examinations
 and the management of programming, 120
exploitation
 economic, coalitions and, 224
 of education, 208
exploitative economic activity, 223–4

foundations, 178–83
 and elite networks, 182–3
 and management of schooling, 180
 and political influence, 181–2
 and production of knowledge, 180
 and steering, 178–83
  educational measurement, 178–9
  social research, 179–80
 and think tanks, 181

hidden curriculum, 107–8

inconsistencies
 in policies and practices, 3
intellectuals
 and steering, 183
interest groups and steering, 185
international agencies, 196

interpretations
 and strategies, 211–12
interpretivism, 11
investors
 and developmental society, 225

management
 and community, 154–5
 and direction of research, 137
 and privatization, 163
 and psychological and social services, 142–3
 and social change, 206
 and social responsibilities, 165–6
 and steerers, 164
 complementary agencies of, 150–1, 156–8
 dynamics of, 152–64
 education, 166
 informal, 154
 intermediate level, 155
 national, 161–3
  forms of, 151, 155–6
  viability of, 151–2, 197–8
 of schools, 154–5
 systems, political, 158–63
 responsibility, distribution of, 149
 structuring of, 149–152, 165
 styles of, 153–154
managers
 social significance of, 205
managing
 structural forms of, 147–8
 techniques of, 148
 undertaking of, 147
material circumstances
 and steering, 187
media
 and schooling, 176–7
modern societies, 201–2

national management, 161–3
 forms of, 151, 155–6
 viability of, 151–2, 197–8

OECD
 and steering, 170–1,
outcomes
 by type of school, 37–9

parenting
    and prospects of children, 68
    and the structuring and operation of societies, 75–6
parents
    advantaged
        and schooling, 78–9
    and school management, 82
    and schooling, 76–80
    and differences in resources and effectiveness, 81
    and differences in resources and capacities, 76–7
    associations of, 80
    differential contributions of, 79
    disadvantaged
        and schooling, 77–9
    selective neglect of, by schools, 81
    situations and circumstances of, 73–5
parents' rights, 68
participants
    and agencies in steering, 186
    and society, 204
    coalitions of, 204–5
    resources and effectiveness of, 190
    and structures and processes, 211
personal strategies
    for developmental society, 230–1
    style, coherent, 231
    styles, multiple, 230
perspectives, 8–10
    and interpretations, 189–92
    and research, 137–8
    and the study of schooling, 8
    and epistemological assumptions, 9
    and evolutionary developments, 9–10
    and moral assumptions, 9
    and ontological assumptions, 9
policy development and planning, 138–41
    and expertise, 139–40
    and management, 139
    and steerers, 139
    political significance of, 140
political
    coalitions and developmental society, 228
    education and developmental society, 228–9
    management of systems, 158–63
    organization and developmental society, 228
    role of foundations, 180–1
    significance of policy development and planning, 140
    strategies for developmental society, 227–9
power
    and social justice, 13
    social justice and participation, 200
predispositions
    and modes of operating, 207–8
private organizations
    and influence, 177–8
privatization
    and management, 163
program
    development and implementation, 108–20
    diversity and type of student, 105–6
programming
    and content, 103–4
    and legitimacy, 116
    and role of the teacher, 121
    and steerers, 117
    and subject communities, 115–16
    and turbulent economic and political circumstances, 118–20
    by specialists, 111–12
    location of responsibility for, 109–10
    management of
        and examinations, 120
    participants in, 104
    political direction of, 117–18
    social dynamics of, 121
programs
    and student development, 107
    and types of students, 122
progressivism
    and programs, 106–7
psychological and social services, 141–3
    evolution of, 141–2
    and management, 142

reality
  of childhood, 74–5
  of schooling, 214
  and social justice, 190–1
regional organizations
  and steering, 170
regulation
  and manipulation, 210
research, 136–8
  and control of schooling, 136–7
  and perspectives, 137–8
resources
  and competence and effectiveness, 199
  strategies for more effective and equitable use of, 219–20
rights
  of parents and children, 68

school
  achievement, circumstances and, 214–15
  community, 194–5
schooling
  advantaged parents and, 78–9
  and political contestation, 5
  and social cohesion, 220–1
  as a system of activity, 192
  as a system of differentiation and discrimination, 58–9
  and protagonists in action, 208–9
  aspects of, 6
  assessment of, by former students, 61
  commercialization of, 4
  differential provision of, 20
  disadvantaged parents and, 77–8
  examination and appraisal of, 4, 10–15
  management of, 27–34
    and distribution of authority and responsibilities, 29–30
    centralized, 28
    localized, 29
    societal, 30–2
    trends in national strategies, 32–3
  organization and operation of,
    historical development, 22–3

outcomes of, 34–42, 59–63
performance and participation in society, 62
prospects for, 209–10
reality of, 214
social
  and cultural elements in, 26–7
  change and, 1–3
  cohesion and, 220–1
  dynamics of, 198–210
  priorities and, 1
  significance of, 191
sponsorship of, 18–21
  by the community, 19–20
  by the wealthy, 19
  Catholic, 20
  church, 36
  commercial, 21
  societal, 20
steerers of, 33–4
structuring of
  and linkages with other sections of society, 27
  and social and economic circumstances, 25
  by gender, 25–6
  by levels, 23–4
  by performance, 24
students' experience of, 51–9
study of, 6–10
  disciplined approaches to, 8
  perspectives and, 8
  social focus of, 8
  techniques employed in, 7–8
systems of, 194
scientism, 10–11
servicing
  and self-servicing, 226–7
  development of, 125–6
  diversity of participants in, 126
social
  background and post-school destination, 63
  change
    and management, 206
    and steering activity, 168
  coalitions and strategies, 206–7
  cohesion and schooling, 220–1

250

conditions for developmental
    schooling, 215
factors and diversity in teacher
    education, 131–2
justice and power, 13
production of children, 69–76
    by class, 70–1
    by ethnicity, 72
    by gender, 71–2
    by religion, 72
    by rural or urban location, 72–3
    by societies, 69
    by type of family, 73
    historically, 70
significance
    of managers, 205
    of schooling, 191
strategies for developmental society,
    221–3
socialism
    as a mode of operating, 203–4
societies
    and corporations, 3–4
society
    and participants, 204
specialization
    and political activity, 146
    and servicing, 125–6, 144–5
specialists
    and management of schooling, 145
    and undertaking of schooling, 145
sponsorship
    and developmental schooling, 219
state
    and steering, 169–70
steerers
    and assessment and evaluation, 130
    and management, 164
    and policy development and
        planning, 139
    and programming, 117
    and strategies, 169–86
    and structures, 168
    and teacher education, 135
    identification and examination of,
        167–8
Steering
    activity, social change and, 168
    and business, 173–8

as model, 174
as employer, 173–4
as provider, 174–5
as sponsor, 175
as subverter of schooling, 176
as supplier, 174
strategies
    for developmental schooling, 216–
        21
    for developmental society
        economic, 223–7
        personal, 230–1
        political, 227–9
        social, 221–3
    maximizing effectiveness, 232
    more effective and effective
        use of resources, 219–20
    social coalitions and, 206–7
    student, 58
    teacher, 95–100
streaming
    outcomes of, 35–6
structural arrangements
    change in, 201
    force and significance of, 201
    persistence of, 40–2
structuralism
    convenience of, 190
structures
    and action, 198
    and relationships, 42–3
structuring
    and participation, 200
student
    achievement and schooling, 64–5
    background and school
        achievement, 62–3
    careers, 57–8
    circumstances and exacerbating
        conditions, 49
    development, circumstances and, 46
    resistance to schooling, 55–6
    strategies, 58
students
    advantaged, 48
    and social arrangements and
        circumstances, 51
    and the structuring of schooling,
        49–50

251

commencing schooling, 52–3
differential effectiveness of, 200
differentiation, categorization and differential treatment of, 53–6
  by class, 54
  by ethnicity, 55
  by gender, 54
disadvantaged, 48
interests of, 45–6
study of, 45
students' perceptions
  of schooling, 57
  of students, 56
  of teachers, 56
systems
  political management of, 158–63

teacher
  career paths, 89–90
  control and reputation, 95
  education, 131–6
    and steerers, 135
    evolution of, 133–5
    political direction of, 134
    social factors and diversity in, 131–2
  position of, 100–1
  preoccupation with control and direction, 91–2, 94–5
  priorities and strategies, 91–100
  role of, 85–6
  situations, diversity of, and responsibilities, 87–8
  status of, 86
  strategies
    classroom, 95
    industrial, 98–9
    school, 97
    specialist, 98
    social, 99–100
teachers
  and knowledge, 90
  and management, 153, 161
  and programming, 114–15
  and social change, 101–2
teaching
  control of, 87, 100
  progressive and traditional, 92–4
  structuring of, 87–91
tertiary institutions
  and steering, 173
traditional societies, 201

UNESCO and steering, 171–2

workforce
  and steering, 184
World Bank
  and steering, 172–3